The Legacy of
R. P. Blackmur

The Legacy of
R. P. BLACKMUR

ESSAYS, MEMOIRS,
TEXTS

EDITED BY

Edward T. Cone, Joseph Frank,
and Edmund Keeley

THE ECCO PRESS · NEW YORK

Published in 1987 by The Ecco Press
26 West 17th Street, New York, N.Y. 10011
Published simultaneously in Canada by
Penguin Books Canada Ltd., Ontario

Printed in the United States of America

Designed by Francesca Belanger

ACKNOWLEDGMENTS

The generous assistance of the Mildred Andrews Fund in support of this
book is gratefully acknowledged.

For Essays and Memoirs

"Notes on a Hypothetical Blackmur Anthology" by Kenneth Burke first appeared in *The Nassau
Literary Magazine.*
"Casella as Critic" by R. W. B. Lewis copyright 1951 by Kenyon College. Reprinted by
permission of the author and *The Kenyon Review.*
"The Horizon of R. P. Blackmur" by Edward W. Said first appeared in *Raritan.*
"Affable Irregular" by W. S. Merwin was first published in *Grand Street.*

For Texts by R. P. Blackmur

"T. S. Eliot." *The Hound and Horn* 1 (June 1928), 291–319.
"Notes on the Criticism of Herbert Read." *Larus* 1 (April–June 1928), 45–58.
"The Enemy." Review of *Time and Western Man,* by Wyndham Lewis (New York: Harcourt).
The Hound and Horn 1 (March 1928), 270–73.
"Technique in Criticism." Review of *Practical Criticism: A Study in Literary Judgment,* by
I. A. Richards (New York: Harcourt). *The Hound and Horn* 3 (April–June 1930), 451–53.

Library of Congress Cataloging in Publication Data

1. Blackmur, R.P. (Richard P.), 1904–1965.
2. Authors, American—20th century—Biography.
3. Criticism—United States. I. Cone, Edward T.
II. Frank, Joseph. III. Keeley, Edmund.
IV. Blackmur, R.P. (Richard P.), 1904–1965.
PS3503.L266Z73 1987   801'.95'0924   87–13516
ISBN 0–88001–152–1

0–88001–153–X (pbk)

Page 325 constitutes an extension of this page.

Contents

v

TEXTS BY BLACKMUR

Preface

This collection is meant to celebrate the legacy of R. P. Blackmur in three ways: through essays about various aspects and implications of his criticism, through memoirs of his presence as a teacher and man of letters, and through previously uncollected texts by him that illustrate his work as a critic and reviewer over a period of forty years. Some of those who contributed to the first section of the volume did not know Blackmur personally but were included because they have been especially discerning about his work in the past. Most were friends or students of Blackmur, as is true of all the contributors to the second section. The editors felt that there were certain insights into Blackmur's contribution to American letters that could be provided best by those who worked closely with him, especially during the years after he left Maine and moved to Princeton to become a more public presence.

It is the editors' hope that these essays and memoirs testify not only to Blackmur's abiding influence as a writer but to those perhaps equally stimulating qualities of mind and personality that he reserved for dialogue—or sometimes monologue—in his home or before a select audience of students and peers, qualities that made him a memorably provocative intellectual force both inside and outside the academy. It is also our hope that the third section of texts will add new evidence to support Blackmur's growing reputation as a major forerunner of contemporary critical perspectives.

Today many critics try to lay claim to the title of creative artist, not in the sense that Coleridge and Arnold were poets as well as critics, but in accordance with a new valuation that would seem to grant to literature and to the criticism of literature equal standing as vehicles of artistic creation. Blackmur would have had none of this. Yet while he would have rejected such a dogmatic claim as outlandish (or, as he would have put it, jackassical), it seems to us that he nevertheless produced a body of essays that qualify, if any critical essays can qualify, as works of art.

I. Essays

KENNETH BURKE

Notes on a Hypothetical Blackmur Anthology

Blackmur was spontaneously and tirelessly interested in the sorts of things that a civilized man should be interested in, the idealities and materialities of human living. He approached such questions cautiously prepared, through the love and close study of notable texts. To have known him is to know why so many of his former students swear by him. To have read his books closely is to realize that they will last. To have heard him talking, at easygoing conversational moments, is to appreciate how much character and equipment he brought even to the lightest of remarks.

If behaviorist tests are any proof, I'll offer this one, as brute testimony of what I, at least, think of Blackmur. When I was asked to review a book of his, I laid everything else aside and spent no less than five solid weeks on the job, reading, re-reading, not just that book but all his others, note-taking, writing, re-writing, and begad! taking Patience Pills on the side, for this to me was serious business. Of course I would still haggle here and there about our differences. But those are nothing as compared with our bonds back and forth beyond the what-is-it.

In re-reading the only things of his I happen to have with me, his *Form and Value in Modern Poetry,* [1] plus some pieces in paperback anthologies (the heavy, hard-cover volumes being at home), I am overwhelmingly convinced that there should be assembled a volume of *pages choisies,* epigram-like bits, with editorial subtitles, variously illuminating the themes on which he wrote. Such an arrangement, I

3

think, could almost saliently point up the sharpness of his comments. What an admirable combination of toil and intuition, of humbleness and sureness, his performances exemplify!

There would be at least three over-all divisions. First, there would be samplings of his exceptional skill at the savoring of texts. Here would be a succession of his discriminating comments on Hardy, Yeats, Pound, Eliot, Williams, Stevens, Crane, Marianne Moore, etc. This section would deal only with poets, novelists, dramatists, and the like (not critics)—and it would be composed of observations that bear most directly upon textual exegesis, subtleties of style, and the like. A smaller, supplementary part of this section would be concerned with "unsavorings." Here would belong some of his comments in "Notes on E. E. Cummings' Language" (287–312). For though they are overly severe, they are quite suggestive—and, as I indicated in *Attitudes Toward History,* they gave me valuable pieces I needed for fitting together, with some chopping here and there, my own puzzles to do with the problematics of "symbolicity."

Above all, he spontaneously knew that a poem is not to be analyzed as *propounding* a doctrine (theological, metaphysical, magical, historical, or whatever), but as using doctrines for poetic effects. I won't say that he always did, for it's a hard point to keep in mind, and even harder at times to make clear. But the perception shows up most directly when he notes how Eliot uses the Church as "a way of handling poetic material to its best advantage" (127). Of the same quality is his reference to "Eliot's one-man job of making a decorum" (162–63).

As regards Stevens, characteristically, while discussing "the approach of language, through the magic of elegance, to nonsense" (187), he is at pains to show how exacting in its use of words Stevens's style is. Having called Pound's *Cantos* "a rag-bag" (in borrowing an early term of Pound's "now excised from the canon" [92]), he gives the trope a quite different twist with regard to "The Emperor of Ice-Cream," thus: "Two ideas or images about death—the living and the dead—have been associated, and are now permanently fused. If the mind is a rag-bag, pull out two rags and sew them together. If the materials were contradictory, the very contradiction, made permanent, becomes a kind of unison" (190). All three articles on Stevens (with their many potential cullings) make one realize how exceptionally close in this case poet and critic were. For nearly every typical poetic invention on Stevens's part, Blackmur had the corresponding critical intuition.

Somewhat in line with the comment on Eliot I have already cited, he says: "Hebrew poetry (not to say the Bible) is used throughout Miss Moore's work as a background ideal and example of poetic language, an ideal, however, not directly to be served but rather kept in mind for impetus, reference, and comparison" (228). Among the comments to be selected on her work would be many notable distinctions made in response to her lines, "Ecstasy affords / the occasion and expediency determines the form" (226–31). But I couldn't help wondering how she felt when reading "Miss Moore rails . . ." etc. (233—"Rails"!) His comments on the word "profane" in Yeats are a splendid exercise all by themselves (67–69).

The article on D. H. Lawrence threatens to break the frame (253–67). For after talk of sex in Lawrence, one wonders why no mention of homosex in Hart Crane (at least one dimension of whose work was involved with the stylistic idealizing of his sexual discord). And if sex in Lawrence, why not also tuberculosis in Lawrence? (I say this because, just having read Cleanth Brooks's book on Faulkner, I realize more clearly than ever that, in poetics, everything must be treated sheerly as devices for the producing of poetic effects—as Blackmur treated Eliot's use of religion. For once you introduce *any* references to the work not just as a work but as the expression of a poet's personality, the gates are opened to a riot of non-formalistic speculations.) Blackmur's use of the term "expressive form" with regard to Lawrence shifts from the non-personal meaning of "significant form" in the aesthetic theories of Clive Bell to a personal or psychological kind of meaning, and thereby moves the issue from a study of the poem in itself to speculations on poem-poet relationships.

In the article on Miss Moore, the "rag-bag" motif gets a further interesting development thus: "You cannot look in the words of a poem and see two objects really side by side without seeing a third thing, which will be specific and unique" (249). It's an observation that could be used to good effect with regard to some theorists of modern music who would ask us to hear individual parts as separate from one another without regard to the relationship that necessarily arises in proceeding from one to the next.

As a title for this first and basic section, I'd suggest either "The Facts about a Poem" or "Judgment by Description." (Both are excerpts from his own text. I particularly like the second because many critics fail to discern the functioning of judgment when it is left implicit in perception. Whereat we might also quote: "Discovery is judgment" (16), and "There should be the beginnings of judgment implied in the rules of thumb which it turns out possible to use; they show what can be measured" (220).

After the savorings and non-savorings (and I must admit that my citations were not all as specifically pointed as they could be, if our hypothetical editor consistently tied each of them to some one particular text), there would be a section of comments to do with matters of method. This might be subdivided into "poetic" and "critical." I'd call the latter half "methodological," if Blackmur had not been prominent among those brilliant pranksters of the Guild who use this term as a Hallowe'en pumpkin to frighten children. In any case, still deriving our subtitles from his own pages, I'd call this whole division "The Persuasiveness of Craft"—and there are splendid entries aplenty.

Naturally, in keeping with remarks I have already made, I'd bring out formulations such as these (33–35): "Magic performs for Yeats the same fructifying function that Christianity does for Eliot, or that ironic fatalism did for Thomas Hardy." . . . Or, "Poetry requires either a literal faith, an imaginative faith, or as in Shakespeare a mind full of many provisional faiths." (Here I see the bridge that Aristotle had in mind when in the *Poetics,* on the subject of "Thought," he referred the reader to his *Rhetoric.*) . . . "We find poets either using the small conventions of the individual life as if they were great conventions, or attempting to resurrect some great conventions of the past, or, finally, attempting to discover the great conventions that must lie, willy-nilly, hidden in the life about them." (Above all, I admire the tentativeness and speculative tolerance implicit in such a statement.)

High among the topics to be included here would be "Expectations," "Intention," "Convention," and "Effect." For they all bear strongly upon questions of form and its poetic persuasiveness. And there would be many entries to do with relations between the abstract and the concrete, "ideas" and "images," as per this item in the essay on Marianne Moore: "She found, as Yeats would say, the image to call out the whole idea; that was one half. The other half was finding how to dress out the image to its best advantage, so as to arouse, direct, sustain, and consolidate attention" (236). (Blackmur's way of saying pointedly what the old rhetoricians would have included under the head of "amplification," or *auxesis.*)

In this section, our hypothetical, ideal editor would strive for terms that helped bring out the concern with *functionality* in Blackmur's essays, though functionality would here still be conceived strictly in terms of poetical and critical technique (with corresponding problems).

The final section, also divisible into two parts, would fall under the head of the Situational. It would contain what, when reviewing *The Lion and the Honeycomb,* I once called "social observations that impart an air of distinction to the life of books" and "statements of policy, quasi-diplomatic releases designed to serve some turn in the rhetoric, or politics, of the republic of letters." Perhaps for this section we might borrow Blackmur's expression, "An Intolerable Disorder." For Blackmur's exacting concern with the intrinsic nature of a poem by no means closed his mind to the advantages and disadvantages that befall writers (the good luck or bad luck that marks their relation to their times).

Some of Blackmur's finest accomplishments in the internal analysis of texts were worked out during the years when Marxist criticism (or what went by that name!) loomed large in the local scene. Though Blackmur was temperamentally immune not just to doctrinaire Marxism but even to any critical frame that would shift the attention from the analysis of the work in itself to a stress upon environmental or genetic factors, the nature of his own experience, coupled with his considerable Yankee shrewdness, never let him forget that literature is a means of livelihood for most of those engaged in the producing, criticizing, or teaching of it.

But though he wrote quite a bit even about the sheer economics of the cultural situation, when he was working with texts the usual point of contact between technique and scene is in such statements as: "There was at hand for Dante, and as a rule in the great ages of poetry, a fundamental agreement or convention between the poet and his audience about the validity of the view of life of which the poet deepened the reality and spread the scope" (35); or, of Yeats and Hardy, "Each had been deprived by his education, or the lack of it, of an authoritative faith, and each hastened to set up a scaffold out of the nearest congenial materials strong enough and rigid enough to support the structure imagination meant to rear" (14). But a writer's situation can be seen in terms that vary greatly in their scope. And thus, in summing up, he says that Yeats "learned how to create fragments of the actual, not of his own time to which he was unequal, but of all time of which he was a product" (77–78).

It just occurred to me when I was writing these pages that when turning from the analysis of particular texts and poetic and critical method, to matters of policy in general, Blackmur developed and frequently employed to excellent effect the secular application of a device originally perfected in the tradition of homiletics. Choosing a *figurative* title as his point of departure, he would gradually extract from it a chain of literal, conceptual implications. The persuasiveness of the device as rhetoric resided in the fact that it automatically infused his abstractions with an extra dimension, as with the use of myth in some Socratic dialogues. Who would think, for instance, that an essay on "The Lion and the Honeycomb" might be *literally* entitled "Rhetoric, Poetics, and Dialectic"? Further, he thus set up the conditions whereby he contrived one of his most ingenious arguments, by equating "methodology" with the horrendous apparition in Yeats's poem, on the "Second Coming." And as arguments come and go, in this case the last details to fade from the memory will be Lion, Honeycomb, and Rough Beast.[2]

Although (despite such remarkably schematic jobs as his work on the prefaces of Henry James), we do not usually think of Blackmur as a "system-builder," I believe that a properly subtitled set of selections from his several fine volumes would build up a well-coordinated *Weltanschauung* on matters of literary appreciation, literary method, and the areas where the literary situation impinges upon the state of mankind generally.

All told, the *pages choisies* would shape up as a tolerant and mellow view of things. Yet by no means self-effacing. Blackmur knew his way around. He could take care of himself with quiet dexterity, in the subtle and circuitous ways of literary politics.

I like to think we had a genuine bond in the fact that both of us had worked out educational routines for ourselves, largely sans the direct aid of schools during many of our formative years, though later, we both, in various ways, became much involved in teaching. At the beginning of our academic careers there was much the same bar sinister.

On such terms I always met him, with a mixture of admiration, armed neutrality, and plain simple fondness. Among the pleasantest memories of my pedagogic wanderings (and along with the morbid streak that is natural to all teaching) is a summer I spent in the same house with him and John Crowe Ransom, when all of us were giving courses at the Indiana University School of Letters. He was unfailingly equable, while quietly and persistently busied with his unusual store of knowledge bearing upon the life of letters.

John Crowe Ransom's recommendation for the *Form and Value* book is totally exact: "Few if any critics live who write better criticism than Mr. R. P. Blackmur; I mean subtler and deeper criticism, and sounder. He probes the poem with a keen instrument." And we might well say of Blackmur what Blackmur said of Yeats: "More than any man of his time he upheld the dignity of his profession" (78).

NOTES

1. R. P. Blackmur, *Form and Value in Modern Poetry* (New York: Double-day-Anchor Books, 1957). Subsequent page references are to this edition.

2. R. P. Blackmur, *The Lion and the Honeycomb* (New York: Harcourt, Brace and Co., 1955), 178–79.

EDWARD T. CONE

Dashes of Insight:
Blackmur as Music Critic

In the spring of 1930 Robert D. Darrell became the managing editor of *The Phonograph Monthly Review,* a magazine with which he had been closely associated since its founding (as *The Music-Lovers' Phonograph Monthly Review*) in 1926. Darrell held that position for more than a year (the magazine folded in 1932), and during that period he called several times upon his good friend R. P. Blackmur to contribute critiques of recent records (and, on one occasion, of a book).

Blackmur, as Darrell well knew, was musically illiterate. He could not play an instrument, let alone decipher a score. He enjoyed listening to music, but I doubt whether it ever represented a compelling interest. Certainly it did not in later years, during the period I knew him. For a long time his only phonograph was an old hand-cranked Victrola in the house in Harrington, Maine, where he and his wife Helen spent their summers. When I visited them there in 1948, I discovered a small cache of select records (78s, of course, at that date), no doubt chosen (or presented) by Darrell. Except for Victoria's *O magnum mysterium,* sung by a Spanish choir in some vast church, I do not recall any specific titles, but I remember that they were not ordinary fare—as the Victoria attests. (That was a favorite of Richard's; so was Monteverdi's *Lamento d'Arianna.*) The records had evidently not been played in a long time; for when I opened the phonograph I was assailed by a powerful stench, proceeding from the carcass of a long-dead dried fish that had been stored there—who knew when or why? (Helen later once inadvertently referred to the phonograph as "the refrigerator.") Eventually Richard did have an adequate hi-fi system installed in his Princeton house; but he bought few records, and he never became really familiar with the standard repertoire. He rarely attended concerts unless he had a special interest in either a composer or a performer.

His true concern with music was, in a word, personal. He listened to certain records because his friend Bob Darrell had recommended them. He enjoyed the evenings when I would play the piano for a small circle of friends (although I suspect that he preferred the conversation afterward—often triggered by his own comments on the music, sometimes shrewd, sometimes irrelevant). He was delighted at my proposal to set some of his "Scarabs" as a cycle for soprano and string quartet, and he showed a keen interest in the choice of poems and in their treatment. At one point he even proposed writing an opera libretto for me, based on the lurid tale of the death of the Provençal poet Guillaume de Cabestan. He talked a lot about it, but he never wrote one word of the text.

It should be clear, then, that Blackmur was never more than a musical amateur, in both senses of the word: a lover of the art (though not a passionate one) and very much a nonprofessional. The approach of such a dilettante was hardly what he had in mind when he wrote the opening sentence of a well-known essay: "Criticism, I take it, is the discourse of an amateur." For, as "A Critic's Job of Work" then proceeds to show, the required love of the subject is one so deep that it is dissatisfied to be mere affection, and therefore persists in acquiring an adequate knowledge for support and justification.

Why, then, would Darrell entrust to the young Blackmur such items as the Solesmes recording of Gregorian Chant, Stravinsky's performance (at the piano) of his *Capriccio* for piano and orchestra, Walton's *Façade* as recited by Constant Lambert and Edith Sitwell, and works by Carrillo and Satie? The most obvious reason, of course, is that Blackmur needed the money; employing him was no doubt at least partially an act of charity. In addition, however, it may well be that Darrell felt that Blackmur represented the readership at which the magazine was aiming: technically uninformed, but eager for guidance. The point of view of a highly articulate member of this group might have seemed valuable, especially with reference to the works offered Blackmur for review. For it is noteworthy that those included no well-known, frequently recorded compositions that would require a comparison of the available interpretations, optimally based on a close reading of the text. Blackmur's assignments were confined to very old or very new music, on which the opinions of an untrained but sensitive listener may have seemed more appropriate. Darrell could be sympathetic with a layman's approach because he himself, although a professional, was one of a new and special kind, possibly engendered and certainly fostered by the phonograph: the professional listener. As such, his approach was closer to the layman's than to the composer's or the performer's. (I once characterized the ideal journalistic music-reviewer as a professional layman; the term can perhaps be applied even more appropriately to record-reviewers. At any rate, I think it defines Darrell's view of himself, and it suggests what he may have seen potentially in Blackmur.)

Blackmur exhibited considerable self-confidence as he went about his task. Only rarely did his lack of technical background embarrassingly reveal itself, as when he discussed Leopold Stokowski's program note attached to Carrillo's *Preludio a Cristóbal Colón*—the conductor's attempt to justify the composer's use of microtones by an appeal to musical history (1). Blackmur's inadequate vocabulary forced him to refer to organum as "composed of intervals of eight, five, and four notes," and to twelfth-century descant as employing "intervals of three and two notes." (Translate: "composed of octaves, fifths, and fourths," and "thirds and seconds.") And when we find him reporting Stokowski as saying that "the 13th and 14th century only began, dimly, the use of single and half-tones," we must guess that the reference is to chromatic half-steps (a surmise supported by a subsequent reference to *The Well-Tempered Clavichord*). Thus Blackmur was certainly in no position to recognize the shakiness of Stokowski's argument that "the trend of music is away from wide intervals and towards ever increasingly small intervals." That, even if tenable, does not follow from premises that (if I interpret correctly) blur the distinction between harmonic and melodic intervals.

It is true that, in a magazine of this type, a reviewer would have little occasion to parade any specialized knowledge of music theory and history. Blackmur could safely avoid such topics as quantitative versus accentual rhythm in Gregorian Chant, the harmonic vocabulary of Stravinsky, or the details of Satie's parodic distortions; in that respect his reviews differed little from those of his colleagues, which likewise favored general impressions over specific analyses. But the reader of such a journal has the right to assume—and certainly hopes—that the opinions to which he is being exposed are based on something firmer than the generalities in which they are couched for the layman. Thus he might well wonder just how Blackmur would have justified, with reference to the score, his description of the Stravinsky *Capriccio:* "A form is let loose, played with, flung free, caught, sucked in and discarded." That may well be suggestive to some; but to one reader at least the overwriting strongly implies an attempt to make up for a basic deficiency, an effort to express an appreciation founded on insufficient knowledge. And nowhere are any grounds offered for the slight condescension that follows: "Several auditions convince the ears that, while integration may not be perfect, the music builds out of itself, and the parts demand each other" (5).

It is perhaps by way of apology, then, that Blackmur voiced his distrust of words about music. After a moving disquisition on plainsong (4), he entered a disclaimer: "These are words and words fuddle music more than not, unless they bring themselves finally to the confession of their poor limits as mere pointing fingers."

Particularly is that true of absolute music in its more intimate forms. In an interesting passage (5), he contrasted such music with two other "orders": "An audience is intended sometimes to witness music as a spectacle, sometimes to share its meaning, sometimes to be a part of it." Dramatic music belongs to the first order; music of ritual and ceremony, to the third. From the context, it is clear that chamber music represents the ideal of the second order. "It is a music as far from subjective as it is from realistic drama or romantic melodrama. Its material is the most objective of which music is capable. It will not translate, without adulteration, into anything but musical feelings. Only harm comes from a literary or visual description—harm and obscurity, with dashes of insight."

If Blackmur had his own music criticism in mind when he wrote that last sentence, he perhaps overestimated the harm. His reviews would have led no one astray: his errors were few and easily corrigible. No, it was rather into obscurity that his shortcomings led him. One can almost measure the difficulty of his subject by the extravagance of his expression. And so in the *Capriccio* Stravinsky appears as a necromancer, raising himself from the dead: "The apparition is not of a ghost, it is not ornamental; it is a gestation, it is parturitive; flesh and blood is being born. The tissue is hard and erectile, there are difficulties of delivery. The labour of this music is full of agony and crying; it is the great labour which is the integration of a system of feelings" (5). And this in the essay that cautions against literary description!

At the same time, even here we find some of those saving dashes of insight that were mentioned as an afterthought. Stravinsky, we are told, treats the piano as "the supreme instrument of percussion, as if he made drums sing." (One can forgive a lot of turgid writing for a phrase like that!) Blackmur noted the superiority of the recorded version, conducted by Ansermet with the composer at the piano, over a recent concert performance by the Boston Symphony under Koussevitzky, with Sanromá as soloist. Whether or not he was right in his surmise that the difference was due to the phonographic medium itself, the suggestion is an interesting one: "The phonograph [may be] better for some music than the orchestra; it allows, perhaps, an easier access of concentrated attention on the small things of which music of this sort is made up." What he sensed, I think, was the chamber-like quality of Stravinsky's orchestration, which might well have been dissipated in the vastness of Symphony Hall, even if the precision of Ansermet and the composer had replaced the probable rhythmic slackness of Koussevitzky and his pianist. For Blackmur placed the *Capriccio* in the second of his three musical orders, along with the Beethoven of the quartets and the later Bartók (not to mention Sibelius!). He was anticipating a view, elaborated by later critics such as Virgil Thomson, of phonographic performance as especially appropriate for chamber music—and vice versa.

In the other essays as well, the dashes are numerous and the insights are keen. Blackmur's receptiveness to new music was admirable; yet he was not taken in by mere novelty. Thus, he enjoyed *Façade* but refused to take it seriously, even as parody (6). He got it just right when he described it as "music into which are recited poems by Edith Sitwell." That "into" was intentional, for he used it twice in trying to catch the essence of the impossible relationship of music and spoken text. Although he did not make the generalization, the trouble he found with *Façade* is one that sticks to almost all melodrama (in the technical sense of words spoken to music): "Certainly there is no merger. The words and music do a preposterous best to hinder each other." In the present instance, "If you try to listen to the poems . . . the music will irritate you, snare you, drag you away. If you try to listen to the music alone, the recited words race through the vivid percussion and somewhat starched rhythms, like a fire engine through orderly traffic. If you try to listen to both together . . . you will find no possible combination of the two distractions, which will permit you to do the two things at once. In short, you will be stung fore and aft at one and the same time." How, then, could he enjoy it? As pure burlesque, for "it has the capacity proper to good burlesque—the capacity to dig up the bawdy elements of the soul and then to set them off—among the solemn virtues—in a loud guffaw." His advice was salutary: "Face the music and let it happen. Or let it rip. Or whatever it is that you think it does. You will not be able to deny that it makes a magnificent disorderly house out of the dim salon of musical appreciation."

Satie was even better known than Walton as a musical parodist. Blackmur recognized an often ignored distinction among his satires (2). At his best, "Satie was a comic in chords and a wit in scales: some of his music brings up a burden of self-applause and then, suddenly, crackles with self-mockery, a self-mockery which is at once the destruction and the bitter apotheosis of the subject in the music." Here Blackmur placed the *Trois Pièces montées,* based on episodes from Rabelais. Unfortunately, "Satie was sometimes lazy and took his laughter easily." In *Je te veux—Valse lente,* "Satie deliberately resorts to the banal, perhaps, sinks into the vulgar for fun. Everything is candied. It is a lollipop this waltz, a very good all-day sucker, worth about a nickel." Here Satie's irony—if that was indeed his aim—does not quite work. One is left in doubt as to the real intention: "May be Satie was trying to write popular music, first-rate music-hall . . ."

There is a third Satie, "the Greek Satie," and this is the best of all. "In the *Gymnopédies* and in the *Socrate* there is the shyness and sweetness of genuine competence, and there is the modest simplicity of mastery . . . Here we may say that it is winged music and let it pass." Those judgments are so apt, and so aptly put, that we can forgive the windy sentences in between, which try to establish the content of the music as "the wisdom of human flesh, and flesh approximating nature." What Blackmur needed was a harsher mentor than Darrell, one who would have asked, pointing to such passages, "Just what does that mean? Where and how is it conveyed by the music?"

That mentor would have been pleased with the critique of the *Preludio a Cristóbal Colón,* for Blackmur discussed the work in terms of what he actually heard (1). Although he may have misunderstood Stokowski's attempted historical justification of Carrillo's microtones, he nevertheless recognized in them "the effect of what we hear constantly without knowing it, the life of machines around us." He elaborated that idea in a pun: this is music for "machined ears, ears adjusted at enormous pressure to intervals so minute as the sixteenth part of a tone," but it is also music for "machine-ridden nerves [that] makes the auditor conscious of many a rhythm to which he had privately, unknowingly, adjusted his flesh and nerves." It is thus experimental music, both in its reflection of the mechanical world and in its attempt to expand the capabilities of the human ear. Blackmur insisted on the value of the experiment, but he admitted its difficulties and limitations. Nevertheless, what is important in such an undertaking is "educating our sense, rather than adding to the sensibility of the heart. The heart will no doubt come later."

Blackmur was struck by the sheer sound of the microtonal ensemble, especially by "the amazing vibratility" (!) of the soprano voice, wordlessly singing in quarter-tones. Very acutely, and with sly (or unconscious?) humor, he ascribed to it "the free purity of the perfectly imagined musical saw." (In view of this fascination, and of the expressed confidence in the "heart" to come, I cannot forbear mentioning John Eaton's setting of Blackmur's "Mirage"—for a less serrate type of soprano—as a notable example of more recent microtonal composition.)

Blackmur's most successful piece of extended writing about music was "In the Godly Modes," subtitled "an appreciation of the Solesmes Gregorian Chant Recordings" (4). Here he expressed his delight in the sheer beauty of these remarkable performances, but at the same time questioned the propriety of his own aesthetic reaction. Blackmur was not a believer; yet it would be incorrect to call him a disbeliever. His attitude was rather that of a reverent non-believer.

(The man who dubbed himself a "Tory Anarchist" in politics might have approved of that religious label.) And so he took sympathetic note of the fact that the Roman Catholic Church had forbidden liturgical use of such records as early as 1910, "when the phonograph still squalled in swaddling clothes." But the reason for the interdiction was not the primitive quality of the recording. Blackmur understood what many fail to grasp: "Like folk-music, and perhaps like the greater symphonies, music of this character on records is a species of aesthetic sacrilege." That is a startling conjunction of musical types, but in each case the separation of the music from its proper occasion is an act of violence—although one that we now commit so frequently that we have almost ceased to recognize it for what it is. But Blackmur did: "The very notion of 'playing' [the chants], of picking them up here and there, and listening to them—or not listening to them—without sharing them, without taking an intimate part in their expression, is foreign to their essence and derogatory to their beauty. The chants were made by and for the congregation of the faithful; the records were made by the Victor Company and by them made for—whoso runs to buy." Plainsong is thus a prime example of Blackmur's third category of music, that which requires the audience's participation. Whereas his second order, as we have seen, finds in the phonograph an ideal medium of private performance, music of the third type demands a community of musicians and audience that only the proper setting can afford.

He compared his own reaction to the chants with a Catholic's response to a Buddhist ritual: "The perfection of experience is beyond him, his admiration, his sympathy, are nothing, because the experience is not his and may not be." Yet the non-believer can perhaps "gain something the early Catholic never had—a sense of the music as art." That can lead on the one hand to "emotional debauch"; on the other, to "the deepest possible form of artistic knowledge."

That knowledge, he cautioned, would come only if the music was approached "with all the intelligence on the stretch." Blackmur stretched his, and produced a moving appreciation of an anonymous, communal art. "There is not the anonymity of an individual or the community of a polity; it is the anonymity of a living church, the community of its congregation in prayer. For these chants deal with man in the arms of God." He realized that in an important sense they

were not composed—even though "no doubt individuals both perfected what they found and invented what did not exist . . . On the
other hand, it is as true and more important that it was not individuals
who made them live or gave them meaning. They grew like a language
with subtle and profound accretions of meaning out of the necessities
of common use. . . . Hence we think of these chants as incorporating
the spiritual form of a civilization where the energy of man burst into
emotion and the emotion was religious aspiration . . ."

In their anonymous and communal character, Blackmur compared the chants to the great cathedrals by which "they had been
replaced as the supreme mode of human expression." When one sees
those buildings, "the sensibilities are exhilarated to the same degree
and in much the same way as by the music of the earlier chants which
filled them." Blackmur's lack of historical precision can be forgiven:
after all, who in those days except scholarly specialists knew anything
of Romanesque and Gothic polyphony? What is important is the
comprehension displayed, both of the aesthetic aspect of religion and
of the religious aspect of art—as well as of the troublesome concept
of religious art. Blackmur was inspired by the chants, which obviously
moved him more deeply than any of the other music under consideration; and he communicated his feelings simply and eloquently.

The one book Blackmur reviewed for the magazine was a peculiar assignment. Milton Metfessel's *Phonophotography in Folk Music*
(Chapel Hill, 1928) was an early contribution to ethnomusicology. It
was a compilation of Black folk songs, specific renditions of which had
been graphed for comparison and further study. As Blackmur pointed
out (3), such a graph is not music; it is a sort of score in reverse. Not
only that: "It goes further. It is a mode of physical analysis of a
particular production. It describes how a given singer, Jones, sang a
particular song, X, on a specified date." Blackmur rightly saw that
abstractions of this kind added little to the understanding of the
music. "But," he added, "it may very well be that the mode of
description here outlined would be of use in the secondary art of the
performer and in the tertiary art of the recorder." At this point his
essay took leave of the book and embarked on an interesting speculation: "Why are some singers bad on the records and some good? and
why, further, do some mediocre singers reproduce better on a record
or over the radio than in a concert hall with *viva voce?*" Perhaps the

Metfessel graphs might be of help here by providing singers with an objective basis for analyzing and improving their recorded sound. Blackmur, however, believed and apparently even hoped that such an experiment would fail; for the performer needs constantly to remember that, despite its technological side, recorded singing is after all an art—related to, but not identical with, the art of actual singing. Like any other art, it demands "the effort of the performer to submit to his instrument, to realize that in a sense his instrument is his master, in the sense, that is, that it imposes conditions on the art which when recognized improve the quality of the art itself." In the long run it is useless to depend on the perfection of the mechanism of recording to produce superlative quality: "The onus of perfect work falls on the performer; he is saddled with the necessity for what many people mildly call genius but what is more effectively called *class.*" That was obviously a term that Blackmur loved, for he shaped his whole essay in order to give it prominence. Class, as he explained it, was not confined to art; it was even more at home in sport. "It is what, other things being equal, makes one man win. Dempsey had class and his successors did not. Sarasate and Pablo Casals have class: the composers they play did not need it. Everybody knows what class is, but nobody knows what it consists of; that is they know what it is by direct experience alone." Class, unlike virtuosity, cannot be taught by pedagogy, only by example; it might better be said to be transmitted.

Today the word in that sense has fallen out of use, partly because of its unfavorable connotations in other contexts. Now we are more likely to talk about "style," but that is not quite the same thing. A loser can have style; that is why not every loser is a failure. Only the winner, as Blackmur pointed out, has class. It is thus not for everyone. Today, therefore, the concept would be considered an "elitist" one. That is another reason why the word is now avoided—and why Blackmur, were he alive today, would continue to rejoice in it.

By now one may well have come to wonder at the temerity of the young critic, utterly untrained in music, who was yet willing to take on the tasks outlined above. But such boldness remained a persistent characteristic of the mature Blackmur as well. Something of the same sort of daring enabled him to undertake close critical readings of books originally written in languages he knew only imperfectly, or not at all. He was excoriated for the occasional blunders that resulted, but his insights—no mere dashes—were nevertheless profound.

Blackmur took chances, yes—but he could afford to because his venturesome opinions were based on an unusually reliable intuition. Shortly after the publication of *The Heart of the Matter,* I happened to accompany him to a party. During a discussion of Greene's novel, he was asked his opinion of the review that had recently appeared in *Time.* He responded knowledgeably and convincingly, evoking nods of assent from his charmed auditors. But I knew better. When we left, I accused him: "Richard! you haven't read that novel!"

He admitted I was right.

"You've never seen the *Time* review."

I was right again.

"Then how could you take those people in like that?"

The characteristic mischievous twinkle in his eye accompanied his answer. "I didn't have to read the book or the review. I knew what the novel would be like and I knew what *Time* would say about it."

NOTES

Parenthetical references refer to the following pieces by R. P. Blackmur in *The Phonograph Monthly Review:*

1. "Quarter-Tones," IV/9 (June 1930), 313–14.
2. "Erik Satie—Three Men in a Tub," IV/10 (July 1930), 351.
3. "That Matter of Class," IV/12 (September 1930), 430–31.
4. "In the Godly Modes," V/2 (November 1930), 45.
5. "Necromancy," V/4 (January 1931), 121–22.
6. "Guffaw," V/7 (April 1931), 224–25.

DENIS DONOGHUE

Blackmur on
Henry James

I

In 1921, at the age of seventeen, Richard Blackmur went along to the
Cambridge Public Library to read, for the first time, something by
Henry James. *The Portrait of a Lady* was out, so he settled for *The
Wings of the Dove:*

> Long before the end I knew a master had laid hands on me. The beauty
> of the book bore me up; I was both cool and waking; excited and
> effortless; nothing was any longer worthwhile and everything had be-
> come necessary.[1]

Blackmur doesn't say what, according to that inclusive formula, was
no longer worthwhile: perhaps he meant everything he had already
read or, in his isolation, tried to write. The everything that now
became necessary is equally unspecified: he may have meant the
vocation of being, as James so evidently was, a writer, a critic, consum-
mately an artist. Blackmur was already moving toward a quirky career
as an artist of some homemade, self-taught, hand-me-down variety. It
might have been said of him, even then, as several years later he said
of James, that he "had in his style and perhaps in the life which it
reflected an idiosyncrasy so powerful, so overweening, that to many
it seemed a stultifying vice, or at least an inexcusable heresy" (20).

In any case it was James, rather than Hardy or Conrad, who laid
hands on Blackmur, an imposition he never ceased to feel and sometimes nearly resented. But for the first several years the hands were
felt as nothing but blessing. It was not enough to say that James was

21

an artist, unless the designation carried the emphasis James gave it, in one of his last letters to Henry Adams, when he called himself "that queer monster, the artist, an obstinate finality, an inexhaustible sensibility." James was, as Blackmur said, "completely the artist," he was "so utterly given up to his profession that he was free of the predicament of the artist the moment he began to write." So much so "that he seems to inhabit another world, that other world which has as substance what for us is merely hoped for" (70). Hoped for, I assume, as we hope for values, convictions, principles, and orders commensurate with the disorders they confront.

It is clear from Blackmur's essay on James's *Prefaces* to the New York edition of the novels—his first essay on James, published in 1934—that he was already a Jamesian on principle as well as at heart. "Criticism has never been more ambitious, nor more useful" (15), he said of the *Prefaces*, without measuring the ambition or laboring the use. The ambition consisted in providing for the art of fiction a set of principles sufficient to strengthen writer and reader in the conviction of serious interests pursued in common. The use consisted in giving readers a critical stance, a vocabulary at once technical, executive, and descriptive, adequate to the issues a novel is likely to raise.

Blackmur admired the use as he warmed to the ambition. James's themes seemed to him the right ones, and good enough to sustain the largest demand upon the novel as implying a form and defining a vocation. Three themes in particular (95–96). The first is "the international theme," which in practice means the contentious bearing of America and Europe. The second is "the theme of the artist in conflict with society," a theme usefully exacerbated by the consideration that while the artist in one light is only an extreme instance of the ordinary individual, in another the man most fully an artist is the man, "short of the saint, most wholly deprived" (88). What he is deprived of amounts sometimes to failure in the art; at other times, when the artist's vision disappears in his work, what seems privation in yet another light doesn't matter. The third theme, that of "the pilgrim in search of society," runs beside the second. Together they make James's work add up to "a great single anarchic rebellion against society—against the laws of society—in the combined names of decency, innocence, candor, good will, and the passionate heroism of true vocation" (110). Alluding to the elder Henry James's book, *Society the Redeemed Form of Man*, Blackmur said that "both Jameses were basic dissenters to all except the society that was not yet; and in both cases the rebellion or dissent was merely eccentric or extravagant in life and manners, but central and poetic in work and insight" (110).

What James did with these themes was his transformation of the novel. "In 1881," as Blackmur said, "with the publication of *The Portrait of a Lady*, the European novel as a form became part of the resources of the English language, and James himself a great novelist, for in that novel his three major themes were for the first time combined in a single objective form" (96). "The James novel," the particular kind of thing he made, became a form as integrated, and as variable within its constitution, as the Shakespearean sonnet. Formally, James turned "not only the English novel but also the French and Russian novel from something relatively loose and miraculous to something relatively tight and predictable" (121). As for the reader of a James novel: he "learns a new game which, as it seems to partake of actual experience, he can take for truth; and which, as it shows a texture of sustained awareness never experienced in life, he knows to be art." To gain that effect, "to make art truth, is the whole object of James's addiction to the forms of fiction; it was the only avenue to truth he could recognise" (122).

Blackmur did not always remain convinced by this game or these rules, but for the first several years of his addiction he never questioned that James's approach to the truth was valid, or that the truth arrived at was everything it ought to have been. He no more doubted those procedures than he doubted James's way, in detail, with words. It has often been maintained that James's later style is the proximate cause of Blackmur's, the quirks of one inciting those of the other. In fact, there is no single cause of either. But it was James who showed Blackmur what riches would drop into his lap if he trusted words enough and lavished enough attention upon them. Think of the attention James lavished upon the word "humbug" in *The Golden Bowl*, or the word "incentive" in nearly any context in which it arose; and then of what Blackmur did with the word "tamper" in his essay

on *The Portrait of a Lady*, which becomes "tamperage"—I'm not sure
that the word otherwise exists—in a comment on *Washington
Square;* or with "incentive" when the theme was *The Tragic Muse*
and the figure in question Gabriel Nash—"He had begun brilliant,
the namesake of incentive and possibility and unaffixed freedom, and
indeed of everything good unless by chance you took it seriously; but
he became bored and boring when commitment showed" (206).

It is evident that Blackmur decided, early on, what kind of work
a novel or a story by James was. His sense of the particular kind was
restrictive: he thought it fulfilled only in part and up to a point by
The Spoils of Poynton, What Maisie Knew, and *The Awkward Age*
and completely and wonderfully by *The Portrait of a Lady, The Ambassadors, The Wings of the Dove,* and *The Golden Bowl.* Among
the stories it was exemplified by "The Altar of the Dead," "The
Lesson of the Master," "The Bench of Desolation"; by, in all, "some
fifteen or twenty tales as well as six or seven novels" (113). Not by
The Princess Casamassima or *The Bostonians,* in which James had
plunged himself "into centers of human conduct and motivation and
obsession—into conditions of behavior—of which he was only superficially aware." In those two novels, according to Blackmur, James
"tried to make what he could see stand for what he could not"
(117–18), an attempt doomed by the scale of both projects. The
higher valuation of both novels, as proposed by Lionel Trilling and
other critics, left Blackmur cold, but mainly, I think, because he had
already decided that a James novel differed significantly from a Conrad novel, and that James should have respected the difference and
settled for his limitations.

Assuming, then, that Blackmur had his own idea, however restrictive, of a Jamesian novel, and that he would not be persuaded to
extend it, we can list its attributes. Blackmur was particularly edified
that James always entrusted the matter in hand to someone's sense
of it. It followed that the meaning of an experience is always to be
found between someone's ignorance and his knowledge, or between
someone's partial sense of it and the perfection of his knowledge,
which might well be purely theoretic or virtual. "What he wrote
about was always present in someone's specific knowledge of it" (19).
Hence in James's fiction the relation between intelligibility and form

is always given as a personal relation. "Thickness is in the human consciousness that records and amplifies" (28). This procedure not only kept the fiction actual and human, but made sure that every question would return to its personal consequence. No merely theoretic possibility would float free from a personal implication.

The procedure would have this further merit, that James could keep the definition of self at full stretch, even to the extent of showing a second self haunting the first. Nobody should be forced to coincide with himself, or to confess in practice where precisely he began and ended. I think this explains Blackmur's special feeling for James's tales of the supernatural. He insisted that the ghost stories would hold no interest for the Society for Psychical Research. James "had no access to and no imaginative interest in the supernatural; his ghosts were invariably the hallucinated apparitions of the obsessions that governed or threatened, or as we say haunted the men and women whose stories he told" (48). As such, they appealed to Blackmur's own unsupernatural sense of hallucination and obsession. He was always drawn to think of something in immediate relation to some unofficial form of it; to the first self in obsessive or haunted relation to a second. So, in an essay on *The Sacred Fount,* Blackmur described conscience as "the created other self of the hallucinated intelligence" (66). In a comment on "The Private Life" he makes much of the scene in which Clare Vawtry's true self is secretly writing the works of genius while the visible figure, Vawtry the second-rate man, is engaged in a social world of sustained boredom and pointlessness. It is typical of Blackmur, too, that he finds the most telling forces a little aside from—or underneath—the places where we have been schooled to find them. Emphasizing that James always struggled to use the conventions of society, and to abuse them when necessary, Blackmur explained that the struggle was always "to bring himself directly upon the emotion that lay under the conventions, coiling and recoiling, ready to break through" (92). There is always, in each of us, the old mole in the cellar. So it was gratifying to Blackmur to say that even when we speak well "we speak with voices not our own saying more than we knew we meant, and with a form—a style—into which we seem to have broken through, as into raw air" (163).

II

In 1940 Blackmur signed a contract to write a book on Henry James. In the event, he didn't write it. One reason was that his loyalties were divided between James and Adams: he didn't complete his book on Adams, but he worked on it more assiduously than he worked on the James. Both projects suffered from a disability, that Blackmur's mind was not qualified for the long haul; it worked best on essays, forays, interventions. But I think there was another consideration. Much as Blackmur admired James, his admiration yielded to moods and circumstances, changing emphases and affiliations. In his later years he made demands upon James's fiction which no fiction could sustain; it was as if he wanted the novels to live his life for him, and foisted upon them the needs he couldn't otherwise have expressed. I think this accounts for the change of emphasis which amounts almost to a change of mind when the subject was *The Golden Bowl*. Blackmur published two essays on that novel, an Introduction to the Grove Press edition (1952) and another for the Laurel Henry James Series (1963). He also included paragraphs on *The Golden Bowl* in three essays on more general topics. I shall run through the various commentaries to show how Blackmur's general relation to James changed, and how his different readings of *The Golden Bowl* provide an index or a graph of the change. But I begin with a few considerations to represent a fairly common sense of the novel and a stable context of reference. The book has provoked readers to lively disagreement, I am aware, but this is not an occasion for insistence. Nothing especially original or contentious is intended.

The Golden Bowl is often interpreted as a story of the triumph of good over evil. I would prefer to shift the viewpoint somewhat and read it as a story about innocence deciding, under the provocation of fear and misgiving, to take every risk of knowledge; and, in the second part, of this knowledge deciding not to drive its lucidity to the end of the line. The crucial issue is the cost of knowledge, which is not merely the loss of innocence.

The story is mainly Maggie Verver's, counterpointed in diverse relations to her father Adam Verver, her husband the Italian Prince Amerigo, and Charlotte Stant who has become Adam Verver's wife without ceasing to be Amerigo's mistress. There are also the Assing-hams, Fanny who is Maggie's *confidante,* and her husband Bob who keeps Fanny steady by listening to the much she has to say. Maggie, to whom the adjective "little" is persistently attached until she out-grows it, is the lady of silences, to begin with: her deepest relation—to her father—is such that it doesn't require much speech and thrives on taking everything for granted. Maggie is determined to know everything about her husband and Charlotte, now that she has started on that track. Of her father, we are only allowed to guess that at some point he comes to know most of what needs to be known and has his own imperiously silent way of dealing with the knowledge. His deter-minations are private even when, at the end, he acts upon them in favor, yet again, of Maggie, and removes himself and Charlotte to America. Charlotte bears something of the relation to Mary Crawford in *Mansfield Park* that Maggie bears, to begin with, to Fanny Price. Charlotte has always gone in for knowledge and for acting upon it, magnificently to all appearances; but in the end she is pitched into bewilderment, since she isn't allowed to discover how much Maggie knows of the affair with Amerigo. She makes the best of her bewilder-ment by pretending to turn it into spirit and determination. The Prince has never been innocent—he is not a Roman for nothing—and his story is one of suddenly realizing that there is infinitely more to little Maggie—to Maggie as she has become—than he has ever al-lowed to meet his eye. Seeing her now, he sees nothing else. His affair with Charlotte was never much, even to begin with, but it was more than his marriage to Adam Verver's treasured daughter.

What complicates this account is the impurity of Maggie's in-tention, when it represents itself as an intention provoked by knowl-edge. She senses the relation between knowledge and power, and feels the excitement of knowing in secret far more than she is supposed to know. She is tempted to act, with full dramatic effect, in the light of that knowledge. When she has won, she knows everything she thinks she needs to know. She chooses not to drive her victory beyond that point, or to torment herself by fixing her mind upon the imagery of her husband's adultery. She retains him, and holds him in her power, while letting the abyss alone.

That is to say: Maggie becomes herself, or a new self, by accept-ing the limitations of knowledge that is neither demonic nor angelic.

She does not demand perfection or insist upon ultimacy: she is ready to settle, in the end, for the smallest degree of victory consistent with its being victory at all. Anything less would be defeat, which she knows she has not deserved. It is a mark of her strength—and it is what the Prince now sees with his eyes opened as strength—that she doesn't insist upon the unconditional surrender and disclosure she might have exacted from him and from Charlotte. She confronts the Prince, but gives him plenty of room to breathe if not quite to escape. Charlotte she doesn't confront at all. Maggie is ready to live in the abeyance of punishment.

Our response to Maggie is partly ensured by our dealings with Adam Verver and with Fanny Assingham. We take Maggie at her father's sublime valuation, to begin with, even allowing for the extent to which it is natural for him to find her innocence and her contained silence quite wonderful. There is nothing sinister in that relation. We take Maggie, too, as everything Fanny wouldn't even think of being: silent, contained, unmeddling. Fanny lives in speech and interference, as Maggie in silent appreciations. Fanny's overt life, married to Bob, is a solid thing: she keeps it stirred by imagining crimes she wouldn't herself commit; and by relishing criminal relations, so long as they are not absolutely lethal to anyone she cares for. Her assertion to her husband— "Just so what is morality but high intelligence?"[2]—is a theatrical vivacity, justified only by the consideration that a morality maintained by being stupid isn't worth having. She doesn't expound the further consideration that the ground common to morality and intelligence, if you hold them to that degree in common, can only be a sense of the beautiful. Blackmur deals with this issue differently by saying of James that "having no adequate tradition to fall back on for morals (values) or ethics (decision or judgment), he had to make the intelligence do for both, had to make it do as the equivalent of order and law in operation; and, not finding enough of intelligence in the world, he had to create it, and in creating it, had to put it in conflict with facts and stupidities it could not face without choice." For to James, Blackmur says, "the height of intelligence was choice; intelligence was taste in action, and the utmost choice taste could make was the choice to live or die" (*Studies*, 115–16). But even if we give remarkable emphasis to "live" and "die" in that sentence, it must make a difference that the exponent of this view, in *The Golden Bowl*, is

Fanny Assingham, who is chiefly known by her meddling—with good if not the best of intentions, admittedly—and by the lurid character of what she takes pleasure in imagining. It is entirely possible to be both intelligent and monstrous: it is not the degree of intelligence that is in question but the quality and direction of its interests, what in the multiplicity of things it chooses to care about.

If we start with *The Golden Bowl* as a story of adultery and deceit, we should be willing to go far beyond the considerations which would make that description at all adequate. If we start with Charlotte as a villain, insistently the demanding "other woman," we should recognize how inadequate the formula is to cover her particular way of being alive. If we think of the book as a story of innocence choosing to go beyond itself and to learn whatever is to be learnt, we find our interest settling upon the issue of the cost, in feelings and lives, of the decision that makes knowledge possible. Caroline Gordon once described Maggie Verver as "the richest and the most fairy-like of James's dream creatures, the arch-priestess of glamor, the mistress of legerdemain," and went on to say that "her particular legerdemain is the converting of 'lower' into 'higher' simply by preserving the beauty of appearances."[3] It is a perceptive thing to say, but we are left in dread if not appalled by everything the deliberate preservation entails. I am not sure I could offer to distinguish between the preservation of appearances and the decision to leave the abyss alone; unless I could say that the second is merely a decision to rub along as best one can without being particularly intelligent about it, and the first makes a far larger claim, that the aesthetic sense is more refined than the moral sense and rightly supersedes it.

During the years in which Blackmur was engaged with James's three last novels, critics argued about them, in part, on the basis of the interpretation which Quentin Anderson outlined in "Henry James and the New Jerusalem," an essay in *The Kenyon Review*, Autumn 1946, and developed in his *The American Henry James* (1957). The gist of the interpretation is that *The Ambassadors*, *The Wings of the Dove*, and *The Golden Bowl* constitute an allegory in fulfillment of the elder Henry James's philosophy—a mixture of Swedenborg and Fourier. I mention the interpretation not to do it justice, but to remark that it left Blackmur indifferent, though it greatly interested F. R. Leavis, Francis Fergusson, and other critics. Blackmur regarded criticism as the formal discourse of an amateur, and he thought nothing of biographical, psychological, or philosophical lore in its presumed bearing upon novels and poems: diversions, at best. What he brought to the reading of a novel consisted of his general sense of life, and his particular sense of language and of the other literature it secreted. Reading a poem, the best preparation you could make was to fill your mind with other poems, and let the most telling relations come forward from that store.

I don't know when Blackmur first read *The Golden Bowl.* His first commentary on it turns up in an essay of larger spread, "In the Country of the Blue" (1943), where the theme is James's imagination and the conditions it had to meet. At that point Blackmur had no doubt that the book was a story of the triumph of good over evil, the cost not being reckoned. He speaks of *The Ambassadors* and *The Golden Bowl* together, and of Lambert Strether and Maggie Verver as "triumphing precisely over the most mutilating conditions of life that could well have come their way." The triumph—and here Blackmur includes Herbert Dodd in "The Bench of Desolation"—consisted "in the gradual inward mastery of the outward experience, a poetic mastery which makes of the experience conviction" (*Studies,* 72). Blackmur doesn't, at that stage, bring the question beyond the achievement of conviction: one's victory is sufficient, apparently, if it is sufficiently inward and makes for conviction. There is no allusion to the cost, or even to the fear that contact with mutilation is likely to deface the one who triumphs over it.

In "Henry James" (1948) Blackmur still thought of Maggie as triumphing apparently at no cost to herself. In *The American* (1877) and *The Portrait of a Lady* (1881), Christopher Newman and Isabel Archer are victimized by Europe, and while they are intact at the end they are also left shrunk: "their strength was in the strength to renounce." But in *The Wings of the Dove* (1902) and *The Golden Bowl* (1904), Milly Theale and Maggie Verver triumph over the Europe that has abused them, triumph "by the positive strength of character and perceptive ability which their experience of treachery only brings out." Neither Milly's death nor Maggie's re-creation of her adulterous marriage "is an act of renunciation or disillusion; they are deliberate acts of life fully realized and fully consented to, done because it is necessary to keep intact the conviction that life has values greater than any renunciation can give up or any treachery soil" (*Studies*, 114). These novels become pilgrimages in reverse: the American girls, all candor, innocence, and loyalty, have to be seen as redeeming old corrupt Europe, if the values to which James's imagination testifies are to prevail. But Blackmur's sense of those novels depends upon our giving "life," in that sentence, a value endlessly emphatic, if it is to hold out without deformity against every threatening condition.

What happened to Blackmur's sense of these matters after 1948, I can't even guess, but the account he gives of *The Golden Bowl* in "The Loose and Baggy Monsters of Henry James" (1951) is for the first time rueful. It begins innocently enough. When Maggie comes to divine what the relation between her husband and Charlotte has been and persists in being, she reverses her role:

> Out of her changed goodness and innocence—no less good and no less changed—she draws the power to make something tragically good and ultimately innocent of the two marriages. The sacrifice that she makes is that she renounces the old ground of her beseeching—the aspiration of her innocence, candor, energy, the innocence of her money—and stands on the new and terrible ground of the conditions of life itself. (*Studies*, 133)

But as if Blackmur couldn't bear to see Maggie standing there, he gives her Dante's privilege. She is "as near the exemplar as James could come to our lady of theology or divine wisdom; she is James's creation nearest to Dante's Beatrice, stern and full of charity, the rock itself but all compassion, in the end knowing all but absorbing all she knows into her predetermined self, not exactly lovable but herself love" (134). Having gone so far, Blackmur had to draw back: the comparison was outlandish, after all. What Maggie lacked—what made the comparison outlandish—was the conviction of unity:

> Maggie has the kind of imperiousness that goes with the deepest waywardness, the waywardness that is the movement of life itself; but she has no capacity for exerting the imperium itself except in aspiration. There is too much fear in her: she feels too much of her new knowledge as chill; she is too much there to be preyed on; she is too much an ideal

ever to take on full power. But she does a great deal just the same; if by her goodness and innocence she cannot make other people good, she can yet by that goodness breed their wrong. (135–36)

But this removes Maggie from Dante and from Shakespeare's last plays—in which the heroes defeat the conditions they have to confront by forgiving those who have submitted to them—and keeps the removal going till it ends up in *Measure for Measure,* where goodness can with at least a show of reason be cited as breeding Angelo's wrong. Blackmur quotes, as if to justify his appalled perception, the dreadful scene—Book II, Chapter 30—in which Maggie explains to Fanny that she has driven Amerigo and Charlotte to move among the two dangers, "that of their doing too much and that of their not having any longer the confidence, or the nerve, or whatever you may call it, to do enough." Upon which, smiling, Maggie says: "And that's how I make them do what I like!" (II, 119–20). Surely such a person, even though she claims that whatever she does she does "for love," can't escape in herself the havoc she causes in others. Blackmur doesn't quite say this.

But he says it in his formal essay for the Grove Press edition of the book (1952). Amerigo and Charlotte "create a lie between themselves which will separate them ocean-wide forever." But Maggie as the agent of this necessity doesn't fare any better. She "accepts life with a conviction so violent that it breaks her to pieces and, at the last moment we see her, is unable to look in her husband's eyes at the cost of the life and loyalty her conviction has created there." These agents of truth and lies and havoc—Lambert Strether, Milly Theale, Maggie—"are indeed dread shades into which, with their creations in the lives and loves of their victims, they dissolve, leaving only a vital or a mortal pang, vital as beauty, mortal as incentive, when set upon by the evil that springs in the dusk of life" (*Studies,* 150). It is not that the good perishes but that it persists only as essence or ideal and always removed from the conditions that abused it.

The incentive of this emphasis—to resort to James's word and to Blackmur's—is, so far as the perception is in question, the passage in the *Purgatorio* (XXI:133–36)—

> Or puoi la quantitate
> comprender dell'amor ch'a te mi scalda,
> quando dismento nostra vanitate,
> trattando l'ombre come cosa salda.

—where the shade of the poet Statius has tried to embrace Virgil, and Virgil reminds him gently that "you are but a shadow, and a shadow only is what you see." Statius answers, in the lines quoted: "Now you may comprehend the measure of the love that burns in me for you, when I forget our emptiness and treat shades as solid things." Blackmur quoted the passage in "The Loose and Baggy Monsters of Henry James," but got it wrong—attributing the words to Virgil rather than to Statius. The translation he favored in that essay takes *l'ombre* as "images" (*Studies*, 138). In the Grove Press introduction to *The Golden Bowl* Blackmur refers to the same passage, and gives it in English as: "Now you may understand the measure of the love that warms me toward you, when I forget our nothingness and treat shades as solid things" (*Studies*, 151–52). In either translation, the motif is apt, because it allows Blackmur to suggest the cost of Maggie's triumph. The dictionaries say that a shade is "the visible but impalpable form of a dead person, a ghost," and the *O.E.D.* refers to Coleridge's line: "Shades of the Past, which Love makes substance." In Blackmur's terms, Maggie might have spoken Dante's words either to her father or her husband: and the "words would have been apter still" if father or husband had spoken them to Maggie. "The shade was the only actual." Or, a few pages later, "The life she could not create, the shade she could" (157). It doesn't matter that Fanny Assingham smashed the golden bowl or that Maggie went through the motions of taking up the pieces and miming the possible, impossible act of fitting them together again. She is already a shade. In the final scene of the novel, when Adam Verver and Charlotte have left for America, Amerigo and Maggie embrace:

> It kept him before her therefore, taking in—or trying to—what she so wonderfully gave. He tried, too clearly, to please her—to meet her in her own way; but with the result only that, close to her, her face kept before him, his hands holding her shoulders, his whole act enclosing her, he presently echoed: " 'See'? I see nothing but *you.* " And the truth

of it had, with this force, after a moment, so strangely lighted his eyes that, as for pity and dread of them, she buried her own in his breast. (II, 377)

Pity and dread, in James as in Aristotle, are the cost of whatever triumph the audience sees the tragic hero achieving. It is a question of the relation, which is bound to vary among individuals, between the constituents of the tragic experience. Amerigo and Maggie make yet another "recognition scene," in which Amerigo dissolves everything he sees in what Maggie sees, and there is for him no remainder. What Maggie sees is the cost, the mutilation, hence the pity and dread. Blackmur says:

> Surely this mode of love grew out of moral beauty and high conscience, but as Maggie applied it, it required the sacrifice of life itself till nothing but the created shade was left.

It is, he says, "a shade embracing a shade" (160).

Blackmur's last essay on *The Golden Bowl* (1963) was darker still. Now everything that Maggie does is seen as done regardless of cost and for the satisfaction of a murderous logic. Blackmur makes much of the great scene—book II, chapter 36—in which Maggie watches, in the smoking-room, her father, Charlotte, Amerigo, and Fanny Assingham playing bridge. Bob Assingham is apart, writing letters. In her mind, Maggie is playing these people as if they were cards in her hand. She thrills to the possibility of confounding them by revealing what she knows:

> There reigned for her, absolutely, during these vertiginous moments, that fascination of the monstrous, that temptation of the horribly possible, which we so often trace by its breaking out suddenly, lest it should go further, in unexplained retreats and reactions. (II, 239–40)

She thinks of herself "as the scapegoat of old, of whom she had once seen a terrible picture," who had been "charged with the sins of the people and had gone forth into the desert to sink under his burden and die." She would not be required or urged to die, but to live on and prove to the others that they had escaped and that "she was still there to simplify." Maggie goes out to the terrace, still watching the players, and wondering why she has been able "to give herself so little, from the first, to the vulgar heat of her wrong"—the straight vindictive view, "the rights of resentment, the rages of jealousy, the protests of passion." These rights seem to her as lurid as "a wild eastern caravan, looming into view with crude colours in the sun, fierce pipes in the air, high spears against the sky, all a thrill, a natural joy to mingle with, but turning off short before it reached her and plunging into other defiles" (II, 241–43).

There is more, but this is enough to suggest what Blackmur meant by saying of the scene on the terrace that it "converts both the symbolic actions of the bowl and the image of the pagoda and the actions of love and marriage into actions of the Psyche, that human Psyche who, as Santayana somewhere puts it, after having surrendered everything insists that she has lost nothing." It is, he continues, "one of those lies by which we extend ourselves beyond humanity and degrade the humanity of others." Blackmur now sees Maggie's actions as in every respect—except their intention—destructive. "She makes everybody—Amerigo, Charlotte, her father, herself—do the wrong things for the right reasons." She sends her father and Charlotte packing to American City, "her husband and herself to what I would take to be the horrible adultery of incompatible isolation." This is the tragedy, Blackmur says, "of those who desert their own values for the sake of the principle (often mistaken for the ideal) which they thought had established the values, but which in the event dumbfounded them." Otherwise put: "There is the tragedy: one is driven to what is not necessary by thinking of necessity" (*Studies*, 224–28).

Blackmur's Grove Press essay on *The Golden Bowl* had Dante in mind on every page. The second and last essay had T. S. Eliot, especially the poet of "Ash-Wednesday," which Blackmur asked his readers of *The Golden Bowl* to read in advance and for no specified reason, stopping for meditation on these lines from the second section:

> The single Rose
> Is now the Garden
> Where all loves end
> Terminate torment
> Of love unsatisfied
> The greater torment
> Of love satisfied . . .

Dante is pervasively in Eliot's lines, especially—as A. D. Moody has shown—through the figure of Beatrice perfected in the *Vita Nuova;* the preoccupation with renunciation and transformation; the radiance of love seen in relation to its final cause and to nothing less. The torment of love unsatisfied hardly needs a comment. Love satisfied makes a greater torment still because it keeps the soul locked in time and removed from its final cause; immersion in the "low dream" removes anyone's desire for the "high dream," and makes the worst of torments when recognized for the privation it incurs. The passage which includes the lines makes a chant, leading the soul to substitute a higher for a lower viewpoint, as from "torn" to "most whole." Their bearing upon *The Golden Bowl* is, I surmise, that what Maggie has never had and can't now have is the aspiration which has Dante and Eliot as guides, the *Vita Nuova* for text, and the "Lady" of "Ash-Wednesday" for final cause. Such love would indeed turn shades into substance, which is the reverse of what Maggie does. Maggie's love is satisfied in the mundane sense that it has removed the obstacles which have beset it: Charlotte, Amerigo's intrigue with her, his need of her. But the end of the book forces the reader to feel that for Maggie now there is only the greater torment, to be felt as lack, such that the very obstacles will turn out to have been missed.

But there is a bizarre fact, too. Blackmur's last words on *The Golden Bowl* are so powerfully and movingly phrased that it hardly matters that they are wrong; as indeed they are. It is not true that Maggie represents the Psyche who after having surrendered everything insists that she has lost nothing. Quite the reverse. The last thing she has wanted to do is to give anything up. In the scene in which she watches her father and the others playing bridge, she rehearses what it would feel like to make a scene, but the narrative has this to say after the rehearsal:

> It was extraordinary: they positively brought home to her that to feel about them in any of the immediate, inevitable, assuaging ways, the ways usually open to innocence outraged and generosity betrayed, would have been to give them up, and that giving them up was, marvellously, not to be thought of. (II, 244)

Indeed, Maggie's tragedy consists in her wanting and failing to reconcile incompatible desires: not to give anybody up; not to punish anybody; to have it known to her husband what indeed she knows; to have her father entirely innocent of such knowledge; to have Charlotte punished only to the extent of being bewildered by not knowing; to ensure that her actions—Maggie's, I mean—are at every moment embodiments of the highest principle.

III

If Blackmur was wrong, in the end, about *The Golden Bowl*, the explanation is, I think, that he gradually developed a sense of James's work as a whole which required him to set many of its parts aslant or askew. There were misgivings from the start, or from as early as "In the Country of the Blue." Blackmur knew that James couldn't have done his work at all without immense faith in his powers; but he thought for such faith, such immensity, one paid a price. It is possible for an artist to be too certain for the good of his art. Besides, Blackmur was temperamentally far more attuned to the mind that doubts itself, vacillates, sees so many sides of a question that it can't repose on one. He liked minds that drift and waver. Montaigne was, I now think, his chief of men: what he couldn't cope with, in Henry Adams, was Adams's insistence on knowing the result in advance of the enquiry. "Only the steady supplication of doubt," Blackmur said in "In the Country of the Blue," "the constant resolution of infirmity, can exercise your values and your principles enough to give them, together, that stretch and scope which is their life." As James's faith in himself increased, "he came less and less to make *fictions* of people and more and more to make *fables*, to draw parables, for the ulterior purposes of his faith." Only the habit of a born novelist kept James from turning into the fabulist he seemed determined to become (*Studies*, 70).

Fable is the giveaway word. Blackmur always suspected the imagination which is content to make fables, parables, and allegories. Even the most poetic fable, Blackmur said in his essay on *The Sacred Fount*, "is supreme only by the way, in passing, in preparation for something else" (59). He meant, I think, that the fable is merely a formula, imaginative as it may well be, and that it allows me to apply it to the other fellow and hold myself exempt. Blackmur associated fables with principles which "fairly itch for action but have not yet run down into the skill of the hand that acts, that in this case writes" (80). The fable allows you to see a lot, but prevents you from seeing the rest and especially the bits that don't fit. So it was too readily available to an imagination such as James's, because James "as he never went backward into the full Christian tradition, but tapped his sense of what underlay it, so he never went back into the whole force of love, only into so much of it as could be conceived morally" (103).

Whatever this amounts to as disability on James's part, Blackmur felt it more generally of American literature as a whole. In his essay on Marianne Moore (1935) he developed his sense of her cultivated distaste, her quiet insistence on keeping reality at a distance, to the point of saying that she is in this a characteristic American. "Poe, Hawthorne, Melville (in *Pierre*), Emily Dickinson, and Henry James, all—like Miss Moore—shared an excessive sophistication of surfaces and a passionate predilection for the genuine—though Poe was perhaps not interested in too much of the genuine; and all contrived to present the conviction of reality best by making it, in most readers' eyes, remote."[4] The idea should have been worked out, I think: did these writers write in this way to make it clear to the readers that reality couldn't be possessed merely by reaching out a hand for it; or that between the reader and the reality in question there is always interposed the writer's imagination, and the more arduous the better?

I speculate; because Blackmur didn't develop his idea into a theory of American literature, I think he felt that American writers didn't know enough, or that they were complacent in thinking that what they didn't know could be floated on what they did. Irritated by *The Princess Casamassima* and *The Bostonians*, he said that James's repeated argument "that the artist should be released from the burden of things as they were ordinarily understood to happen, probably came from his ignorance of ordinary things in general" (*Studies*, 118). The fact that James's argument was in favor of the romance as an occasional resource and of Hawthorne's practice more specifically didn't count for much with Blackmur.

But I think I can be more precise about the occasion on which Blackmur's adherence to James became the intermittent and qualified sentiment we find in his later essays. In "The Loose and Baggy Monsters of Henry James" he quoted the famous passage in the preface to *The Tragic Muse* where James speaks of the necessity of what he calls composition:

> A picture without composition slights its most precious chance for beauty, and is moreover not composed at all unless the painter knows how that principle of health and safety, working as an absolutely premeditated art, has prevailed. There may in its absence be life, incontestably, as *The Newcomes* has life, as *Les Trois Mousquetaires,* as Tolstoi's *Peace and War,* have it; but what do such large loose baggy monsters, with their queer elements of the accidental and the arbitrary, artistically mean?[5]

That passage didn't trouble Blackmur when he read it for his essay on James's Prefaces (1934), but in "The Loose and Baggy Monsters of Henry James" (1951) it troubled him enough to make him insist that *War and Peace*—he wondered aloud about James's getting the title in reverse—has "every quality James here prescribes: composition, premeditation, deep-breathing economy and organic form, but has them in a different relation to executive form than any James would accept. Indeed,"—Blackmur went on to say—"put beside *War and Peace, The Ambassadors, The Wings of the Dove,* and *The Golden Bowl* are themselves 'large loose baggy monsters' precisely because an excess use was made of James's particular developments of executive form, and precisely because, too, of the consequent presence of James's own brand of the accidental and the arbitrary, and because these together make access difficult to James's own 'deep-breathing economy and an organic form' " (*Studies,* 129). In another context it would be necessary to explain Blackmur's distinction between executive form and theoretic form, but here and now it is enough to see that James's kind of fiction is taken as one of many kinds, and not as a privileged kind.

The easy part of the explanation is that by 1951 Blackmur had read far more novels, and novels having many more kinds of force, than he had read by 1934. The work gathered in *Eleven Essays on the European Novel* (1964) sufficiently makes the point. But Blackmur's misgiving about James was in one respect radical. In "Henry James" (1948) he referred to James's "final decision at full maturity that in the very passion of pleading for full life in others, for him life had to be sacrificed to art" (*Studies,* 93). It may be that James was too close to Art for Art's Sake for his own good, but in any case Blackmur suspected that in James himself there is a perverse instinct that "attaches itself to life as directly as a leech or a tick to your arm; it means to do something with life—even with the life that has slipped or been taken away—that will in the end seem to the actor triumphant and an act of love" (225). In yet other words:

> The pity and the dread indeed. Pity for the torment of love unsatisfied, dread for the greater torment of love satisfied, the turmoil and the waste. In Eliot's poem the phrases are part of a prayer for release from these torments. In *The Golden Bowl* the two torments are enacted as ends in themselves, and the greater torment as a supreme end worth any loss and any surrounding waste to attain. (229)

But when Blackmur says, in the same place, that "the temptation to annihilation in James's mode of love has only to be named to be at hand," he doesn't mean merely that James was imaginatively sympathetic to people who are willing to sacrifice life to a principle or an ideal supposed to transfigure it; but that some motive in James himself took sinister pleasure in seeing them do it.

IV

The pleasure is not further examined, possibly because Blackmur thought it would lead him out of the novels and into biographical or psychobiographical speculation. But the fact that he mentioned it at all suggests that the three last completed novels stayed in his mind as unitary evidence of some motive he didn't care further to trace. If this is so, it would account for the curious fact that Blackmur doesn't distinguish the three novels one from another: it is not that they make a trilogy but that he read them in the same spirit and as pointing to the same enabling or disabling condition. The discriminations which F. R. Leavis made, by which *The Golden Bowl* was retained as far superior to *The Ambassadors* for critically producible reasons, didn't occupy Blackmur's mind.

But even a cursory examination of the novels is enough to show that the pattern which Blackmur ascribed to the later James is far more evidently active in *The Ambassadors* and *The Wings of the Dove* than in *The Golden Bowl.* The spiritual majesty of renunciation—to call it that for the moment—is a telling motive in Lambert Strether, who sacrifices Madame de Vionnet and Maria Gostrey so that he can feel at ease with himself—"not, out of the whole affair, to have got anything for myself." In *The Wings of the Dove* Milly Theale's spirituality reaches from the grave with the effect, if not the intention, of separating Kate and Densher forever—"We shall never be again as we were!" But there is no such absolute in *The Golden Bowl;* and the fact that Blackmur thought he saw an absolute, a principle of spiritual ambition quite dire in its consequence calls for a further explanation.

During the years—or many of them—in which Blackmur was reading Henry James, critics close to him were preoccupied with certain related questions. What constitutes a valid human image? What is the proper relation between ordinary life as we live it and the aspirations embodied in art? What credence should the human image in a work of art give to images which rest upon nothing but our desire? These questions were usually considered in a religious context and by recourse to religious terminologies. I am alluding to Francis Fergusson's book on Dante, Father William Lynch's *Christ and Apollo,* Allen Tate's essays on the imagination. Tate's essays, in particular, proposed to distinguish between the symbolic imagination and the angelic imagination. The distinction amounts to this. The symbolic imagination—Dante its greatest exemplar—"conducts an action through analogy, of the human to the divine, of the natural to the supernatural, of the low to the high, of time to eternity." Such an imagination works willingly and unresentfully with the body of the world. But the angelic imagination resents every human limitation, denies man's commitment to the physical world, and sets itself up in an assertion of independence. Such an imagination rages for essence, for direct and unmediated knowledge of essences. "I call that human imagination angelic," Tate said, "which tries to disintegrate or to circumvent the image in the illusory pursuit of essence."[6] The distinction is well known, and fully clarified in Tate's essays on Poe, his chief exemplar of the angelic imagination. He calls it angelic because, according to Aristotelian accounts of states of being, only the angelic state of mind has direct knowledge of essences.

Tate's distinction between the symbolic and the angelic imagination was supported by several books to which he paid due tribute:

especially to Charles Williams's *The Figure of Beatrice* (1943) and Jacques Maritain's *The Dream of Descartes* (1944). Much the same emphasis can be found in Francis Fergusson's *The Idea of a Theater* and *The Human Image in Dramatic Literature.* So much for a particular context. But of course I am not suggesting that this context exactly coincides with Blackmur's: for one consideration, his relation to Christianity was never orthodox, as Maritain's was or even as Tate's was for a few years. His thinking never relied, as Tate's did, upon the Incarnation, upon the birth, life, death, and resurrection of Christ as the central event in human history. But suppose we were to retain Tate's distinction and to construe it now in a secular or humanistic form, wouldn't the angelic imagination issue in the perversion that Blackmur ascribed to James? In that version, the human image would be most complete when it had ceased to be human and become something other than human life. What other? Something entirely abstract—and we recall how critics in Blackmur's generation took abstraction as the most sinister of principles, even though Wallace Stevens spoke up for it as a refined pleasure. *The Golden Bowl,* Blackmur said in a rather flat sentence, "is a novel of the daily world James partly knew and partly created; and if it goes beyond the human it does not go to God but to the inhuman" (*Studies,* 222). At the end, Blackmur took Maggie Verver's "mode of love" as yet another example of "that ever-present possibility, man's inhumanity to man." "That it may also be," he continues, "in our circumstances, an approach to charity is what commands us to read the book" (230): a perfunctory concession, on Blackmur's part, since he didn't for a moment believe that Maggie's mode of love had anything to do with charity. He thought it had to do with logic, and therefore with perversion. I think it had most to do with an entirely human muddle which could not have been foreseen, given the presumed resources of lucidity and strong intentions.

NOTES

1. R. P. Blackmur, *Studies in Henry James,* ed. Veronica A. Makowsky (New York: New Directions, 1983), 161. Subsequent page references to this edition are given parenthetically in the text.
2. Henry James, *The Golden Bowl* (New York: Grove Press, 1952), I, 90.

Subsequent page references to this edition, volumes I and II, are given parenthetically in the text.

3. Caroline Gordon, "Mr. Verver, Our National Hero," *Sewanee Review,* 63 (Winter 1955), 38.

4. R. P. Blackmur, *Language as Gesture* (New York: Harcourt Brace and Co., 1952), 285.

5. Henry James, *Literary Criticism: European Writers and the Prefaces* (New York: The Library of America, 1984), 1107.

6. Allen Tate, *Essays of Four Decades* (Chicago: The Swallow Press, 1968), 428.

R. W. B. LEWIS

Homages to Blackmur

My own acquaintance with R. P. Blackmur came about as a result of an essay I devoted to his writing in the winter of 1951, entitled "Casella as Critic: A Note on R. P. Blackmur." Re-reading this piece today, I am struck, as who would not be, by a certain archness of style, a palpable straining after intellectual effect. If I present it here virtually unchanged, it is because the straining is in some sort a tribute to Blackmur himself—it was due to the effort to cope with as formidable a literary mind as his, and as magisterially wayward a manner of expression.

To an extent, the essay is a period piece: a token of the early 1950s, a note to that golden age in American literary criticism. It was a moment that, on the Princeton scene, was the age of Richard Blackmur. In an afterword, I will say a little about how, in the wake of the essay, I came to know that scene and its magus.

. . .

The prose of R. P. Blackmur reveals a mastery of the unsprung paradox—the paradox which never quite gets uttered, the paradox lurking in the syntax, content perhaps to remain muted and anxious anyhow not to distract attention. This provides one of the chief difficulties of Mr. Blackmur for the reader: not his paradoxes, but the submerged manner in which they exist; and I am greatly concerned in this note with Mr. Blackmur's difficulty. I intend to suggest, however, that the paradox, like the difficulty, is not primarily a question of style; I suspect it to be indicative of Mr. Blackmur's "position," at the moment of writing: a position which is shifting and expanding, so that the moment must be stressed. The position I refer to involves a very unusual variant on the ancient dialectic of religion and art.

I begin with this matter of the paradox because I have a couple of my own—by way of a hasty assessment of Mr. Blackmur as critic—and they appear as all the more crude and pushing in view of the refinement of their subject's. The first is this, put as plainly as possible: that although Mr. Blackmur is one of the most obscure, often the most irritating and superficially one of the least engaging of contemporary critics, he seems to me pretty well assured of being one of the two or three very likely to endure. (There is a minor or derivative irony here, since Mr. Blackmur is the one who holds it to be "most regrettable" that some criticism "remains alive . . . long after the generation, or even the age, in which it was written.")[1] I can easily imagine Mr. Blackmur's essays being read at almost any future date, as we continue to read, say, the Elizabethan critics or the great exegeses of the Bible; and if that should be so, it will be not only because the obscurity will prove to have been largely inescapable, the irritation largely due to his putting us secretly to shame by doing what we are always only promising to do, the inability to engage us due to his merciless regard for the work rather than for us. Another man of our time writing about literature and likely to endure is Kenneth Burke. The authors of *The Theory of Literature,* meaning (I take it) to distinguish and not to evaluate, tell us that Mr. Burke is a "literary theorist," and Mr. Blackmur is a "literary critic." I should suppose that both men are literary theorists, and much more than that; they are very nearly theologians; and while that "very nearly" may turn out to be the whole story, it can be so only if it is that kind of story. It is precisely the ventures towards, if not into, theology that may guarantee both Mr. Burke and Mr. Blackmur continuing attention.

Whatever his position—and I hope I have given an anticipatory hint of it in the title—Mr. Blackmur inches towards it with what seems to me to be a remarkably full awareness of the uniquely American dilemma from which it might arise. This brings me to my second paradox, and a less verbal one than it sounds: that the author of "The Good European: 1945" is very much of an American. The capacity and the habit which would, at first glance, appear to mark him as a

European in cultural temper are exactly those which declare him a good American: the capacity to move with ease among the major epochs of the history of Europe; the habit of invoking the greatest of western names—Plato, Dante, Montaigne, Coleridge—to symbolize clusters of ideas, attitudes, feelings. The habit, of course, is Emersonian—perhaps Emerson's major contribution to democracy; and one that is virtually impossible for the good European to acquire. The European (who is usually a Frenchman or a Dane in the first place, and only a European by opposition) is at once too close to and too remote from those epochs and those names; and this is why the capacity is no more easily come by. For beyond his traditional consciousness of the history, the language and the scholarship insulating the saving document—and which the protestant mind is skilled in dispensing with—the European nowadays shows signs of being fatally at odds with his own past. I am not speaking of the professional scholars, the priests of the routine, who continue to generate theses about Goethe and Petrarch and for whom Heine and Leopardi already constitute radical risks; but (granting the comforting exceptions to this and any other generalization) of the more ambitious and adventurous intellectual who came of age between the wars. This is the person who betrays a kind of dazed disinclination towards his own past; this is the new dispossessed. So it is no longer he, it is much rather his American counterpart who can canvass the past with assurance—who is apt to find vital meaning in Thucydides, quote Dante as a gloss on Baudelaire, cite Montaigne as a model for the contemporary critic. This is the special sense in which Eliot appears to be an American poet; and it is not surprising that the educational doctrine of the Great Books of the West should originate and thrive in Chicago.

The learned critic in America, like the learned poet, has presently, I am suggesting, a double advantage over the European: he can feel a genuine and living relationship to the European tradition, and he can feel the relationship to the whole of it. He even enjoys revising it occasionally: a protestant tactic; Mr. Blackmur, along with several of his colleagues, has offered some fairly startling reconstructions of the past. But it is just the sense of a relationship to Europe that persistently forces a critic as sensitive as Mr. Blackmur into exploring, weighing, defining the relationship; for he knows that the American is related in his difference as well as in his sameness; he knows that the American may win himself a relationship to the past without possessing it. Mr. Blackmur speaks out of his awareness when he says, as recently, "It is not that I wish to go back and not that I wish to separate our adventure from the history of what we have been through."[2]

What Mr. Blackmur is talking about in that passage, what he cannot very well help talking about in any such discussion, is what he has to find in the heart of the past, at the core of the tradition: Christianity and a Christian civilization (they are not the same). This discovery is what has bothered and fascinated him from the earliest days of his ambiguous involvement with T. S. Eliot; and he is at it again in his in many ways extraordinary essay on Thomas Mann's *Dr. Faustus*. There he confronts over several pages the title of the book and the quotation from Canto II of the *Inferno* which follows it: "Lo giorno se n'andava . . ." What the title and the verse mean, what they may have meant originally and in themselves, what they can mean to an elderly modern German humanist, what they can mean to an American reader in 1950: these are the questions asked and the relationships weighed; and part of Mr. Blackmur's answer is in his summary of the verse: "Half of the Greco-Christian world is here, and very nearly all that remains of it: what is human and invocably human."[3] Mr. Blackmur's contention with the past—something possible for him exactly because of the vital relationship (as against the contemporary European) and perhaps indeed composing that relationship—is a contention with Christianity. I do not mean to say so with the air of one who delivers the *coup de grâce:* I say only what I learn from Mr. Blackmur.

But I am not ready even yet to engage this question, the question of Mr. Blackmur's position; though I should admit at once, what may not be obvious in the preceding paragraph, that the binding of Christianity to the past and to Europe (as, most blatantly, in the substance and the title of Hilaire Belloc's *Europe and the Faith*) seems to me an almost scrupulous inversion of the claimed fact. But it is time now to remember that, whatever else he may be, Mr. Blackmur is also and always a critic; and so it is time to ask how a critic, especially as dedicated a critic as Mr. Blackmur, can get himself into a position at all. This is to remind ourselves of the qualities of Mr. Blackmur's criticism and the nature of his success. Stanley Hyman has done much of our work for us, in his interesting and invaluable, though somewhat frustrating, essay in *The Armed Vision* (1948); and I should certainly direct the reader there for the general account. Little more need be said about Mr. Blackmur's remarkable acuteness of perception, his conscientiousness or his taste; and as to his stature, Mr. Ransom lectured us all on that many years ago. I agree more or less unreservedly with Mr. Hyman and Mr. Ransom, and I disagree with Granville Hicks, who once alluded to Mr. Blackmur as a passionate quibbler, and with Alfred Kazin who called him the sedulous shadow of Henry James. But just as there is much passion and some quibbling, so there is undoubtedly the James aspect; as for James himself there was what Eliot defined as the Hawthorne aspect. You have to combine a lack of sympathy for James with a belief in discontinuity (as Mr. Kazin used to) in order to consider the James aspect a bad thing.

What Mr. Blackmur found in James is suggested in the opening sentences of his chapter in *The Literary History of the United States*[4] (all in all, probably the best single essay on James, though partly a pastiche which should be read in connection with some of Mr. Blackmur's other studies of the same subject, especially "In the Country of the Blue"). Mr. Blackmur speaks of James's "reality" as embodying his response to "the human predicament of his generation . . . the predicament of the sensitive mind during what may be called the interregnum between the effective dominance of the old Christian-classical ideal through old European institutions and the rise to rule of the succeeding ideal, whatever history comes to call it."[5] I myself do not believe that this is an exact statement of our predicament, though conversely the predicament may be traced in part to statements of this kind; but I am sure it is an exact statement of the condition of Henry James, and I suspect it may be autobiographical as well. It is very likely this predicament, or the sense of it, which accounts for the element in the fiction of James and the criticism of Mr. Blackmur which has most annoyed and tantalized their readers: the element I would like to call, without too much frivolity, the hidden-ball play. (The criticism and the position will not, we see, stay separated very long.) Now William Faulkner is the acknowledged living master of the hidden-ball play, and some of his novels are quite apt replicas of a football game in which everyone is running, tackling and being tackled at once, and almost no one, especially the spectators, has any idea who is carrying the ball. The surrealist novel, for example *The Cannibals* by John Hawkes, has employed the device even more extensively; but long before Faulkner and American surrealism, Henry James demonstrated his genius in this respect, and for reasons hinted at by Mr. Blackmur. An example from James ought to help us to get closer to Mr. Blackmur.

The situation towards the end of the eighth book of *The Wings of the Dove* is this. The three main figures are come to Venice: Millie Theale, the dying fairy-princess from New York; and the impoverished English lovers, Kate Croy and Merton Densher. The strategy of the lovers, as shaped by Kate and executed by Densher, suggests a final brilliant stroke. It has operated all along to lead Kate's wealthy dragonish aunt, among others, to believe Densher somehow involved with poor Millie; and Kate with a Lord Mark. Borrowing the useful method of Stephen Spender in his commentary on *The Golden Bowl*, we might say that the true situation is: A (Millie) BC (Kate and Densher) and D (Lord Mark); but that the strategy creates an illusion of the situation AC and BD. The action now proposed is for Densher to marry Millie and so inherit her enormous wealth when, as she must do before much time passes, she dies. Some four hundred and fifty pages have been expended to build up the complex and moving patterns of real and illusory relationship in which the proposal might produce its maximum vibration. As a matter of fact, in James's unending process of generation and corruption it is already too late for the act; Lord Mark has already revealed to Millie the true situation, though the lovers are unaware of this; an irony providing a final vibration. So it is that Kate Croy plants the idea in Densher's mind, the idea of his marrying the dying American heiress: an idea Densher will not even acknowledge until Kate in turn promises to come to his rooms and give herself to him—a realization and recognition of *their* relationship to ensure the falseness of the others. The account proceeds. Kate is trying to force Densher to articulate the proposal.

> Encouraged visibly by his glow of concentration, she looked at him through the air she had painfully made clear. Yet she was still on her guard. "Don't think, however, that I'll do *all* the work for you. If you want things named, you must name them."

He had quite, within the minute, been turning names over; and there was only one, which at last stared at him there dreadful, that properly fitted. "Since she's to die I'm to marry her?"

It struck him even at the moment as fine in her that she met it with no wincing or minding. She might, for the grace of silence, for favor to their conditions, have only answered him with her eyes. But her lips bravely moved. "To marry her."

"So that when her death has taken place I shall in the natural course have money?"

It was before him now and he had nothing more to ask.[6]

I do not say that this is the climax or the "high point" of the novel, only that it is one of the most memorable of the moments in which a deed or an object, hitherto concealed, is finally exposed and named for us. James did not share the belief of his younger colleague, Joyce, in the magic of names; he did not believe that things come into existence and are known (and possessed) by the act of naming them. It was much rather that things could be named only when existing and known, only when created by the pressures and repercussions of human relationships. I have not looked up all the meanings of the name "marriage"; but I believe it is or has been an honorable estate, an institution, a sacrament. And yet, exactly because of the predicament, it was not to be expected that either James or his characters could respond to marriage in any of those phases, and so they could not name it prematurely. What James had to do, what he was wonderfully gifted in doing, was to create the "reality" of the thing (marriage, for example) by enacting its place in the dynamic pattern of relationships. The ball may have to be hidden a long time, but the aim is not to tease.

Something of the James narrative method has been taken over by Mr. Blackmur and adapted to the uses of criticism. The grounds are no less arguable, for critics and novelists are presumably eligible for the same predicament, and in this case, the results are generally happy ones. The first impression, on reading one of Mr. Blackmur's essays, may be unfavorable: a very usual first impression must be that one has no notion what he is talking about. The impression is exact enough, since what the discussion is *about* is often just what Mr. Blackmur finds it misleading to name, and sometimes he never gets around to marriage at all, but counts, as Kate did not, on the grace of silence. I will not offer an example at length: examples in plenty can be found, especially in the essays on fiction and on criticism—on Mann, Dostoyevsky, Tolstoy, Melville; on Winters, Trilling, Eliot, and on the "burden," the "job," the "enabling act," the "feather-bed" of critics. They account for our sense of the compressed and the oracular in Mr. Blackmur's style. For Mr. Blackmur, the hidden-ball expert among critics, seems to leave out the object, direct or indirect. He will propose "models for our consideration," without telling us what they are models of. He talks about "parody," but not about what is being parodied. He bases an interpretation of Tolstoy upon a theory of "incarnation," but he is careful not to confess what it is which is made flesh.

The examples are chosen at random, for I am not leading up to a suggestion that what is being imitated, parodied or made incarnate is God or a Platonic Idea. I am contending, for the moment, only that Mr. Blackmur's systematic omissions are both warranted and critically effective. Stanley Hyman's image for Mr. Blackmur's criticism is that "of a stage magician sawing the woman in half. During the perform-ance one has the illusion that she is cut up, but afterwards she springs up whole and untouched to take a bow."[7] Mr. Blackmur does not touch the "heart" of the work; he deliberately probes around it, wielding what Bronson Alcott used to call the murderous knife of analysis with caution and love. So the labor of violation, as he remarks in an essay on Melville, seems to deepen our intimacy with the substance:

> The dramatic form of a novel is what holds it together, makes it move, gives it a centre and establishes a direction, and it includes the agency of perception, the consciousness set up in a book upon which, or through which, the story is registered. Dramatic form cannot in prac-tice be wholly isolated from other formal elements; form is the way things go together in their medium—and the medium itself, here language, may be properly considered the major element of form; but we may think of different ways in which things go together in a given work, and strangely, the labor of abstraction and violation will seem to deepen our intimacy with the substance of the work and, more valu-able, to heighten our sense of how that substance is controlled. The sense of control is perhaps the highest form of apprehension; it is understanding without immersion.[8]

A Jamesian passage, of course; but an accurate description of what Mr. Blackmur accomplishes in practice.

It must be admitted, in a kind of parenthesis, that there are some purely stylistic difficulties that have only superficially to do with the James aspect. I have suggested that the so-called evasiveness of James and Mr. Blackmur may instead be a most resolute way of confronting the object, given a certain sense of predicament; in both instances then, it is creative rather than evasive; but this does not entirely mitigate the syntactical arthritis which Mr. Blackmur occasionally discloses. The clauses in some of his sentences seem to come in from opposite directions and get firmly glued together without having very much to do with each other. They appear to clasp hands, as it were, while looking over each other's shoulders. Sentences of this kind have an assumption of logic, but they are not even enthymemes. We meet a similar difficulty in whole paragraphs or in single words; it is a matter of unequitable distribution of meaning. Mr. Blackmur knows many, often all possible, meanings of a given word; but he has an excessive admiration for the dictionary, and he is not always in full command of the old, conventional meaning which the dictionary can never give but which must be present in order to lend power to peculiar and distorted uses.

Mr. Blackmur may reply at once that we do not know the old, conventional meaning any more than he does; that, he may say, is precisely the meaning which can no longer be known. What we do, of course, is to perform an imaginative act of memory: an act which Mr. Blackmur appears to distrust profoundly. One of his ways of associating himself with Henry James has been to quote, with regard to James (in the *Literary History*) and to himself (in "A Burden for Critics"), the phrase of Santayana: "an ignorant man, almost a poet." In the case of James, Mr. Blackmur is highly successful in tracing the broad acres of genuine ignorance; in his own case, the phrase recovers its original irony. Mr. Blackmur is the type of learned critic; but he remains adamant about a special condition of ignorance, which is a part of his contention with the past.

According to scholastic theory, doubt may be resolved by making a distinction; the romantic temper is inclined to remove difficulty by tracing a development. Those of us who are concerned with literature are incurably romantic; and so, in the face of the apparent contradictions in Mr. Blackmur's discussion of criticism over the years, I am going to attempt the sketch of a development. For Mr. Blackmur has surely been developing: he is in the middle of a journey, or even (who knows) nearly home. It is not primarily a development in sensibility; nothing need be added, at any rate by Mr. Blackmur, to the essays on Marianne Moore and Hart Crane which he composed more than fifteen years ago. The journey and the development must be plotted, and understood, along different lines. One way to describe them would be to speak of an adjustment between the enterprise of criticism and other possible high human enterprises. Mr. Blackmur, though regularly given to speculation about the critical act, rarely alludes to the role of the critic. But while the act has been continuously defined as important, serious, complicated and exhausting, it is only recently that the role of critic, as Mr. Blackmur performs it and comments on the performance, has approached the roles of Prophet and Fool.

It is perhaps inevitable, in a time when the artist is being ever more easily accommodated to the Christ figure, that the critic should assume the function of the prophet, dispatching himself to cry in the wilderness: Prepare ye the way of the Lord. But the *critic* as prophet must accept the correlative role (I shall return to this) of fool; it is part of his commitment to disappear in the fourth act. How this all comes about, is still a question. In the case of Lionel Trilling's "liberal" critic, for example, there is not much mystery, for Mr. Trilling has insisted all along that reality itself is a dramatic composition of men in action; that the creative imagination must address itself to reality in this social sense; and that, consequently, the critic is concerned with the values of the good *polis*—with political values, taken as images of truth and destiny. It is interesting that Mr. Blackmur so far mistook Mr. Trilling's meaning that he has argued against a literature of government: as though Mr. Trilling had advocated Fair Deal literature or Council of Europe literature, or perhaps the poetry of the minuscule Socialist majority.[9]

The comment on Lionel Trilling is pertinent and suggestive, for it is a contribution to Mr. Blackmur's twenty-year-old discussion of the relation between pure criticism and criticism with an ulterior purpose; and it is within this relation that the adjustment has occurred and the prophetic role has emerged. In the fine discriminations between pure and tendentious criticism of a series of essays in the thirties, Mr. Blackmur seemed to be saying that tendentious criticism was all very well, it was simply not his concern. He displayed an Eliotesque charity towards those other possibilities; with the difference that Mr. Blackmur's charity was not the product of conviction and was insofar the less persuasive. Eliot's conviction about the Christian Church, indeed, was one of the tendencies Mr. Blackmur was being charitable towards; a conviction about the socialist state was another. But in those days, Mr. Blackmur made few special claims for his kind of criticism; he was only, as the saying goes, trying to get along.

What has happened, I think, is that Mr. Blackmur, in the course of distinguishing himself from the other major possibilities, has been compelled to absorb more and more of their essential revelations. He by no means stands alone in this regard; but he goes about the business of absorption in a more secretive and, I suppose, a more disarming manner. Still, absorption is not something you can keep quiet about forever; and there is always the danger that the absorbing agent will grow fat in the process. Mr. Blackmur's criticism is not fat, but it is growing all the time. It is presently concerned, for example, with larger and larger chunks of experience—with great long novels rather than with intense short poems. The "double agent" of 1935 has become triple: "a triad," Mr. Blackmur writes in 1943, "is the only tolerable form of unity."[10] The more or less simple opposition between the pure and the tendentious has expanded (by 1946) into "Four Categories in Criticism,"[11] with the "symbolic imagination" occupying a position of anagogic insight, and with the linguistic and the formal as successively higher stages beyond the criticism of ulterior purpose. And (by 1950) the New Criticism which Mr. Blackmur has been practicing in common with Mr. Ransom, Mr. Brooks and Mr. Burke is discovered to be partial criticism: it is rhetoric; and criticism is enjoined to strive for wholeness by bringing into play dialectic and poetic as well. These are some of the steps by which a dedicated critic, in the interests of pure criticism, manages to build himself a position. I am sure there are intimate relations between the triads, and various schemas suggest themselves. But probably the significant thing to notice is that each of them has the quality of totality; criticism, ceasing to be one of several intellectual acts, is becoming the entire intellectual act itself.

And this is not only possible, this must be so, *if* the object of the critical act is the ultimate object of comprehension. The constant object of intellect, someone used to say, is *being;* whether so or not, I quote it as an example of the ultimate: and there is a sense in which Mr. Blackmur is saying that poetry is being. He is willing, we may observe, to offer the *Phaedrus* of Plato as a model of the total and interrelated action of the mind: as a model for criticism (in "The Lion and the Honeycomb").[12] Now the *Phaedrus* is undoubtedly a dialogue about rhetoric and its proper subservience to dialectic; but true rhetoric is illustrated by Socrates in a myth about salvation—about beatitude accomplished by kindling the energy of mind and spirit to a highest intensity of awareness. Mr. Blackmur wants to keep the rhetoric and dispense with the salvation. Here, too, there has been a development. In 1935, proposing "the early Plato and the whole Montaigne"—uneasy colleagues—as paradigms for the critic, Mr. Blackmur asked rhetorically: "Is not the inexhaustible stimulus and fertility of the Dialogues and Essays due as much as anything to the absence of positive doctrine? Is it not that the early Plato always holds conflicting ideas in shifting balance, presenting them in contest and evolution, with victory only the last shift?"[13] Mr. Blackmur is no longer so positive about the absence of positive doctrine; but now he intimates that the dialogue may be the doctrine. I do not have the *Phaedrus* beside me, but I believe it is there (though more explicitly in the Seventh Letter) that the merit of written dialogues is assessed: they provide amusement for old age, Socrates says, and serve to remind their author—of what? Not of the vision, which was unforgettable, but of the path to the vision. It is Mr. Blackmur, we might say, who has forgotten the vision: or perhaps he thinks it is only a vision of the path.

But here the most subtle kind of distinction is required of us. In all this discussion of being and poetry and vision, I do not mean to imply that Mr. Blackmur, in any simplified way, is following Matthew

Arnold in the notion that poetry can become the substitute for religion. This is of course, the issue, for religion is the tendency of tendencies, and it is the Christian apologists and the Dante-affirmers from whom Mr. Blackmur has absorbed the most. Mr. Blackmur speaks for himself in "A Burden for Critics" (1949):

> It is getting on towards a century since Matthew Arnold suggested that poetry could perhaps take over the expressive functions of religion. Possibly Arnold only meant the functions of the Church of England and the lesser dissenting sects. Whatever he meant, it did not happen, it could not and it cannot happen. All poetry can do is to dramatize. This it has done. It has not replaced or in any way taken over the functions of religion; but it has been compelled to replace the operative force of religion as a resource with the discovery, or creation, of religion as an aesthetic experience. The poet has to put his religion itself into his poetry along with his experience of it.[14]

Alongside which exceedingly admirable and provocative observation, we may place another remark, from the essay on *Dr. Faustus;* but first Mr. Blackmur's contention ought to be rehearsed. It is not only that poetry cannot do the work of religion; but also that religion itself can no longer do the work of religion. Religion was one human way of coping with a human situation—*the* human situation, perhaps; but something "has happened" to the religious way; it is no longer available to us. Poetry is however not a modern substitute; it is a different strategy altogether. From the essay on *Dr. Faustus:*

> It is we northerners always who understand the *ground of appeal* to the resources of the Latin and Catholic spirit; we need them more. I do not say this was so for Dante's time, certainly not for Augustine's; but it is so for us. We know what is corrupted and what corrupts, and how the relation may become tolerable: we know what we must acknowledge, although we do not wish to acknowledge it: the terms of an everlasting and vital predicament; and it is characteristic of our age that the acknowledgement should be attempted in the works of art.[15]

The ball is kept hidden there with uncommon agility; but that is what the passage is about. Mr. Blackmur is not being immodest in saying "we know." What distinguishes him from most critics of T. S. Eliot, for example, and especially from the hostile critics, is that so few of them betray the slightest understanding of Christian doctrine. The peculiarity of Mr. Blackmur is that he has a pretty large understanding of that doctrine and that his understanding is expressed in the act of rejection, as an insistence upon ignorance. Mr. Blackmur's ignorance is like the ignorance which was so fashionable from the 14th through the 16th centuries—the ignorance of men who, like Petrarch and Nicholas of Cusa, grasped the doctrine well enough but took much singular pleasure in demonstrating how men could know nothing about it; a very learned ignorance indeed, and culminating in the familiar phrase and the erudite essays of Mr. Blackmur's friend Montaigne. Mr. Blackmur rejects the atonement and demands ignorance about the revelation; he will preserve only "what is human and invocably human," so the revelation granted and absorbed by him can be nothing else than the revelation of an "everlasting and vital predicament."

Now *this* revelation (as against the other revelation, which was intended to make this one look like darkness itself—in Allen Tate's words, "the daysky fell to moonless black") can of course be attempted only in works of art. If "religious experience" is acknowledged chiefly these days in literature, it is not only because it has been more and more driven out of formal theology and is unwelcome anywhere else; it is also because very frequently it is not religious experience at all, but rather the experience of the lack of religion. I do not imagine I am in any essential disagreement with Mr. Blackmur on this point. The difference is that Mr. Blackmur makes his point as a humanist; in his own fine phrase about Yeats, he is "tragically content" with the situation; and I do not suppose it is possible to be content, tragically or otherwise, unless there is the conviction—secretly, it may be; for all I know, unconsciously—that Christianity is a mere historic phenomenon, of whatever enormous and mythical proportions. It is this conviction and this contentedness which lead to the elevation of art, in however guarded and humble a manner, to the place of the ultimate object of comprehension.

Mr. Blackmur is fond, as I am, of the saying of Montaigne in "Of Experience": "Sit he on never so high a throne, a man still sits on his own bottom." I think he takes the saying too literally; but this is the same story. In any case, to Montaigne's celebration of the absence of grace, Mr. Blackmur would add his factor of the "symbolic imagination," the best and the most he can rescue from what he regards as the decaying Christian imagination. The symbolic imagination is the special quality of the critic as prophet, announcing to the ungodly the communication of men with ultimate reality. There is no higher calling, except that of creation itself; and it is the requirement of humility before the creation which marries the Prophet to the Fool. For if it is the task of the critic to bring the artist back into contact with those who might understand him, and to bring him back to his own senses, it is none the less imperative that he should not be around at the finish.

Like all journeys, Mr. Blackmur's journey is a quest for final cause: a quest for, as he says in an essay on *Anna Karenina*, "that force greater than ourselves, outside ourselves, and working on ourselves, which whether we call it God or Nature is the force of life, what is shaped or misshaped, construed or misconstrued, in the process of living."[16] Mr. Blackmur knows that it makes a difference whether we call it God or Nature; but until he completes the journey, he must put the case that way: he must not spring the paradox. But if I have plotted the journey with anything like accuracy, I have the feeling that Mr. Blackmur's journey to God (or Nature) will end with Dante—a Dante humanized and secularized, a Dante who would have put himself into his own hierarchy of sinners. We know exactly where, because Dante felt the same temptation and overcame it in the person of his friend Casella. The attempt to embrace Casella and the song they began to sing together, on the shore east of Mount Purgatory (Canto II), may have constituted the most dangerous moment in the entire vision; certainly the whole poem was at stake, and for this poet that could mean the whole universe. It was precisely the danger of accepting the aesthetic experience and letting the religious experience wait; or it was the equivalent danger of taking the latter as an allegory of the former. But at the first words of the song ("Amor che nella mente mi ragiona"), Dante's Cato sent the lot of them flying. So Casella too was to hear the laughter.

·   ·   ·

A few months after the essay appeared, Blackmur wrote to me. He said he had finally got his face back in working order, after reading the flattering things (as he called them) that I had said about him. He had other observations to make, but he ended by disavowing the notion I had attributed to him, that "poetry is being." What I had meant of course was that in my view he took literature too seriously; I then shared the attitude of Marianne Moore about poetry, that there was something important beyond all this fiddle. I am less sure of that opinion today. What I am more sure of is that R. P. Blackmur moved about, in conversation and on paper, in the world of literature—taking that word in its broadest imaginable meaning—with such authority as to persuade us that it *is* the domain of ultimate human discourse.

Later in the fall, Blackmur invited me to Princeton to discuss an appointment there. With the expert connivance of Whitney J. Oates, Professor of Classics and then head of the Special Program in the Humanities, an arrangement was made whereby I would hold a Humanities fellowship for a year and then an appointment as Resident Fellow in Creative Writing. It was a football Saturday, I remember, and Princeton, led by the dazzling Dick Kazmaier, was slaughtering what was to have been its most dangerous opponent by something like 60 to 20. This news, received as we passed through the library turnstile on our way out, thoroughly exasperated "Mike" Oates, who remarked that no one in the university could think about anything, and especially about literature, until the season was over.

In fact, literature, the making of it and the interpreting of it, loomed on that local landscape, then and for some years to come, as it rarely has anywhere in the country. During the first year my wife and I spent in Princeton, the Creative Writing program was being run by Delmore Schwartz and Saul Bellow (the latter just finishing *The Adventures of Augie March*). Ralph Ellison came down frequently for the night (*The Invisible Man* had recently been published). John and Eileen Berryman lived in town (Berryman was writing "Homage to Mistress Bradstreet"), as did the Irving Howes. Allen and Caroline Tate showed up periodically. Robert Fitzgerald was no longer in residence, but his wise and warming presence was much felt. The Gauss Seminars in Criticism, on which Fitzgerald had made a report, were flourishing, with Francis Fergusson sapiently in charge. One of the seminars that year was given by Edmund Wilson, who presented what became key chapters of *Patriotic*

Gore. In another, Dwight Macdonald continued his exploration of popular culture. Theodore Roethke was on hand from time to time; on one boisterous Sunday afternoon in our apartment, after asking if he could use the phone, Ted put in a long-distance call to Dylan Thomas in Wales.

Blackmur was away in Europe during most of 1952–53 (we sublet his apartment on Princeton Avenue), but he was back in the fall of 1953, and we could watch the literary community gather around him. Our perspective was inevitably a partial one. I was only briefly and peripherally a member of the Princeton University faculty, and cannot attest, as others are doing in these pages, to Blackmur's role therein. The community we were aware of was largely composed of non-academic folk; or to put it more accurately, its constituents related to one another in essentially non-academic ways. This was true even of those who actually were on the faculty: for example, to refer to them, as we never did, by their full names, E. B. O. Borgerhoff, Edward Hubler, Tom Riggs, Edward Cone, Edmund Keeley. These various people related in particular through *talk:* lively and insistent talk, sometimes heated, even combative. There was an enormous amount of talk in those Princeton days—and evenings, when there was likely to be a fair amount of drink, and some shouting. At these several activities, no one in the community came close to outdoing R. P. Blackmur: he was the talking center of the perpetual talkfest; and if one shouted at him, it was sometimes to break into his onflowing monologue.

But it was brilliant talk; all things considered, the most brilliant I have ever heard in my life. It ranged over literature and politics, personal reminiscences (to hear him, Blackmur had at one time or another worked at any job you could name) and the human condition. As the evening drew on, Blackmur tended to grow aphoristic, and my wife got the habit of writing down his sayings on the inside of a matchbook. Blackmur enjoyed reading them the next day, often expressing amused astonishment at his cleverness. These trophies have, alas, been lost.

The wife of one seminar leader, after listening for a couple of months to Blackmurian talk, became disaffected. When asked one day what she thought of him, she replied after only a little hesitation:

"Oh . . . arrogant, wistful, brilliant, boring." She was shrewd to detect the wistfulness; the arrogance was obvious, though it was easy to exaggerate; and the brilliance unmistakable. I myself cannot recall ever finding R. P. Blackmur boring. In the image I retain of him, he is sitting up straight in an armchair, moustache trim, eyes twinkling, drawing on the ever-present cigarette and coughing through its smoke; holding forth, murmuringly, with unmatched intelligence and wit, salted with irony and superbly quirky turns of phrase.

A bibliographical footnote. As the 1950s recede sufficiently to be subjected to scrutiny, reports on the literary period in Princeton have begun to come in. Russell Fraser's biography of Blackmur (1981) struck this reader as rich in information but curiously wrong in narrative tone. Irving Howe gives an account of Princeton (which he didn't much like) and a fine little portrait of Blackmur in his "intellectual autobiography," *A Margin of Hope.* Eileen Simpson's memoir of the time, *Poets in Their Youth,* is engaging and illuminating. But it is in Robert Fitzgerald's *Enlarging the Change* (a portion of which appears in this volume) that R. P. Blackmur is allowed to give his most recognizable performance.

NOTES

1. R. P. Blackmur, *The Lion and the Honeycomb* (New York: Harcourt, Brace and Co., 1955), 184.

2. *The Lion and the Honeycomb,* 179.

3. R. P. Blackmur, *Eleven Essays in the European Novel* (New York and Burlingame: Harcourt, Brace and World, 1964), 101.

4. Reprinted in R. P. Blackmur, *Studies in Henry James* (New York: New Directions, 1983), 91–124.

5. *Studies in Henry James,* 91.

6. Henry James, *The Wings of the Dove,* Laurel edition (New York: Dell Publishing Co., 1958), 387.

7. Stanley Edgar Hyman, *The Armed Vision* (New York: Alfred A. Knopf, 1948), 264.

8. *The Lion and the Honeycomb,* 132.

9. See "The Politics of Human Power," *The Lion and the Honeycomb,* 32–42.

10. R. P. Blackmur, *Language as Gesture* (New York: Harcourt, Brace and Co., 1952), 250.

11. See "Notes on Four Categories in Criticism," *The Lion and the Honeycomb*, 213–25.

12. *The Lion and the Honeycomb*, 176–97.

13. *Language as Gesture*, 375.

14. *The Lion and the Honeycomb*, 201–02.

15. *Eleven Essays in the European Novel*, 101.

16. *Eleven Essays in the European Novel*, 3.

VERONICA A. MAKOWSKY

Blackmur on
the Dove's Wings

R. P. Blackmur's favorite novel was Henry James's *The Wings of the Dove*. His initial reading, at age seventeen, left him "both confident and desperate in the force of art."[1] He felt "excited and effortless; nothing was any longer worthwhile and everything had become necessary" (*Studies*, 161). One notices the characteristic Blackmurian paradoxes, and one thinks of Blackmur's lifelong emulation of the Master's high-mandarin style. Blackmur undoubtedly cherished a nostalgic fondness for this novel as the instrument of his introduction to James, but why did *The Wings of the Dove*, rather than one of James's other masterpieces, remain Blackmur's favorite?

In his 1958 introduction to the novel Blackmur provides a summary of the plot.

> The story is simple. Kate Croy and Merton Densher wish to marry but are prevented because of Densher's poverty and because Kate's aunt wishes her to marry money and position. When Milly Theale, a millionaire American princess, appears in London and is discovered to be mortally ill, Kate plots that Densher shall marry Milly, inherit her money when she dies and then marry Kate. Milly learns of the plot, but at her hastened death leaves Densher her money just the same. Densher refuses the money and also refuses to marry Kate. It is a melodrama of renunciation and remorse . . . (*Studies*, 172)

A consideration of Blackmur's chronic fascination with this "simple" story will demonstrate two recurrent themes or patterns. One is the

Jamesian motif of the sacred fount, which concerns the mutual exploitation inherent in the relations of men and women. The second is a major theme of Blackmur's own criticism, the interaction of art and life.

The chapters on Blackmur's early life in Russell Fraser's recent biography provide the information necessary to suggest what so attracted the adolescent Blackmur to *The Wings of the Dove*. I believe that he saw some aspects of himself in each of the three main characters, Kate Croy, Milly Theale, and Merton Densher. Kate Croy is the product of a once-good family which has come down in the world, a circumstance of acute humiliation for Kate. Blackmur, too, descended from good stock, particularly his mother's family, the clerical Palmers. His father, however, like Kate's, couldn't keep a job, and his mother was reduced to keeping a boarding house. The young Blackmur may well have felt a pang of recognition at the opening scene of the novel which finds Kate and her father in a sordid boarding house where Kate "tasted the faint, flat emanation of things, the failure of fortune and of honour."[2] The Blackmur boarding house was at the wrong end of Boston's dignified Irving Street, a source of rankled pride for young Richard. He may well have sympathized with Kate's unaided efforts to remove herself from the wrong side of London to the better quarter of her Aunt Maud.

In some ways Blackmur's identification with Milly Theale is at once the most simple and the most complicated. What James calls her "freshness of the first and only prime" (*Wings*, 150) would attract the interest of any young person. Milly, though, also has a more curious trait. Like Henry Adams, another of Blackmur's youthful and lifelong enthusiasms, Milly believes she lives a posthumous existence and will become truly alive only when she is dead. "Since I've lived all these years as if I were dead, I shall die, no doubt, as if I were alive" (*Wings*, 145). Milly hastens, if not wills, her own death by "turning her face to the wall"; it is a longing to be immured in solitary stillness or stasis that Blackmur often expresses in his poetry. An island off the coast of Maine, Jordan's Delight, is his "flowering desert dark, soul's ease," of which he declares, "men do not come to live here."[3]

Merton Densher, though, would be the character with whom

Blackmur most closely identified. Young Blackmur, recently expelled from high school and making his way by a series of odd jobs such as soda jerk, may have empathized with Densher's Venetian isolation. "He had never been, as he judged it, so down. In mean conditions, without books, without society, almost without money, he had nothing to do but wait. His main support really was his original idea, which didn't leave him, of waiting for the deepest depth his predicament could sink him to. Fate would invent if he but gave it time, some refinement of the horrible" (*Wings*, 425). This description also demonstrates Densher's passivity, what he himself considers "his so extremely manipulated state" (*Wings*, 339) and "his own incapacity for action" (*Wings*, 375). The manipulators or catalysts are always women, first his mother, then Kate Croy, Aunt Maud, and Milly Theale. In his biography, Fraser states that Blackmur was his mother's favorite child and that he remained devoted to her until her death two years before his own. Fraser comments, "Early boyhood in Cambridge begot in Richard his fatal lassitude, his conviction of apartness that fostered helplessness no less than independence, and his willingness to let someone else do it. Mostly, 'someone else' was a woman" (20–21).

The protagonists of *The Wings of the Dove* seem to resemble not only Blackmur himself but his parents as well, which is not surprising when one considers the influence or imprinting of parents upon their children. Like Merton Densher, Blackmur's father was an Englishman, but, unlike Densher, he actually managed to marry the American girl, Helen Palmer. Fraser describes Blackmur's unemployed father as continually sitting in the back parlor, motionless and speechless (8), a state much like that of the passive Merton Densher as he sits in his *pensione* awaiting Milly's death.

Of Blackmur's mother, Fraser writes that "awareness of her family's distinction aggravated her sense that life hadn't turned out as it should have" (9). In this way, she evokes Kate Croy, but Blackmur may have identified her more closely with that great advocate of renunciation and sacrifice, Milly Theale. Of Helen Palmer Blackmur, Fraser says that "for the children she was willing to lay down her life. This is what she did. But she made their lives a casualty of her unrelenting affection" (15). Milly Theale lays down her life for Kate

Croy and Merton Densher, but, similarly, their guilt made their lives "a casualty of her unrelenting affection." Life in the Blackmur household may indeed have been "a melodrama of renunciation and remorse," R. P. Blackmur's epithet for *The Wings of the Dove*.

Even more curious than the ways in which *The Wings of the Dove* seems to parallel young Blackmur's past and present are the ways it seems to predict his future, particularly his relations with women. Merton Densher, an amiable but ineffectual intellectual, is drawn to Kate Croy because "he had admired and envied what he called her direct talent for life, as distinguished from his own, a poor weak thing of the occasion, amateurishly patched up" (*Wings*, 340). Delmore Schwartz called Tessa Gilbert, Blackmur's first love, "a beautiful instance of vitality" (Fraser, 43). Fraser states that Blackmur and Tessa Gilbert "were polar opposites, so they made a pair . . . Tessa lived in her body and rejoiced in the world. The body was Richard's torment, and he defined the alienated man" (43).

A similar pairing of opposites occurred in Blackmur's marriage to Helen Dickson. Like Tessa Gilbert, Helen Dickson could confront and enjoy the material and practical sides of life. As Fraser depicts their relationship, "where he dithered, she coped. Anything Helen tackled, she was sure to do well" (69). For Merton Densher, Kate "had always simplified, and it brought back his sense of the degree in which, to her energy as compared with his own, many things were easy" (*Wings*, 439). Kate's energy, though, had something animalistic about it. She is described as "brutal" (*Wings*, 133) and a "panther" (*Wings*, 202). Helen Dickson is similarly characterized by those who knew her as a "natural," a "primitive," and even a "caged animal" (Fraser, 70).

The circumstances leading to Blackmur's engagement to Helen Dickson present an almost uncanny parallel to the ending of *The Wings of the Dove*. In accordance with Kate's plan to gain Milly's fortune, Densher pretends to love Milly and encourages her love for him, but by the end of the novel, the hunter has become the victim. Densher recognizes the despicable use to which his pliant nature has been put; he has fallen in love with Milly and cannot bring himself to marry Kate. Blackmur also met his second love through his first. On the rebound from Tessa Gilbert, he was introduced to

Helen Dickson at one of Tessa's parties. According to Fraser, who quotes Blackmur, "at first he had egged himself on to fall for Helen. Abruptly the real thing confronted him, 'realer than I had imagined possible. . . . She has said and done enough for me to make it impossible . . . for me to leave her' " (66). What Blackmur wrote of James he could have said of himself: "The act of jilting was for James, throughout his work, an act of moral abasement, for in performing it one damaged one's integrity" (*Studies*, 52).

In Blackmur's work, as well as his life, themes from *The Wings of the Dove* continued to appear. Kate Croy and Merton Densher use sexual intimacy to assuage their guilt about Milly; they were possessed by "the need to bury in the dark blindness of each other's arms the knowledge of each other that they couldn't undo" (*Wings*, 487). The poet seeks a similar "dark blindness" in Blackmur's "Scarabs for the Living, xvii": "Oh, love is lusty blind / but wakened is abased; / in darkness kind finds kind" (*Poems*, 47).

James's trope of the sacred fount also appears frequently in Blackmur's writing. In James's novel by the same name, "the sacred fount is like the greedy man's description of the turkey as an 'awkward' dinner dish. It may be sometimes too much for a single share, but it's not enough to go round" (quoted by Blackmur in *Studies*, 62). James uses the image of the fount to characterize the finite amount of vitality in a sexual relationship and depicts each partner's attempt to gain as much as he or she can. In *The Wings of the Dove*, Kate Croy feasts on Merton Densher and Milly Theale, and Merton preys upon Milly and Kate; Milly, however, may be the ultimate feeder since she drains Kate and Merton's relationship of its meaning, energy, and love.

In *Studies in Henry James*, Blackmur writes, "There is not one of us who has not felt, suddenly in the midst of the indifferent ease of intimacy, the sense of having been battened upon to the point of exhaustion by his friend, his lover, or the ominous stranger; and there is not one of us, either, who has not felt the opposite, that he has taken fresh vitality, drained all the season's sap from the other fellow" (61). By the evidence of Blackmur's poetry, he certainly had felt the operations of the sacred fount. One verse is entitled "Too Much For One: Not Enough to Go Round" (*Poems*, 99). In the second section of

"Dedications," called "Wind and Weather," Blackmur characterizes two lovers in terms that could easily apply to Kate Croy and Merton Densher.

> What can be shared seems never a full share
> until by justifiable grand theft
> each in his guilt has tenderness to spare.
>
> (*Poems*, 55)

"Wind and Weather" also contains lines which evoke Milly Theale and Merton Densher in the great autumn storm in Venice.

> I gave that I might measure my own lack,
> she hers. The rest was social wind and weather:
> the storm that forced still holds our lives together.
>
> (*Poems*, 56)

The sacred fount represents lovers' mutual exploitation, but that mutuality forges an unbreakable bond in Blackmur's poetry and James's fiction.

The Wings of the Dove also suggests that love is not best in the present, but in memory. At the end of the novel, Merton Densher finds his recollections of Milly Theale's love much more enthralling than the living Kate Croy. In Blackmur's poetry a similar theme appears, as in "A Labyrinth of Being" where he writes that "passion once shaped should be imagined dead" (*Poems*, 64). The second section of that poem expresses the futile regrets, not of one who has loved and lost in the grand manner, but of a man who has lost because incapable of loving enough. He was, and remains, imprisoned by his mocking thoughts.

> Because one face had meant
> exile for a year
> to manual labours of the heart,
> exile from the mind's content
> the mind's slow-moving certain gear,
> he lost the patience of life's art
> and settled in that corner
> where the soul is disciplined and taught
> by memory the mourner
> how much more bitter than dead beauty is

> the funeral business
> of the holy ghost of thought.
>
> *(Poems, 59)*

Merton Densher, at the end of *The Wings of the Dove*, is alone with his holy dove of thought, the memory of Milly Theale.

The notion that love is better in memory has as its corollary that it is a diminished thing in the present, as are each of the lovers. The last line of *The Wings of the Dove* is Kate Croy's "We shall never be again as we were." Kate might have elaborated with these lines from Blackmur's "A Testament on Faith."

> Once two people talked;
> now two others think of them who passed
> when their first darkness fell, a mask
> forever glued upon them;
> now two others grieve.
>
> *(Poems, 128)*

In a synopsis of his unpublished novel, *The Greater Torment*, Blackmur returns to Kate's words when he paraphrases them to describe the state of his protagonists (Fraser, 158). Indeed, even the title of this novel reprises Blackmur's obsession with James's theme, for in T. S. Eliot's *Ash-Wednesday*, "the greater torment" is not unsatisfied love, but love satisfied.

As one might expect, Blackmur's early identification with the protagonists of *The Wings of the Dove* emerges in his criticism of the novel. In 1943 he wrote this account of the tale's resolution:

> I think of Milly Theale in *The Wings of the Dove*, whom we see actually killed by the conditions of life, acknowledge them how she will, but who yet so transcends them that her image—the image of the lost dead—brings to Kate Croy and Merton Densher, who had betrayed her in life, an unalterable unutterable knowledge of what life is under its mutilated likeness. Things could, as Kate told Merton at the end, never again be the same between them; all because of the freshness and candor which had not perished but been discovered in the death of Milly Theale. *(Studies, 71–72)*

Blackmur emphasizes the beauty of sacrifice, of renunciation, and of death, perhaps thinking of his mother's sacrifices or of his own desire to find a still place of refuge from "what life is." His interpretation is also consistent with the principles of the New Criticism, which Blackmur helped establish and exemplify. Milly becomes art, an image purged of life; the form of her life has emerged from what Blackmur liked to call "inchoate chaos" and has become a text for others to read.

With the passing years, though, Blackmur changed his interpretation of the novel. In "The Loose and Baggy Monsters of Henry James" (1951), Kate begins to rise in his estimation. Milly concomitantly falls, until she begins to resemble that fallen angel who tempted Christ in the desert.

> Kate is criticism which does not destroy but modulates: under her impact we see the nominal heroine of the novel, Milly Theale, for what she is, an aspiration impossible of realization; she is that temptation seen on the high places which is the worst temptation, once seen the most corrupting, appealing with the best impossible appeal to the worst in our natures. . . . The wings of the dove are still clean and silvery, but the sheepfold is fouler than ever; for the dove has created its dirt. (*Studies*, 135)

In his last comments on this novel, in the introductions to the Laurel Editions of James (1958–64), Blackmur posits that Milly's renunciation for love "seems to involve clear suicide or some form of dehumanization" (*Studies*, 227). He concludes that "the infection drawn from the good is worse than that drawn from the evil. It is a curious psychology with which James provides us in his late novels" (*Studies*, 223).

Blackmur's altered interpretation of *The Wings of the Dove* reflects changes in his life and in his criticism. His marriage had failed, and perhaps the virtues of renunciation and sacrifice seemed less honorable and more empty. As life's span diminished with each passing year, he may have wanted to run toward life instead of away from it. What is certain, though, is that his late criticism, found in *The Lion and the Honeycomb* and *A Primer of Ignorance*, emphasizes broader cultural questions, particularly that of art's relationship to society. As Blackmur grew beyond the New Criticism, he became dissatisfied with Milly, an icon removed from life, and developed more respect for Kate, who did not seek to evade life's turmoil, but to use its elements to make her own life a work of art.

Blackmur's change of heart about *The Wings of the Dove* suggests a reason for his inability to complete his long projected work on Henry James. He now had two Milly Theales, each appropriate to a stage of his own development, and he would not sacrifice or renounce either. One might further speculate that a similar pattern held in his incomplete *Henry Adams*. He refers to the effects of Marian "Clover" Adams's suicide in much the same terms he used for Milly Theale's turning her face to the wall. Of Adams he writes, "In his wife's death died a part of him, and by her death a new part lived in him, living backward and forward like memory, with that double force of the richness of the possible and the devastation of the actual which memory alone gives."[4] Blackmur never did write the portion of the manuscript concerning Clover Adams's suicide. Perhaps when he no longer found virtue in Milly Theale's renunciation or believed love best in memory, he was compelled to reevaluate Clover Adams as well. Once again, his older and younger selves had conflicting heroines, and he would sacrifice neither.

From Blackmur's intense response to *The Wings of the Dove*, we cannot simply conclude that you are what you read. We can see, though, that a work read with passion and sympathy is endless in its ramifications on a life and a career. To paraphrase what Henry Adams said of teachers, such a magnetic and suggestive work affects eternity; one can never tell where its influence stops. Change can replenish and enrich as well as damage and dwindle. After all, "We shall never be again as we were" could be read as a declaration of growth for R. P. Blackmur as well as Kate Croy.

NOTES

1. Russell Fraser states that *The Wings of the Dove* was Blackmur's favorite novel in *A Mingled Yarn: The Life of R. P. Blackmur* (New York: Harcourt Brace Jovanovich, 1981), 149. Blackmur describes his response to *The Wings of the Dove* in the introduction to that novel in his *Studies in Henry James* (New York: New Directions, 1983), 161. Subsequent references to these books will be indicated parenthetically in the text.

2. Henry James, *The Wings of the Dove* (New York: Signet, 1964), 9. Subsequent references to this edition will be indicated parenthetically in the text.

3. R. P. Blackmur, "From Jordan's Delight" in *Poems of R. P. Blackmur* (Princeton: Princeton University Press, 1977), 3. Subsequent references to this collection will be indicated parenthetically in the text.

4. R. P. Blackmur, *Henry Adams* (New York: Harcourt Brace Jovanovich, 1980), 86.

SERGIO PEROSA

Blackmur's Criticism
of European Fiction

It was R. P. Blackmur, I believe, who opened my imagination to literature, shaped my attitude of mind, and formed, at least partially, my style. My schooling had been formal and my readings systematic. The whole of Dante and Virgil, Homer and Petrarch, Leopardi and Manzoni at the *liceo;* most of Shakespeare, rows of Elizabethan plays, the major poets and novelists of the canon at the university (modern writers were then read on the side and on one's own). But it was Blackmur, in the late fifties, in his graduate seminars on "Poetics" (I took two, at the risk of spoiling my academic chances) who opened my eyes to the inner workings of literature and my imagination to a proper appreciation of it. (As he wrote, "the imagination requires images, as vision requires fables, and thought requires formulas, before conceptions can be realized" [2, 123].)

He accomplished this in his mellow and unassuming way, through the authority of his formal attitude (I called him "Sir" and for a while he reciprocated), the weight of his thoughtful disposition, and his wide range of references. But he did so mostly through his insistence on flashes of thought, poignant definitions, turns of phrase—often culled and quoted, sometimes in modified form, from other writers—that became illuminations almost in a Rimbaud-like manner, that made you reconsider all you knew (or thought you knew), that sent you back to read familiar books in a totally new way.

I still own a thick brown notebook where I recorded his aphorisms. Fellow students and followers of Blackmur will easily recognize them (that's why I dispense with quotation marks). Art gives to feeling theoretic form (from Croce); by expansion, the novel gives to life theoretic form. Form is the limit whereby we know and apprehend identity. Verse is what is regular and contains what is irregular. In successful writers we see deep difficulties braved; they break through language into style. Reason is logic aware of imagination. Reason generalizes poetry, poetry specifies reason. Poetry casts light on the hidden forms of things. Words unveil the permanent analogies of things by images partaking of the life of truth . . .

The reference to Shelley in the last example is one of many allusions to the somewhat obscure but revealing dicta of the great masters: inspiration is the reward of daily work (Baudelaire); poetry exhibits a state of more than usual emotion and more than usual order (Coleridge); art bitten by poetry longs to be freed from reason (Maritain); or (with Santayana) we behold the Spirit that chills the flesh and is itself on fire. Most of these definitions are found scattered and applied in all of Blackmur's books, and I shall attempt in a moment to explore the nature of their logic (or the logic of their nature), to describe the possible figure in the carpet which accounts for the lesson of the master. What I wish to stress and evoke here, if at all possible, is the kind of intellectual energy which was released by their subdued recitation around the table, by their sudden appearance at the crucial moments of discussion, by their application to unexpected areas or contexts.

After the Princeton experience, Blackmur took me with him to a summer session of the Indiana University School of Letters. In the sweltering heat of that summer, he would meet his students with perfect composure and sharp lucidity of mind in the morning, rehearsing and deepening the tentative wisdom of his intellectual search. In the evenings he kept a sort of open house for friends and devotees: poised on straddling legs and leaning against the mantelpiece, chain-smoking, he bestowed on us the unforgettable experience of night vigils during which the range and sharpness of his mind enveloped and cut through us. I have been grateful to him ever since, and told him so on my last visit with him, a year before his death. I think that pleased him.

Some such testimony as the above from a European scholar is needed, I believe, to express the sense of his influence before I embark on a brief assessment of his criticism of fiction—my chosen topic, though by stipulation I shall eschew as much as possible his crucial criticism of Henry James and concentrate rather on his criticism of the European masters of the novel.

Most of the pregnant quotations I have cited point to an underlying principle in Blackmur's criticism (the principle that also shaped my attitude of mind and my way of looking at literature). It is the concept of homeostasis—the precarious equilibrium of an unstable state, as Blackmur put it—that directed his view of literature and was applied to most of his readings. This concept involves a compulsion, as it were, to keep opposing ideas, principles, and perceptions balanced in one's mind, in order to be able to perceive meaning and form, depth and extension of reference, the burden, drift, and momentum of literary expression.

Not only in Blackmur's view and practice does the reconciliation or balance of opposites become a guiding principle. In rhetorical terms, his basic attitude and practice may be termed chiastic, i.e., focusing on cross arrangement—and I believe that he owed this more than anything else to the example of James. Blackmur's mind was trained—and he trained our minds—to live not in uncertainties, but in the unstable and uneasy condition of *opposing* certainties, in the delicate balance of opposites, in homeostasis. This element, in turn, provided the force, the momentum, and the exaltation of literature, in fiction as well as in poetry. Blackmur's sharp distinctions were meant to reconcile, combine, reconstruct, or reach towards ultimate or pristine unity. "I do not mean to differentiate so much as to join," he wrote (1, 307); while the domain of the arts "is precisely the actual experience of what goes on between the idea and the reality" (2, 29). He loved to work with opposites, cherished the very word "between"—a connective rather than a separating condition with him, which seems present openly or implicitly in so many of his titles and exegeses.

I think we should start from here. His chiastic (as I have called it) critical perception is at work whether he is writing about Ara Coeli and Campidoglio, or the Logos in the Catacomb, or Reason in the Madness of Letters (one need only look at the subtitles of these essays), or a possible theory of literature located "Between the Numen and the Moha." The Numen and the Moha are the two contrasting principles of a power other and greater than ourselves: the aspiration and force of the sublime, and the baseness and stupidity in our souls that bring us down and make us see beauty and attraction in Sodom. Blackmur's avowed wish was "to combine them, to make them compose, in the interests of beautiful reason" (1, 296). In this essay he quotes Coleridge's dictum that poetry exhibits a state of more than usual emotion and of more than usual order, and he stresses that "we associate tragedy with the idea of goats and the idea of katharsis" (1, 292), that we "crave *and* shun" emotion (1, 295), that an artistic representation "is a generalization with the particulars kept in" (1, 300). He speaks with relish of "violent charity" and "predatory compassion" (1, 302). All this belongs to a chiastic imagination and bears directly on Blackmur's conception of fiction, to which I'll turn in a moment; and it is precisely in "Between the Numen and the Moha" that the transition is made clear.

Blackmur's original—or early—conception of fiction was shaped by and derived from Henry James's. In all his essays on the master, though particularly in "The Loose and Baggy Monsters of Henry James" (1951), Blackmur worked on dichotomies and divisions, on the relation and balance of opposites so amply provided by James: between art and life, art and morality, life and the ideal, reality and imagination, abstractions and human values, appearance and reality, general vision and limited point of view, expansion and foreshortening, "platitude of statement" and ambiguity, regionalism and internationalism. In James, Blackmur found the example and the model of the novelist who combined and reconciled, particularized and composed—a splendid balance and blend of opposites. But he also found, in James, the basic ideas for "the underlying classic form in the novel," as runs the subtitle of "The Loose and Baggy Monsters," an essay to be read in connection with "Between the Numen and the Moha" if we want to grasp Blackmur's articulated view of fiction.

If we thought he drew from James mostly a *technical* lesson we would be grossly mistaken. There is nothing (admittedly) of the strict New Critic, even less of the Narratologist, in Blackmur. Technique is subservient to the incarnation and the discovery of meaning; it is a means of showing or expressing life, to compress, sharpen, or enliven "the amount of felt life" (in James's own phrase). Once more, it is a way of balancing the claims of vision and the claims of reality, the "theoretic form" imposed by the writer and the pressure and sweep of the actual. In each case these opposing terms are, if not of equal importance, of strictly related and interwoven relevance. From "The Loose and Baggy Monsters":

> All that I have to say here springs from the conviction that in the novel, as elsewhere in the literary arts, what is called technical or executive form has as its final purpose to bring into being—to bring into performance, for the writer and for the reader—an instance of what life is about. Technical form is our means of getting at, of finding, and then making something of, what we feel the form of life itself is: the tensions, the stresses, the deep relations and the terrible disrelations that inhabit them as they are made to come together in a particular struggle between manners and behavior, between the ideal insight and the actual momentum in which the form of life is found. . . . There is a mutual interaction. There is a wooing both ways; what is found is in some respect affected by the tools used; . . . what is found affects, for the instance, the medium in which it emerges. . . . (1, 268)

In this view, Tolstoy is as much a master of composition (in spite of James's strictures) as James is a writer enveloped, provoked, and inspired by the enormous lap of the actual (in spite of his stress on purely personal relations and on consciousness). The artist is caught —or is at work—between the actual and the ideal, between turbulence and form; he is " 'against' his time" and yet he has "necessarily to collaborate with it" (1, 285). He requires a technique that "articulates and joints and manipulates" (1, 282), as well as a feeling for life that *animates* his view and his perspective.

Poetry is a complex of images, I remember Blackmur saying, but it is also the feeling that *animates* them; never an abstraction or a mere intuition, it is always concerned with feeling and with a sense of life. The same is true of fiction. In "Between the Numen and the Moha" we read that "the novel is ethics in action. Feeling and action. What is felt and what is in action . . . This is because the novel, and every other form of literature, is a confrontation of behavior" in which "morals are compelled to respond to the turbulence of actual life" (1, 289–90 and 305). If the novel gives theoretic form to life, it must first confront actual behavior, "the deep contest of adverse wills" (1, 307) in society and in morality. Thus its underlying classic form is neither the conceptual, nor the executive or technical form, nor the symbolic form: "what the novel is really about [is] the everlasting struggle, the concert of conflict, between the two realities of aspiration and behavior" (1, 306). Chiasmus is overwhelmingly present in these definitions, and so is a consideration of its basic elements: the drama of extremes in conflict, "how behavior gets into literature and what it does to morals when it gets there" (1, 289).

Moving away from James's technical lesson, Blackmur entered the realm of the great masters of the European (and only partially American) tradition of the novel. I say "only partially American" because Blackmur seems to deal with American novelists mostly in terms of, or in the context of, their European *confrères*, and often to their disadvantage. James he considered as standing in between, a mid-Atlantic novelist, concerned with the ethos of American life and society in the complex context of the American literary expatriate. His interest in Henry Adams's two novels must be seen as part—and only part—of his interest in Adams's crucial cultural preoccupations and symptomatic ideological stance. The two novels are seen as significant in connection with Adams's life in that they prefigure his later concern with power and weakness; but they lack precisely the dramatic view of the conflict, the sense of the necessary struggle.

Blackmur's essay on Melville gives a reductionist reading, as is known: "He added nothing to the novel as a form" (1, 125); in spite of his "perception of dramatic fate," Melville's work "constantly *said* what it was doing or was going to do, and then, as a rule, stopped short. . . . To put it sharply, he did not write of characters in action; he employed the shells of stock characters. . . . This is, if you like, the mode of allegory" (1, 129–30). I feel that the two essays on Adams and Melville are written very much in a Jamesian mode: if James had written on Melville, I suspect he would have written in this manner, and one might even say that Blackmur on Melville reads at times like James on Hawthorne in his 1879 monograph (this is, incidentally, one of the few cases in which Blackmur attempts a stylistic analysis, mostly in deprecatory terms). In a similar way, when writing of Faulkner in his "Reason in the Madness of Letters," Blackmur was led to inquire "why it is that [Faulkner] has deliberately surrendered the advantages of syntax" (3, 25); and I suspect that he saw him, ultimately, as a second-rate Dostoevsky.

The "dramatic attitude," the full sense of life *and* style, of feeling and form, the balance of character and action, daring forms of what he called "rival creation": these Blackmur found in the great masters of the European novel. He was aware of the mimetic tradition, of the type of novel mostly concerned with the actual, relying on the existence of a knowable, recognizable world: Zola and Dreiser, Balzac (with his great *élan*, though he could not write) and Hemingway (whose power to write in actual scenes attempted timidly and inconclusively the imposition of symbolic patterns). But this was not his cherished tradition. It lacked "the deep contest of adverse wills," the moral and symbolic complexities, the probings into the dark sides of the soul—those elements, formulas, or clichés that in his Prefatory Note to *Eleven Essays in the European Novel* Blackmur listed as essential to his "great tradition."

As one might expect, these were, first, theoretic form imposed on life; second, the creation of new psychologies; third, "a speculation in myth which reaches into the driving psyche" (2, vii). These ultimately converged into the formula that combines, once more, the requirements of plot and character, of outer behavior and deeper psychologies: "A man's *ethos* is his *daimon*" (the terms were of course used in an Aristotelian sense) (2, v–viii).

This "great tradition" of the European novel reaches backwards in time only for springs and tentative historical roots (in Fielding and Smollett, Richardson and Austen). It is basically a pre-Modernist and Modernist tradition: the great nineteenth-century founding fathers (Stendhal and Flaubert, James and Tolstoy) and their culmination in the early twentieth century (Proust and Joyce, Gide and Thomas Mann, Kafka and Pirandello). In between the two moments fall the shadow and the influence of Freud and Jung ("the two greatest allegorists of the present time," in my notes), with their stress on the dark side of the mind and on a dramatic view of life in which tragic confrontations spring not only from conflicts in society but from lacerations in ourselves. Yet Blackmur's conception is not strictly historical, and the great nineteenth-century forerunners of the Modernist tradition—notably Dostoevsky, but also Henry James—seem just as aware and in as full possession of deeper psychologies and "rival creations" as their twentieth-century followers.

Both *Madame Bovary* and *War and Peace* show the disruptive workings of society on individuals whose new psychologies unfit them for acquiescent life, whose ethos (again in the Greek sense of character and behavior) involves them in inescapable situations or *mythoi.* In both novels the presence of the actual directs and distorts behavior; behavior, in turn, thwarts and warps morals to tragic ends. Based on the actual, the experience of their heroes and heroines shows the craving for and the discovery of the real, and reaches for eventual collapse and destruction; but this experience is dramatized in tightly composed and controlled forms, in symmetrical structures.

"In the nineteenth century the novel of Flaubert, Dostoevsky, and Tolstoy took on the risk of drama and was forced into objective imagination" (2, 50). *Madame Bovary,* in particular, is "the history of one of the great ways by which we accommodate our inner or our true selves to the bruise and press of society. . . . It is also the history of that kind of damnation which comes when we are unable to accept the conditions of life" (2, 49). As for Anna Karenina, "her tragedy is that she has destroyed too much of the medium, too many of the possibilities, of actual life, to leave life tolerable" (2, 25); and this in a novel which is seen and analyzed as an almost perfect system of symmetries and reversals.

Moving forward in time, Proust's *Recherche* strikes Blackmur as an "enormous rival creation of the world." "His whole book is morals in action," showing "a continuous approximation of moral progress" (3, 26). In Proust, as in the other great figures of Modernism, the central character is often an artist—mostly baffled, frustrated, exposed, crushed as much in his confrontation with the drive and drift of society as by the dark forces at work within his psyche. Though this is never openly stated, it seems that for Blackmur there are ordered, structured, and imposing ways of representing this ordeal and its counterpoises; there are also forms that lean towards or rely on entropy and dissipation, that mimic fragmentation and loss of identity.

To the first instance belong the great examples of Thomas Mann and James Joyce. Mann's "greater magnitude" in *The Magic Mountain* "depends precisely upon that power of prophecy which comes to the artist who dramatizes the actual thought—thought in all its senses—of his own time" (2, 77–78). His artistic and intellectual force lies in the picture he gives of the transition between two worlds and two periods of time—a "legend of the *haut-bourgeois* at the climax of the nineteenth century"—and in his grasp of the darker, demonic drives within the individual: "if the mind is honest in some dark corner it finds it cannot abide on its own practice." The task of the mind is "making full assent to the conditions of life with will and choice, with reason and imagination"; yet it is beset by the horror of reality, by the "cultivation of hallucination and phantasy" (2, 77–78). In his essay on *The Magic Mountain* Blackmur works brilliantly with the balance of opposites, and in homeostasis; but in *Doktor Faustus* the strange, the unfamiliar, and the demonic get the upper hand and make it almost expressive and reflective of post-Modern times and sensibilities: "Adrian Leverkühn's music is the naked human voice of the actual world and collapses at the apocalypse of the world to come" (1, 49).

Blackmur's study of *Ulysses* seems to me the apotheosis of his balanced and chiastic view. Joyce's novel is declared "the book that *made* an order out of the substance of the dadaist imagination" (3, 24), out of fragmentation and dissipation, by combining the big gap of the unconscious *and* the enormous lap of the actual. "*Ulysses* is the most structured book in English since at least Milton and it does as much to maintain and develop the full language as anybody since Shakespeare." It is described as a Pythagorean reduction of the many to one—and what a relief, after all the loose talk about the stream-of-consciousness technique! Blackmur goes to great length to show the perfect correlation of its characters, the "mythical" background that holds the structure together, the rhythm of the narration and of the language. "There are weights which answer each other," and there is a triple means of commanding attention: universal patterns, characters that are "parallel and completing each other," a story "gradually told in immense bursts of vivid detail" (3, 61–62).

In the longer essay "The Jew in Search of a Son," the breakdown of our world is seen to force itself as a theme and "to present an inordinate mass of detail," which the writer has to accept and master. Yet in *Ulysses*, "there is both repudiation, by Stephen, and acceptance, by Bloom; and also, by Molly, a gesture of surpassing indifference." Much is made of this triadic pattern, of Stephen's need for Bloom, of his pride, hubris, and consequent damnation; of Bloom's acquiescence in life and his final salvation; of Molly's cultivation of herself. But it is their correlation that matters, so that "the waywardness or high jinks of the book is order pushed, the chaos is order mixed, the disgust is order humiliated, the exile is order desiderated or invoked" (2, 31–32).

The breakdown of the picture so vividly painted by Mann, the dissolution of identity so bravely restored by Joyce in his triad, the loss of a structure that would keep our souls and our lives together, are accepted and presented (or exploited) *as such* by Modernists of the other type: Gide, Kafka, Pirandello, Camus, Woolf. Blackmur took cognizance of, and analyzed, their work and their impact, but never, I dare say, with real relish or full adhesion. In Pirandello we witness the *play* of modern psychology, "the kind of movement and the kind of withdrawal the psyche makes in its craving for that form which determines identity" (3, 27–29). In Kafka, "what happens cuts down everything but the indestructible principle of the self," and we are left with "an inner shriek of the deracinated quick of spirit"; we have "religious novels of rebirth where only the agony, not the birth, takes place" (3, 27–29). In André Gide—another author "loved with aversion" by Blackmur—we find the lighter touch, even a touch of frivolity, and the struggle for an individual culture (3, 27–29). The personality created in *The Counterfeiters* is "so frail and precarious that it is at the point of extinction" (1, 48). There is no higher vision, no higher dream, in Gide; perhaps not even in Woolf, in whose world, according to Blackmur, "human relations disappear in the very technique of sensibility in which they are supposed to be lodged and to be understood"; certainly not in D. H. Lawrence, in whom "the hysteria of direct sensual experience destroys every structure of the sensibility" (3, 24). Just as he was against expressive form, Blackmur was skeptical of diffusiveness.

He was undoubtedly less at home with, and felt less sympathy for, these writers who mimicked, expressed, or exploited entropy and dissipation and who did not struggle to reconstruct an order, however precarious, out of chaos. Behind both types of Modernist writers he saw, however, the presence and the lesson of perhaps the greatest nineteenth-century forerunner, mentor, and indeed representative of the modern novelist: Dostoevsky—who is with James, perhaps, the object of Blackmur's greatest love. That Blackmur cherished and studied both these writers so much and so consistently speaks once more for his chiastic critical imagination, for his need to work with and balance opposites. But within Dostoevsky himself he found or posited a powerful dualistic force at work: the fascination with the torments, the lacerations, the debris of conscience, on the one side, and, on the other, a driving need to hold the scattered and shattering pieces of the mind and of the world desperately together. In Dostoevsky Blackmur found the epitome, or the greatest example, of the chiastic creative imagination at work—a rage for order in spite of, or thanks to, the inner and outer chaos: "All Dostoevsky's great novels form a drama of the two extremes in conflict" (1, 294). And in his articulated analysis of the major novels (which forms Part II of *Eleven Essays in the European Novel*) he worked with that principle constantly in mind. In *Crime and Punishment*—we read at the beginning of that study—Dostoevsky had depicted what Shakespeare called "the point where two prayers cross, where, in the human heart, good and evil are created in one gesture" (2, 125); in *The Brothers Karamazov*, we read towards the end, the notions of guilt and innocence are inextricably linked.

In his great novels the Russian writer can offer contrasting moral values and opposing views of society brought to a crisis or to a climax by the driving urges of torn, lacerated, aspiring characters. He was perhaps the greatest discoverer of deep and dark new psychologies at work in the context of society, morality, or religion, of characters divided and composed by the highest aspirations and the basest corruptions. Yet his characters are never solitary or in isolation: they react to the life of the senses and the life of the spirit, human relations and human oppositions, social struggles and utopian dreams. Above all, they are presented as part of complex patterns—psychological, social, intellectual, and ideological patterns—in which each has a relative value and lives in structured connection with the others.

Dostoevsky's dualisms and oppositions—the clash or the balance of opposites—are seen to work on the level of structure, of characters, and of values. Each action, condition, or movement has its counterpart; as in *Crime and Punishment*, "There is a synergy—working together back and forth—between these counterparts." Collateral form and homeostasis become guiding principles:

> This working together takes place, and the resultant unity is seen, not because there is any logical connection between the parts, but because, quite to the contrary, the conflicting elements are dramatized in associ-

ation, in parallels that, as they say, never actually meet except as opposites. . . . What we get is a kind of steady state precariously maintained between the conflicting elements. The balance tips, but it recovers in the act of tipping. . . . Dostoevsky's imagination arrests, for the maximum possible amount of attention, the moments when the balance does tip from love to hate, from pride to humiliation, from idea to deed, from image to tension . . . We seem to see deeply what they make together by seeing wilfully what they are apart. (2, 130–31)

In turn, characters are "doubles" in themselves (humble and proud, damned and blessed; the saint is an epileptic, the atheist a believer), while each has his or her double on the level of plot: "In any pair, the one may be taken as the idea of the other, and the other the reality of the idea, and the only alternation is as to which, at a given moment, is idea and which reality" (2, 130). For instance: Raskolnikov is "self-willed and will-less" in himself, and "balanced in turn against the other characters in this novel" (2, 130–31). In *The Idiot* we have the dramatization of "God's gift of the good and perfect individual man" beating down the evil of society, and "quite the opposite" (2, 141). In *The Possessed* we find the "only true concert, the concert of conflicts" (2, 166). These two novels deal in fact with opposing themes, but each theme works through dualisms and oppositions: in the former, the epitome of the good man suffers from *le grand mal*, in the latter, the vision of Christ "creates the vision of the anti-christ" (2, 169).

Dostoevsky "not only gave the devil his due; he knew that the devil lived in his own heart unexorcisably, whether by saint or peasant" (2, 171). What Blackmur says of Stavrogin can then be taken to express his deepest view of the Russian writer: order and disorder are balanced on the knife's edge. Though oppositions are sometimes reconciled, no new order is achieved in his novels: "He could not bring himself to envisage as united what he felt as separated by a great gap" (2, 171). On the level of values, his stories are concerned with the tearing down of order, but without proceeding to balance "the sense of several disorders—the tensions of chaos—against each other so as to form a new order" (2, 122). As for his "doubles," he met them side by side "each impervious to the other, each lost in his own temptations . . . with a kind of incommensurable equivalence in their disparate momentums" (2, 183).

The culmination of these unresolved dualisms is found in *The Brothers Karamazov*, the novel on which Blackmur worked harder and more extensively—not so much, I think, on account of its greater depth, as for the way in which a complex structure of characters and ideas, types and feelings, rages and values, was made to work *as* a structure and as a pattern ("separately they are nothing, it is the bringing together that counts" [2, 188]). In this structure of interrelations and in this pattern of contrasting values we witness force transformed by sin into motive, an inner beat of systole and diastole, a dialectic of parallels. All characters are recognized as "doubles," with "the potential of reversing without altering their roles"; they are on the "teeter of reversability" (2, 192). As for values, "virtue and shame, honor and lust, love and murder, all seem to come together—as for simultaneous interconversion" (2, 202).

"Simultaneous interconversion" seems to me to express admirably what Blackmur saw and appreciated in Dostoevsky. As we, moreover, identify at the deepest level with these "brothers in baseness" (2, 213), doubleness and homeostasis invest all values: the positive side of vision rises out of the negative side, and we are "faced with such an equilibrium (essentially, the sudden weightlessness of our contrary beliefs)" (2, 216). This is another key definition. In this novel, only the experience of absolute guilt can "create the utopia of forgiven man" (2, 170). Thus we catch a glimpse of the "other truth" whereby the guilty are acquitted and the innocent are convicted: "This is how it is that in *The Brothers Karamazov*, the plain and overwhelming story of a murder is lifted into the condition of miracle, mystery, and authority" (2, 243).

I take it that in the structured correlation of the brothers Karamazov Blackmur saw the same principle at work that he had recognized in *Ulysses:* the complexity and total sum of man shining through correlated and opposing characters, a pattern emerging out of chaos, separation reaching for unity. But let it be remembered that Blackmur's was not a relativistic view. He saw that intellectual and religious values—in the broad and deep sense—were at the bottom or at the core of Dostoevsky's inspiration: "Art in the long run is as good a measure of honesty as we have; moving in the actual, it plays on truth," he wrote (2, 215). But he also saw principles and beliefs tangled and contradicted—as they should be—in the life of the novel in action, in behavior that alters morals: "It is in the novel, more than in any settled form of art, that our thoughts and tendencies—the dogmas by which we catch momentum day to day—come into their own true concert, the concert of conflicts" (2, 166). We reach here full circle.

In the case of Dostoevsky it is rather hard to extract Blackmur's views, because he follows Dostoevsky step by step in a kind of close reading that is almost symbiotic, piling *his* dualisms and contradictions on Dostoevsky's dualisms and oppositions, thriving on complexities and reversals. His essays on Dostoevsky seem his most deeply felt and complex in language and style, as if for once Blackmur had himself succumbed to mimetic form and wrote critically about Dostoevsky as Dostoevsky wrote creatively in his novels. This may be taken to represent, on the level of language and expression, an example of almost perfect symbiosis: the chiastic imagination of the critic finding the most complex embodiment of a creative chiastic imagination, or the latter determining the former.

Apart from this, Blackmur makes of Dostoevsky the perfect case of a writer who offers a prefiguration, perhaps an anticipation, of the plight of modern man, of the sense of loss and separation and tragedy inherent in our contemporary condition. Neither the New Critic nor the neo-humanist, neither the cold analyst nor the muddled moralist, Blackmur saw the value and the extension of that prefiguration, yielded to it but rose to clarify and describe it in his critical pages. I believe that finally he was fascinated by the way in which Dostoevsky made the catharsis coexist with the goats of tragedy: "Hurrah for all the Karamazovs!"—Blackmur cries out at the end of his essay—"for here is the condition where all are guilty and none are guilty. To live in that condition, and to love life, is to endure the tragedy of the saint. In this novel the saint is migratory among the three brothers, nowhere at home" (2, 243).

It was so with the critic of the European novel: migratory among his books, nowhere at home, not so much divided in allegiance as invoking the wealth of possibilities that fiction and literature can evoke and embody. In his studies of Dostoevsky we see how his critical faculty was raised—but he remained lost in amazement.

NOTES

Page references are to the following editions, introduced respectively by the numerals 1, 2, and 3:

1. R. P. Blackmur, *The Lion and the Honeycomb* (New York: Harcourt, Brace and Co., 1955).
2. R. P. Blackmur, *Eleven Essays in the European Novel* (New York and Burlingame: Harcourt, Brace and World, 1964).
3. R. P. Blackmur, *A Primer of Ignorance* (New York: Harcourt, Brace and World, 1967).

F. D. REEVE

Blackmur's Craft

Can you like a writer whose work you don't admire? De Tocqueville pointed out that "among democratic nations, a writer may flatter himself that he will obtain at a cheap rate a meager reputation and a large fortune. For this purpose he need not be admired, it is enough that he is liked." The forecast expresses an antinomy of our literary life to this day, a sort of warfare between popularity and excellence in which Blackmur himself intervened by trying to persuade middle-ground culture—for example, *The New York Times Book Review*—to upgrade itself, to respect the integrity of dissent as much as an artist's enabling vision. In Blackmur's world, admiration was a kind of friendship, and some people maintain that his personality was more important than his poems. Some admire his criticism; some find it eccentric and elitist; and some support their objections by citing Wallace Stevens's remark to Henry Church that Blackmur had no lack of ideas but didn't know what they were. Filled with sea imagery, Blackmur's poems are put down as a Maine man's response to common themes of love, loss, loneliness. Such crude treatment assures a diminished result, and perhaps by putting Blackmur down the teachers make themselves feel taller.

Others, including me, esteem Blackmur as one of the most percipient and gifted literary men of the twentieth (and, therefore, of any) century, and regard the three volumes of published poems and the recently collected scattering[1] as the embodiment not of his critical procedures but of his critical intentions.

In each poem Blackmur's lyric self temporarily puts his formidable criticism in the service of verbal toughness, the bones of structure. Proceeding from experience as if it were a text—"It's always a help to speak from a text"—not from insecurity or iconoclasm but from fullness of mind, he drums the resonances of words, weaves patterns of reusable images, shores up the scenery of indeterminacy. His whole mind goes into motion round a central moral gesture. Contextual measures adequate in themselves but, like any uncertain measure, uncodifiable and untranslatable, the poems appear as fragments of longing for completeness. "The only kind of meaning poetry can have," he wrote, "requires that all its words resume their full life: the full life being modified and made unique by the *qualifications* the words perform one upon the other in the poem."[2] He himself admired Eric Heller's *The Hazard of Modern Poetry,* from which he quoted: "Experience is not in the impressions we receive; it is in *making* sense. And poetry is the foremost sense-maker of experience. It renders *actual* ever new sectors of the apparently inexhaustible field of *potential* experience."[3] The poems exceed the criticism by their mobility, their ambiguity and their ironic mode. As word houses—houses of and for words—they preserve the possibilities of skepticism better than criticism and protect against loss by doubt. Valéry asked, "Whenever you think do you not feel you are disarranging something?" Blackmur twice quoted the query and Elizabeth Sewell's observation on it: "Words are the only defense of the mind against being possessed by thought or dream."[4] Poetry, he said, is the means to knowledge of the complementary relation between order and chaos.[5] His last poems achieve the clear strength of earned emotion.

The poetry begins by expressing the continuity of the tradition to which it belongs and the changes in the sorts of experience that it's making sense of. "Phasellus Ille" (43), an Italian sonnet, opens as a translation of the first line of Catullus's fourth poem—"Phasellus ille, quem videtis, hospites"—

> This little boat you see, my friends, has not,
> as once Catullus' pinnace could repeat,
> a history of deep-sea peril sought;
> for her no honoured peace, no earned retreat.

The two craft are two possible forms of the mind's expression, the omniform American mind that knows "that every individual must do the job over again, in token form, in his own life but that he cannot do it at all without the co-operation of cultures he only partly grasps and of ideas of which he misses the original point," as Blackmur wrote in the 1954 issue of *Perspectives* that he edited.[6] His boat—as opposed to his craft—has not traveled so widely as Catullus's—his ordering must be different—but the chaos on which the order works is different, too:

> I do not need the bluster and the wail
> in this small boat, of perilous high seas
> nor the blown salt smarting in my teeth;
> if the tide lift and weigh me in his scale
> I know, and feel in me the knowledge freeze,
> how smooth the utter sea is, underneath.

Blackmur forgoes Catullus's amiable prosopopoeia but uses Catullus as source for the paraleipsis in the first half of the sestet; that is, Blackmur's boat doesn't tell him its history but stands in for him, as awkward and vulnerable as any contemporary. The images of stormy seas and windblown spray that Blackmur sets beyond his present experience are presumably recalled from other days afloat but they're also taken directly from Catullus's poem. Catullus's Jupiter-controlled ocean becomes Blackmur's personified tide. But what Blackmur extraordinarily adds to Catullus, that poetic increment which renews the life of the Latin and is the new life of the American, is the profoundly ironic perception, offered as full knowledge extrapolated from partial experience, that the power of the sea is smooth, submarine and mysterious. The closing tercet is exquisite in the musical movements corresponding to the intellectual. "The utter sea" lingers as an image and as a definition close to symbolism. The more I read the poem, the more its technical excellences astonish me, the deeper sound the reverberations of emotional intensity and moral integrity. Even in other, imperfect examples, Blackmur's is a poetry of perfection.

Like all craftsmen, he displays the qualities of his tools, making his verse realign vocabulary, as October frost quickens "the richened air" (34); or hold an ineffable image in which the words become reality, like the sea-island sheep's "faint, fog-cracked cough of half

surprise" (21); or uncover layered meanings by syntactic rearrange-
ment, illuminated by "the light the night at last breaks both ways
through" (57). No singer of self, Blackmur doesn't use his language
as advertisement. "What can't be said doesn't exist," Baudelaire
remarked, and Blackmur's report is similar, poetry being the supreme
effort with words to push back the edge of darkness even a little, to
admit doubt and to accommodate uncertainty. It's the imagination
becoming its own music. As She says in "The Cough":

> —Words verge on flesh, and so we may,
> someday, be to ourselves the things we say. (41)

The other half of the idea (in Blackmur's dynamics, each verse draws
its apposite opposite with it) follows; he asks that

> God forbid
> there seem more beauty in a word
> in that it's said, and heard,
> than lies in the still body hid. (42)

"All that has been said," wrote Melville with comparably great generosity, "but multiplies the avenues to what remains to be said."

The modesty of such a mind is spiritual, not social. It delights
in the immediately sensual—"the sea herself . . . spreading her lazy
thighs" (25)—and respects the force perceived in presence, the invisible power of a pendulum made visible through its reversings. In
"Witness of Light" (33), the language patiently educes the power—

> See all we see
> weakness and strength
> without feud without faith
> mirror the mystery
> light in the light

—building, through a sophisticated catalogue of antinomies and puns
("lightning in light") balancing the actual and the symbolic, to a
transcendent illumination:

> Humbled from confusion
> the cumulus words:
> O charitable heart
> see all we see

> the witnessing art
> light in the light

The ecstatic vision affirmed by verbal inventiveness is the substance of the imagination. The witnessing art observes, beholds, gives the news or evidence of it, attests, authenticates, indeed presages it. It delivers it. Words in the world are clouds in the sky—wandering, meaningless. Art's office is to humble them—to bring them down—into significant, or real, life. As God can't deny mercy to the properly penitent, so the heart must be charitable even in a time of

> the hunger for bloodshed
> and rape as release

when presented with everything that the imaginative mind grasps and, in patient humility, orders—what Blackmur, combining Aristotelian ethics and Christian spirituality, calls "the inward mastery of the outward act" (82).

The brilliance of the light comes from the hardness of the art. The love behind it is all earned emotion, a full projection. Blackmur's compass is so wide, his antennae so responsive, his mind so accurate and his standards so demanding that you can't trespass your own integrity in coming to a judgment of his work. The poetry includes his uncanny ability to allow for variation and to correct for deviation. The "anni mirabiles," those miraculous years 1921–1925, formed him; the values they affirmed he reaffirmed in his verse. He reformed the American tradition, forecast America's literary weather. One of our finest Collectors of Customs—exposing fraud, taxing imports, encouraging domestic invention—he was both native and natural. As he put it,

> My innocence, like my guilt, is radical,
> and strikes a taproot down you cannot sever. (80)

A harsh, even hostile country, America, for such an intelligent, self-reliant, unforgetful man. A poet in America who keeps his vision seems doubly strong. Indeed, reading Blackmur's verse, I sense a burdened poetry seeking to shift its weight to song, as if to sing in spite of the facts.

As a king dwells in royalty, can't put it off for the life of him, so Blackmur inhabited imagination. The opening stanza of "Petit Manan Point" (36–37) shows how his exemplary literary mind took reality by device, from complexities of prosody to local pronunciation—

> At last from the thick mile of brush we six
> came out to sea-light in our summer tan,
> came out on the last flat hand
> of seaward land,
> issued in eager company
> on the full solitude of Petit Manan.

—shoring up its generalizable self against the ultimate

> mountainous white waste
> of the great storm to come.

One could gloss key words (for example, "waste" as in the Shakespearean "waste of shame") or elaborate on a verbal inversion such as

> in this flat hand
> the laying on of death

thereby enhancing the poem's central image of the Point that comes to nothing, from beyond which nothing comes. A metaphysical sorrow shapes this and other heavy poems. As real as the world on Atlas's shoulders, it's a melancholy no man gets rid of:

> Beware this bleak elation.

Measured against the stars or against men's collective power, a man is small, is worth only as much as he believes. Impotent against massed nature, the best believer keeps repairing the "injured imagination," but the here-and-now, the Point where

> one could lay impossible keel and frame
> for half the hulls upon the Gulf of Maine

is the self's boneyard inhabitable only in imaginative reconstruction. The office of doubt is to assure constancy; the complete world is the equilibrium of imagined reality:

> O friend of shadow, friend of brimming silence,
> come walk with me, come slowly by my side.

> We shall, if we walk long enough, and turn
> as the sun turns us, burning in our eyes,
> at last see the red river fold that sun
> to rest, and have ourselves such peace of earth
> as evens out those strangers, night and day.
>
> ("River-Walk," 53–54)

There being two kinds of death as there have been since Genesis, the facts contest the vision. That is, there's

> Death, or its equivalent in knowledge,

each brought to harmony in the poetry. One side of harmony is mastery; the other is mystery: Mystery is unmasterable, the knowledge that there's no further knowledge, a final ignorance to which one comes by training and sensitivity. As Blackmur wrote elsewhere, "One has to possess one's ignorance like knowledge."[7] But the birds, whose perfect song is beyond our language, the poem says, can't know our music,

> nor is their silence our despair. We are
> (in this desert judged, impeached, identified)
> the straight shadows of separated stars.

The cosmic unity that to Dante six hundred years ago seemed natural, to Blackmur (and to us) is incredible. Language is our bridge across "the bottom of our silence"; the compact elegance of poetry, the limits of control.

Blackmur's great critical mind revitalized Western tradition and adapted American literature to modern sensibilities. The past was the grand setting for the present, but there was no Calliope to help nor Alma Venus to bless the present poet, who had, essentially, to remanufacture his language. Blackmur's criticism gave a modern reading of the classics and explained his contemporaries, including himself. Understanding that poetry wasn't antithetical to socio-political life but greater than it, in the process becoming the experience it made sense of, he grasped the opposition between conventional values of American life and the values expressed through the literary tradition. He invested himself in that tradition—for example, in the work of Henry Adams—which he studied for itself in relation to poetic meaning. From that comes his repeated perception of an intellectual discovery, or triumph, as a social failure. Adams's pattern seems to be his own, and his reading of Adams's Clarence King could easily yield to my version of Blackmur:

> King was perhaps the clearest of all the symbols Adams created for himself as lodged in the welling, shifting ambiguity of an individual human being. His figure was human, his stature created out of the human. He stood for what oneself could do at the utmost and, at the same time, for the riddle of why the effort failed. . . . Clarence King, from his first manifestation onward, meant to Adams that a full response to life in his own country and time was possible, and that all assent and revolt and despair were alone meaningful in terms of that possibility.[8]

Life in art is the largest possible life, recreating the processes of experience without violating them, embracing contradictions and desire, and including the world of wonder. It houses a man in his belief, suits him with his talent. Adams's or Blackmur's "effort failed" only in the profound sense that genuine art is testamentary. Imperfectly understood in its own time, its excellence bespeaks its legacy.

Blackmur's poetry is double-threaded. Some of the poems— "Before Sentence Is Passed," "Twelve Scarabs for the Living: 1942," "The Good European: 1945"—are as harshly political as his essays and reviews. In general, however, it takes to a point beyond the criticism the perceptions and relations by which literature lives. Not that he wrote to principle; rather, he wrote from necessity, and the canons structuring his criticism were procedural guides in writing and revising the verse, building its skeletons, measuring its proportions, shaping its rhythms, beating its resonances. Why haven't his shorter poems with their surprising, apt diction and crafted simplicity become widely popular? As popular as, say, "Stopping by Woods on a Snowy Evening"? Blackmur's "A Second World" (73) is brief and elegant, but it boldly expresses his skeptical, faithful mind. The poem grows larger but no less unsettling the more we read it:

> Who that has sailed by star
> on the light night air,
> first hand on the tiller,
> second, the nibbling sheet,

> who, looking aloft and then aback,
> has not one moment lost
> in the wind's still eye
> his second world
> and the bright star
> before the long shudder fills on
> the windward tack?

Caught between states of being, in an actual moment when opposite directions, like time past and time future, are possible, we're turned through the eye of the wind to the eye of the mind. This is the vortex that discovers and conceals the second world; it's the circling spirit of water recurring throughout Blackmur's poetry, transforming itself with ultimate conviction into "eddying, bodiless faith" (11). The poems are its enactments.

Difficult because of their expressed intelligence but always intelligible, they take on what, in a review, Blackmur called "the regular everlasting job of making over again the absolute content of sensibility with which we get on, or with which we acknowledge our failures to do so."[9] They acknowledge, modify and improve the rules of prosody, at the same time becoming the activity they describe. "Poetry *thinks,*" Blackmur wrote, "by giving the actual experience—the *make-believe*—of thought."[10] Fact and fancy complected, the perfect representation:

THE SKIN OF THE SOUL

> If righteousness without its faith is sin
> and faith without its sin is empty act,
> how shall the armed man plead? or soul save skin?
> Between the lover and his murder pact
> there is the third lost face, self looking in. (91)

Least egotistic of men, Blackmur lived by poetry and its criticism, a way of life to be extended as widely as possible. Ironically, he who understood Stevens's work, explicated it and generated Stevens's respectful audience, wasn't understood by Stevens. Like Roethke and others, perhaps Stevens was too megalomaniacal to accept Blackmur's discriminations and to honor his ambivalences. In the years since Blackmur's death in 1965, the subtleties of his poems and the strengths of his standards have, like lighthouses, grown even more attractive in isolation. His work is of a piece, distinguished by assiduity and skill, by wisdom, courage and generosity. We can now see that he accomplished what, in a lyric written when he was twenty-three, he proposed doing from the start:

> I would meet
> Between the midnight and the first succeeding bell
> One hour brimful as the sea,
> One body deep as my breath in me:
> So I would do my last things well. (134)

NOTES

1. See *Poems of R. P. Blackmur* (Princeton: Princeton University Press, 1977). Subsequent page references are to this edition.

2. R. P. Blackmur, *Language as Gesture* (New York: Harcourt Brace and Co., 1952), 323.

3. R. P. Blackmur, *A Primer of Ignorance* (New York: Harcourt Brace and World, 1967), 60–61.

4. *A Primer of Ignorance,* 39 and 47.

5. *Language as Gesture,* 357.

6. R. P. Blackmur, "Editor's Commentary," *Perspectives* 6 (Winter 1954), 135.

7. R. P. Blackmur, *Henry Adams* (New York: Harcourt Brace Jovanovich, 1980), 193.

8. *Henry Adams,* 92–94.

9. *Language as Gesture,* 255–56.

10. *Language as Gesture,* 259.

EDWARD W. SAID

The Horizon
of R. P. Blackmur

Not an inch measure nor a yard stick, but a compass bearing:
the focus of scope, great enough initially to absorb any amount
of attention, wide enough eventually, one thinks,
to command a full horizon.

—R. P. BLACKMUR

I

Few things in intellectual or aesthetic life are more unattractive and
dispiriting, and yet more common, than the orthodoxy to which a vital
and significant performance can be reduced by a programmatic admiration and uncritical codification. Flaubert's *Dictionnaire des idées
reçues* is of course the parodic monument to such a fall, but so too
on a modest and quotidian level are the definitions, tags, markers
employed to theatricalize and grasp the work of critics, particularly
those whose writings are perceived as influential. To think of Matthew Arnold and T. S. Eliot, for example, is virtually impossible
without getting past a whole set of by now automatic labels like "the
best that has been thought and said" or "dissociation of sensibility."
The irony, of course, is that such labels give currency to work whose
density might otherwise render it unread, although we should also
allow that a direct connection does in fact exist between populariza-
tions of Eliot and Arnold and their intention to make their ideas
prevail.

Some usually unstated (or unstateable) balance between critical
performance and critical influence can be found at the heart of every
major critic's work. The critic feels, and even intends, the balance,
without being able to say whether it works. This is not just a matter
of empirical verification, of actually trying to ascertain whether readers find, for example, that insights delivered by a given critic are useful

or practical for them; nor is it a matter of calculated strategy by which the critic launches a few slogans while also reserving a part of his thought for really difficult work. Critics write, of course, in order to be read; to change, refine, or deepen understanding; to press evaluation and revaluation. Yet rare are the critics for whom criticism is its own justification, and not an act for the gaining of adherents or for the persuasion of larger and larger audiences. Rarer still are critics whose work at its center cradles the paradox that whatever criticism urges or delivers must not, indeed cannot, be replicated, reproduced, re-used as a lesson learned and then applied.

Even among such a tiny minority of critical practitioners R. P. Blackmur occupies a position of intransigent honor. Not that he does not teach. Rather what he teaches, or whatever his reader gains access to, appears to be incidental to the main department of his concern. His earliest essays in critical explication were exploratory and wayward, marked by the frank amateur's enthusiasm, the autodidact's diligence, the private reader's inwardness. Much of the time he seemed to locate himself at the source of the poet's creativity, as it deployed forms, idioms, figures to negotiate the disorder of modernity. Blackmur was especially sensitive to the dangers besetting modern poetry in an inattentive culture, dangers stemming from a felt incompleteness and lack of support in the environment that drew the poet (and by implication the critic) to the invention of machinery or of a system whose job it was to supplement poetry with the rigor, the stability, the discipline of universal order. Like the early Lukacs, such poets—among them Yeats, Eliot, and Pound—regarded with nostalgia a lost age of integrated life, thereby condemning themselves in the present to overcoming what Eliot called "the immense panorama of futility and anarchy which is contemporary history."[1] This they could do themselves by providing various therapies for the afflictions of modernity in the form of insights or systems that gave coherence on the one hand, but repelled readers on the other. Blackmur's seminal point of departure therefore was this fact, perceived not as a disability but as an enabling condition of great modern poetry:

> It is almost the mark of the poet of genuine merit in our time—the poet who writes serious works with an intellectual aspect which are

nonetheless poetry—that he performs his work in the light of an insight, a group of ideas, and a faith, with the discipline that flows from them, which taken together form a view of life most readers cannot share, and which, furthermore, most readers feel as repugnant, or sterile, or simply inconsequential.[2]

The difficulty the reader experienced with the great moderns resided only partly in the esoteric language, complex homemade schemes, and what Blackmur was later to call the "irregular metaphysics" on which these writers depended; difficulty also derived from the reader's negative reactions to them, which Blackmur was one of the first to recognize as an obstacle purposely designed by the writer. Modernism therefore was like a customs barrier erected to force through the bits of modern life that could be shaped by technique and the symbolic imagination into aesthetic order, and it was also a way to compel readers to pay out parts of their full being as humans in order, perhaps, to gain a new sort of aesthetic insight. This technique worked in odd ways and, as Blackmur was to show in *Language as Gesture,* very often it did not work at all. Yeats expected too much from magic, Hardy from his "ideas," the late Eliot from his Christianity, Stevens from his abstract fictions, Pound from his "intellectual attitudes."

Unlike Arnold and Eliot, however, Blackmur did not see his role as suited principally to emphasize the modernist writer's failures, and consequently, the reader's feelings of repugnance, sterility, and inconsequence. What he constantly kept referring to instead was the imagination, which, when it was employed to decode modernist instincts, he called the provisional imagination, an energy rather than an organ, as it wrestled with the passage from "life" to "art." Thus, he wrote, "criticism keeps the sound of . . . footsteps live in our reading, so that we understand both the fury in the words and the words themselves."[3] This is one of the many definitions of criticism scattered throughout Blackmur's work; it is typical of them all in that inflections and emphases are on processes, energies, turbulences. Criticism took from modernism the struggle to get matter into language ("getting into" is one of Blackmur's most frequent idioms), although it was of course the critic's job to do the work over, and to see whether or not life actually made it into art, how much was exacted by technique and aesthetic ingenuity, how little or how much that was necessarily left out could be recalled, or at least felt, in what poetic language delivered.

No one who has read Blackmur will fail to be impressed by how hard he worked at giving his chosen writers their due. He is without question the finest, the most patient and resourceful explicator of difficult literature produced in mid-twentieth-century America; he ranks with such differently virtuosic European readers as William Empson and Georges Poulet, although unlike them he is not deflected into the antinomian stabilities provided even by categories like "ambiguity" or "human time." For all his sporty quirkiness Blackmur took seriously the central polarity of nineteenth- and twentieth-century high culture, the one theme that provided continuity for him from romanticism up through modernism: the relationship between "Life" and "Art." Because he saw the relationship between this pair of terms as encompassing every possibility from opposition to absolute correspondence, he read poetry, fiction, and criticism as processes giving provisional resolution to the differences and similarities between art and life. Criticism for him therefore dramatized and re-performed the mediations by which art and the symbolic imagination actualized life, but of its very nature criticism also undermined itself. It did not define ideas, taste, and values so much as it set them back into the Moha, "the vital, fundamental stupidity of the human race,"[4] from which as art or as Numen they then emerged. Criticism is best seen as a provisional act, as perhaps even a temporary deformation of and deflection from literature, which itself is approximate, tentative, irresolute. "Literature," Blackmur writes in the title essay of *The Lion and the Honeycomb*, "is one of our skills of notation of the incarnation of the real into the actual."[5]

The consistency of Blackmur's criticism is that from the beginning to the end of his career he read literature as secular incarnation, a word he used frequently to represent the powers of life to reappear in art, or, as he spoke of it in reference to *Anna Karenina*, "the bodying forth in aesthetic form by contrasted human spirits of 'the terrible ambiguity of an immediate experience.' "[6]

It was enough for him to take stock of literary actuality—incarnating, realizing the real, whether that was society, culture, the unconscious human behavior. Beyond that, he said, "the mind acknowledges that the force behind art exists outside art, and also that the work of art itself almost gets outside art to make a shape—a form of the forms—of our total recognition of the force that moves us."[7]

The deliberateness of Blackmur's language, its studied *lenti* and detours should not, however, obscure its remarkable generalities, its frequently imprecise terminology, its plainly impressionistic dependence on the vocabulary of theology and mysticism. In Blackmur, there is a surprising concordance between the great technical proficiency in deciphering modernism, and the lesser homegrown (because random and unpredictable) bourgeois humanism in a churchyard. It is as if the idiom of I. A. Richards were constantly being drawn back toward, and then soaked in, the subjectivity of Montaigne, amplified by, say, what could be imputed to such differently Christian writers as Dante and Maritain. Blackmur's terms allusively map a field, however; they do not hold down things, or territories. He speaks of soul, spirit, art, artist, society, and life, with familiarity, not with the decorum of a trained cleric. Then, suddenly, he moves into the verse of a finely calibrated poet like Marianne Moore in order to register with astonishing precision the nature of her actuality, as it gets formulated in a line: "She resorts, or rises like a fish, continually to the said thing, captures it, sets it apart, points and polishes it to bring out just the special quality she heard in it. Much of her verse has the peculiar, unassignable, indestructible authority of speech overheard—which often means so much precisely because we do not know what was its limiting, and dulling, context."[8]

This combination of precision and allusiveness, of relentless poetic accuracy and often sloppy soul-mongering, is, I think, of the very essence of Blackmur's genius. He should be read as constantly reinscribing his fidelity to the discipline and the impurity of serious intellectual work, in which one eye is kept on a repeatedly invaded and turbulent world, while the other eye follows the processes of aesthetic composition with an unswerving interest in its redemptive and extra-worldly ambitions. The result is a criticism whose "labor is to recapture the imaginative burden and to avoid the literal like death."[9]

Not surprisingly then, Blackmur is the least influential, the least doctrinal, the least serviceable (in the base sense of the word) of the New Critics, a group of eminent interpreters with whom he has always been associated. Conversely, no one of them—not Ransom, nor Tate—had his range or anything like his power. His intellectual world was as much European, classical, and metropolitan as Erich Auerbach's or T. S. Eliot's, but without Auerbach's narrative and relational explicitness or his capacity by training and conviction to enact philological presentations like *Mimesis*, and without Eliot's conservative sense of tradition or his austere canonizations of European monuments. The point to be made here is that unlike all the other New Critics Blackmur *could* make use of Auerbach and Eliot in ways that emphasized either their wildness or their interesting shortcomings, despite their weighty authority. He sensed in Eliot's work its unappeasable restlessness, which ran directly counter to its Anglo-Catholic proclamations; in Auerbach's readings of Pascal and Flaubert he commended the man's fine erudition and his account of the *topoi*, by which these authors placed life into literature, even as Auerbach gave "too little credit to the actual material that got into the work with their aid." What Auerbach forgot, according to Blackmur, is

> that every writer who survives is constantly wrestling with a burden of actual experience by no means amenable to anything but disposition (disponibleness) by the method. Thus he [Auerbach] not only missed but denied the wrestling, swindling authority of life itself, apart from all categories, in the series of images that lead to the whiff of all human ill in Emma's soul—a whiff looking out its home in the smoking stove, creaking door, sweating walls, damp floor, and above all in the odor of the food; and missed, too, our chance at that whiff while Emma pecks at the hazel nuts or marks on the oil cloth—those creases that come and go—with her knife. No; for him it is *bêtise à la bête,* with a further cruel judgment in Flaubert's *style.* That was Auerbach's; and it is true that he has made it present; it must be taken account of.[10]

The return to a generous assessment of the great *Philolog* at the end of this otherwise critical passage is characteristic of Blackmur, as much his style as the impressive appeal in what precedes it to the minute details of everyday life so grindingly actual in Flaubert's prose.

(It is worth mentioning that Emma's tongue reaching deep into the bottom of the glass from which she licks the very last drop is one of the recurring motifs in Blackmur's criticism: it signifies "a touch of the actual" used by the major artists to "put in" and to "leave out" just enough of instinct and institutions in the representations of reality.[11] But the closer we look at Blackmur's work the more we shall find that back-and-forth restlessness, that oscillating and shuttling between text and reality which, in his one major attempt at a theory of literature, he called "between the Numen and the Moha," that transforms his work from the mere explication, to the *performance*, of literature. Wherever Blackmur finds a reification, a hard definition, a system, a strident tone, an overly busy label, a conception forced into overwork, a scheme running on by itself, there he methodically introduces the "uncontrollable mystery on the bestial floor." To the claims of Auerbach's seminar, given at Princeton in 1949, there was opposed not only Flaubert's stubbornly middle-class Emma imported by Blackmur into the discussion so as to provoke Auerbach, but also the presence of Ernst Robert Curtius, hardly less trained and formal than the author of *Mimesis*, but a man who was "relative to Auerbach, a deep anarch of the actual. Every blow he struck at Auerbach was meant to break down the formulas whereby we see how unlike things are like. . . . He understands why it is that the textbooks *must be wrong:* because they are designed to take care of the reading we do not do: a legitimate enterprise when provisional, fatal when permanent. . . . It seemed to me, then, that Curtius was potentially always on the verge of breaking through into Emma's life itself, or into the moving subject or locus of literature."[12]

As in so many other places in his criticism, Blackmur here outdistances anything we might still recognize as New Criticism. There are not only the concerns about "life" and worldliness, but the tense impatience with any attitude that does not see literature—no matter how well-wrought, how much "itself"—as poised uneasily between anarchy and form. Moreover Blackmur was concerned not just with literature but with the nature of the aesthetic; a true theorist of art, his interests and instruments were theoretical, cultural, social, even political, all of which have appeared to me to be quite unconnected with the comparatively modest, even tight world of New Critical ideology. In trying to understand Blackmur as someone interested in the "moving subject or locus of literature" we should remember that he intended criticism to be as quick, as moving, as theoretical (in the Crocean sense), and as nomadic as literature itself, at the same time that it retained a "tory" cast of form and perceivable order.

Let us now examine the historical and intellectual conjuncture that seemed misleadingly to have aligned Blackmur with the New Criticism, and then let us reappraise his place in American criticism as it appears two decades after his death. Then, finally, we can go on to discuss Blackmur's significance as perhaps the greatest of native American critics produced in the first half of the twentieth century, and certainly one of the very greatest anywhere in the contemporary West.

II

Blackmur's oddities of background and manner have been noted often enough: they require only the very briefest of rehearsals here. With the exception of Kenneth Burke, Blackmur had the least dependence on formal education of any of his contemporaries who wrote what we might call "high" as opposed to journalistic or popular criticism. This is not only because, obviously enough, he had no formal university training, but because he resolutely made no effort to compensate for that fact. None of his work pretends to scholarly completeness or to exhaustiveness, at the same time that it is both learned and openly grateful to the best that scholarship has to offer. Neither did Blackmur use the word "academic" to stand in for expressions of contempt or dismissal. On the other hand, immediately after he came to Princeton in 1940, he did learn how to exploit the academic world with great success. Clearly he did not fit easily or comfortably in an academic Department of English, but that is where for the longest part of his intellectual life he functioned, and it is there that he must be evaluated.

What distinguishes Blackmur's style from the very beginning, well before he became a university academic, was the freedom and errantry of his explorations of literature. Biography certainly mattered very little in his critical apparatus, except when he studied Henry Adams; then it mattered too much. Although Blackmur generally focused on the literary text, he was strikingly different from Brooks, Warren, Tate, and Ransom in that he wandered very far afield from it. As we shall see presently, midway through his career he became much more of an intellectual, in the Sartrean or Gramscian sense of the term, than any of the New Critics. Yet he seems to have only guardedly admired Lionel Trilling, and in his consideration of *The Liberal Imagination* had much to criticize in Trilling's elevation of "mind" and "intellect" as models for, and contents of, literature. Trilling, Blackmur said, was too much indebted to Arnold and Freud, "masters" of extremism and power. In his concern with society, power, and mind as regulators of literature, Trilling, according to Blackmur, disregarded "the true business of literature, as of all intellect, critical or creative, which is to remind the powers that be, simple or corrupt as they are, of the turbulence they have to control. There is a disorder vital to the individual which is fatal to society."[13] And this criticism is levied much more harshly against Irving Babbitt's Humanism, a doctrine that made for itself "a mind that was restricted to general ideas, and general ideas that could not refresh themselves, such was the severity of their order in the monkish sense, in the fount of disorder."[14]

As against the official learning and disciplinary rigor either of scholarship or of the committed intellectual, Blackmur occasionally offered a sometimes uninspired blend of turbulent, unfocused, and badly misappropriated doctrine, drawn seemingly at random from his recent reading. Blackmur's slips—there are a fair number of them—cannot be overlooked, because they do really count as signs of the daring logic that governs his overall performance. His rehash of Coleridge and Aristotle towards the end of the essay "The Lion and the Honeycomb" has in it much of the sliding and slipping of someone unable to do much with a general idea like "crisis" ("Turning," Blackmur writes, "is a kind of decision. *Crisis* is the intellectual act, *and* its occasion, of decision.")[15] and equally unable to move from general to specific because he refuses to let traditions of scholarly argument and intellectual sequence support him. Consider the following passage from this essay as an example of what I mean, and note how his handling of general ideas falls either into unconvincing repetitions of what he has said much better elsewhere, or into the jarring irrelevance of some ridiculously trivial observation that does not help matters at all:

> Mimesis, I take it, is the mind's action, and there is no question that, richly understood, any single full mimesis operates in deep, but widely variable relation to poetics, dialectic, and rhetoric. For myself, I see a sequence or relation whereby the mimetic act is the incarnation into actuality of what we can grasp of reality; which is the reason why we pay enormous salaries and devotion in Hollywood and why in my boyhood Bernhardt was the divine Sarah, and which is also a good part of the reason for the lasting power—and greatness—of great literature.[16]

What remains of this flailing and clutching, however, is the reaching out and crossing over and, underneath that, the rhythms of chancy investigation governed by Blackmur's finely responsive sense of "the moving subject or locus of literature." Here, as I said, the effort doesn't work, but elsewhere it does. Thus if for Blackmur literature was about movement, if the place of literature was not restricted to a fixed spot (or *topos*), then it behooved the critic somehow to remain attuned to that fact, to describe literary experience as a zone rather than as an inert place—above all, not to remain bound or in any serious way inhibited by the barriers and protocols of academic or literary specialization. Even so, the field was not an open one to Blackmur; he had to take stock of what styles of writing on literature already existed so that he could then go on to devise his own mode.

We must try to recall, I think, what Blackmur was offered as a set of models for writing criticism, most of which he refused. There was first the academic scholarship produced by the universities; this entailed editing, textual criticism, historical periodization and, when it was done as brilliantly as it was by Livingston Lowes, important studies of influence and reference. Second, there was the style of criticism perfected by Edmund Wilson, a form of literary portraiture indebted to Sainte-Beuve, versatile, journalistic in its directness and address to the reader, serious and engaging at the same time. This seemed not to have interested Blackmur, probably because narrative lay at its heart, and narrative gave Blackmur very little leeway for the exfoliation of impressions and musings. Third, there was also the nationalistic historiography underpinning the criticism written by Van Wyck Brooks, and this was too programmatic and tense for Blackmur's much more leisurely mode; like the New Critics—and this is why he has always been lumped together with them—he avoided the explicit teleological moralizing that drove Brooks's and Parrington's "ages" of American literature, preferring instead to concentrate on texts. My conjecture is that Blackmur's neglect of F. O. Matthiessen and Perry Miller is traceable back to his discomfort with the earlier generation of tendentious Americanists, although I am certain that had he more carefully read the newer generation he would have favorably noted the difference.

As for the criticism associated with *Partisan Review* or with the New York intellectuals, as they have been called, Blackmur's treatment of Trilling, respectful and interested as it is, nevertheless stands for the larger impatience he had with a critical mode that operated on what he seems to have considered to be the principle of authorization, which took one back all-too-dutifully to Freud, Arnold, Marx, and other critical masters for validation and accreditation. Some of this impatience is much more pronounced in Blackmur's pawing of Granville Hicks, not as formidable or polished an intellect as Trilling, but seen as a representative of politicizations of criticism that were disabling in Blackmur's eyes. Perhaps it is for that reason that Blackmur's avoidance of the English critical scene (always excepting Richards, Eliot, and Empson) is so total; neither Leavis, nor the Bloomsbury group, nor individualistic practitioners like Read and Aldington figure in his mature work at all.

On the other hand it would be too simple to say condescendingly that Blackmur's work is merely provincial; his provinciality was altogether too interesting and self-conscious to be dismissed. He was certainly more aware of European literature than all the above critics except Trilling and Wilson, even if like all of them he was completely unaware of the major schools of twentieth-century Western Marxism, some members of whom, like the early Lukacs, Ernst Bloch, Benjamin, and Adorno, he would certainly have found suggestive for their path-breaking aesthetic criticism. Likewise he seemed to have had little working knowledge of French philosophical criticism (the *Nouvelle Revue Française* school, Bachelard, Ramon Fernandez), although I recall from my student days at Princeton the respectful references he made to Marcel Raymond, which were to turn up later in "Anni Mirabiles" (reprinted in *A Primer of Ignorance*); similarly he spoke admiringly of the early Erich Heller.

I mention these gaps and lapses as a way of underlining how thoroughly Blackmur tried to cultivate his own manner, which he grounded in a kind of studied provinciality, methodically eccentric and outside the main vehicles of critical expression available to him in America during the thirties. His early *Hound and Horn* essays seem to come from direct encounters with poets whose bewildering discontinuity with predecessors is their first characteristic; Blackmur registers their startling achievements without many predispositions except the willingness to be surprised and to follow them, sometimes playfully and at other times sternly, wherever their vocabulary and rhythms take them. More than any other critic in English (more than Eliot, Richards, or Empson, more than the Southern Fugitives) Blackmur's critical *askesis* was to shed as much as possible of his ideological or philosophical beliefs in order to concentrate on poetry as language, not as belief, vision of the world, or truths—which, as I said above, he also studies, but as interferences in poetry. In this view he anticipates some critical attitudes of the 1960s. Hence of course the attractive originality of his voice, and the large spaces created in his essays for patient interpretation and sometimes ingenious speculation. This is the explicative trend or movement embodied by *Language and Gesture*.

Although it contains essays from as early as the thirties, *The Lion and the Honeycomb* (1955) strikes me as opening out Blackmur's critical practice very dramatically. I am not speaking here of a development tied to a later chronological moment in Blackmur's career, but rather to a quite marked attempt occurring right across his work to expand his horizon. Nevertheless one should mention some important events that bear directly on this development in Blackmur's work. First of course is his affiliation with Princeton, which dated from the early forties. A major university thus enabled him to tap its resources, and from it to move out into the world of institutions. Second, is the centrality to him of European modernism as a coherent movement, embodying a set of ideals, a canon of works, and a series of references that predominate in his writing henceforward. Joyce, Mann, Eliot, Yeats, Gide, Pound, Faulkner, Stevens, Kafka are the main figures (except for Rilke, Baudelaire, and Lorca, the absence of major Continental poets is puzzling), and with them came philosophers like Jacques Maritain and Benedetto Croce. Blackmur's major statement on modernism, surprisingly minus an extended consideration of Proust, was formulated in the set of four Library of Congress lectures, "Anni Mirabiles, 1921–25," which remains, I believe, the most sophisticated and brilliant of all the many critical works on modernism, far in advance of its time, dazzling in its close analysis as well as in its general adumbration of the limitations on the artist's role in modern society.

Inevitably, the work on modernism led him back into the nineteenth century to study and write about the great realistic novelists— Flaubert, Dostoevsky, Tolstoy, Stendhal, Melville, Henry James. Some of this work emanated, I believe, from his teaching at Princeton, where I can recall that on occasion he gave public talks, or class lectures as a visitor in various courses taught by colleagues. (One in particular was a bravura and densely associative lecture on *Humphry Clinker,* in which Blackmur's leitmotif was Smollett's predilection for smells!) This communal aspect of his work indicates a much larger concern of Blackmur's years immediately following the end of World War Two, his role as a quasi-public, or in Gramsci's sense an organic, intellectual, involved in the life of society at a fairly high level of integration with it. This is the third important "event," or new bearing, in his critical thought, and since it is quite evident in *The Lion and the Honeycomb* we should look at it a bit more closely.

The recent publication of Robert Fitzgerald's *Enlarging the Change: The Princeton Seminars in Criticism, 1949–51* provides us retrospectively with the first sustained opportunity to see Blackmur at work as a cultural intellectual. The impressive thing about Fitzgerald's memoir is how in it Blackmur seems to have situated himself at a number of extremely interesting intersections. He was crucially engaged with the early history of the Princeton Institute for Advanced Study, and instrumental in getting Robert Oppenheimer to consider a program in the humanities for the Institute; this was a direct consequence of Blackmur's institutional presence at the University. Secondly, Blackmur was really one of the pioneers in devising an interesting (as opposed to a dead) cultural space to absorb the unhoused energies of that great generation of refugee European philologists that included Auerbach and Curtius. He seems to have sensed—perhaps because of the vantage of his own lack of formal university training—what a formidable background in tradition and learning these refugees carried with them, and how it was imperative in postwar America to give them a direct and appropriate role in intellectual life here. Thirdly, and most importantly, he seems almost instinctively to have understood that the tradition of European bourgeois humanism could not be accommodated to conventional academic demarcations in America, and that an extradisciplinary venue, enabled by foundations and corporations, would be best for acculturating this still lively tradition in the United States. Hence the seminar format, which was later to be institutionalized at Princeton University as the Christian Gauss Seminars in Criticism, certainly the most impressive of such series carried on at an American university.

In all of this Blackmur was the moving figure, helped by his fortunate association with John Marshall of the munificent Rockefeller Foundation. But I do not think that Blackmur's role was mainly entrepreneurial. In saying that culturally and theoretically speaking he stood at a number of intellectual as well as institutional intersections, we are, I think, much closer to a description of his actual role, precisely because his own critical *praxis* had already chosen for itself a sectoral or zonal attitude towards literature and culture. Later, I shall speak of how his attitude derived from, and remained perfectly congruent with, his lifelong commitment to the essay. He had situated himself in a relatively independent position to be able to study literary texts as constantly moving in and charting a novel space between history, society, and the author, a space whose verbal actuality or incarnation was paradoxically both an extension of the real, and a powerfully constituted defense against it. His model for such a critical attitude was Henry James, whose executive powers as a creative writer were matched in their own intellectually distinct form by his critical faculties, as those were exercised most effectively by the public interpretation of his own novels. Blackmur's statement in *The Lion and the Honeycomb* that James's Prefaces were "the most sustained and I think the most eloquent and original piece of literary criticism in existence"[17] was originally made in 1934, but if we try speculatively to reconstruct a rationale for including so exuberant a claim for the Prefaces in a 1955 collection of his essays, we might learn a good deal about the older Blackmur who was developing the Princeton seminars.

In James's asseverations of the novel's value (as an emanation out of its author's "prime sensibility" and its corresponding ability to develop its own moral sense out of its form) Blackmur found statements that offered James a chance to declare his own genius as novelist, and, no less important, "to explain the serious and critical devotion with which he made his Prefaces a *vademecum*—both for himself as the solace of achievement, and for others as a guide and exemplification."[18] Although James did not share Melville's failure as a novelist who relied on imputation from the outside rather than rendering from the inside, he was nevertheless, like his predecessor, an American writer confronting a world of cultural forms fundamentally alien to the new and overburdened sensibility. James's success in the writing of fiction and of a criticism adequate to his practice as a novelist depended on his conception of "underlying form," which gave art its "deep-breathing economy" and its organic texture.[19] This achievement, Blackmur points out, occurs at a time when the "disestablishment of culture" was fully accomplished, and this in turn obligates the artist to the duty of "creating consciousness" laden down with the massive weight of that "whole cultural establishment" no longer carried by social institutions.

America, however, was still tied to Europe, although much sooner than Europe it had moved towards that "formless" mass society in which "the disinheritance but not the disappearance of the individual" had already taken place. How then to accommodate the past, Europe, culture, and the present in an actuality which had at its disposal only consciousness for such a task? Such a dilemma was further underscored by the extreme urgency with which James treated the question of form in the novel. Consequently, Blackmur's consideration of James stressed the relationship between consciousness and form as a social, and not just an aesthetic, issue. Is there any way, Blackmur says, that we can conceive of how "things are held together in a living way, with the sense of life going on," now that "there is no longer any establishment, no longer any formula, and we like to say only vestigial forms, to call on outside of ourselves?"[20]

I would suggest that this way of phrasing James's predicament is also the central question of Blackmur's later work. As he articulates this quandary one can see how Blackmur's reflections on the problem were a way of linking his actual condition in America—as a teacher, critic, and cultural force at Princeton right after World War Two—with his worldly as well as imagined role as an intellectual who has no close political or social affiliations to carry him along but who nevertheless feels himself committed to a position of authority and a site of privileged intensity as an heir of the ages. I do not intend any irony here. Blackmur's postwar criticism is I believe directly tied to a sense of American responsibility for the world after the dismantling of the old imperial structures. This sense fueled his most extraordinary essays, and, alas, the astonishing ignorance and condescension about the non-Western world in his worst ones. It allowed little or no sympathy for the problems faced by the new postcolonial states of Africa and Asia (quite the contrary, as a reading of the first essay in *The Lion and the Honeycomb,* "Towards a Modus Vivendi," quickly reveals), and it seems to have blinded him completely to the possibility that Europe's (and America's) colonial role in the peripheral world was not always up to the claims of Greco-Roman civilization. But, much more important for our purposes here, the seriously mulled-over problems of the new and relatively isolated consciousness impinged on Blackmur's work so strongly as to enliven his criticism with a skepticism and experimental alertness that prefigured all the tremendous theoretical changes that were to occur in American criticism in the decade following his death in 1965.

So long as Blackmur wrote and acted then, the imperialism latent in his sense of the American creation of a new consciousness was constantly held back, undercut, reduced by radical doubt and by theoretical self-consciousness. All his portraits of intellectuals and artists in the world are either morose, severely judgmental, or downright pessimistic: his lifelong fascination with Henry Adams is the strongest case in point. Unlike Kenneth Burke or the younger but still contemporary Northrop Frye, Blackmur devised no cosmic schemes, had no centralizing or, as the current expression has it, totalizing vision, no completely useful methodological apparatus. "The prescriptive *mortmain"* of codifications of insight were, he thought, especially to be wary of; it is the case now, he said, that there is a "hardening of the mind into a set of unrelated methodologies without the controlling advantage of a fixed body of knowledge, a fixed faith, or a fixed purpose."[21] The created consciousness—his as well as James's—was not really a substitute for fixed knowledge, faith, or purpose, since consciousness was condemned to perceptions and re-perceptions of its vulnerability, its historical situation, and its lucid partiality. Instead of doctrine and fixed method there was a pliant and constantly mobile awareness of the "tory anarchy" provided by art and culture, and in the public sphere, a more complete sense of humanism—without orthodoxy or imposable dogma—than official Humanism allowed:

> The true business of Humanism, since it works from intellectual bias in even its most imaginative moments, and since it takes for itself the function of mediation, is to mediate the ravenings of the intellect; to feel the intellect as elastic, plastic, and absorptive; to feel the experience on which the intellect works as ambiguous, present only provisionally, impinging, vanishing, above and below, known far beyond its own mere grasp; and thus to restore to the intellect its proper sense of strength and weakness in necessity, that in setting up its orders and formulas of order, it is coping with disorder. It should remember that an order is not invalidated by disorder; and that if an order is to become imaginative it must be so conceived as to accommodate disorder, and indeed to desire to do so, to stretch itself constantly to the point where it can envisage the disorder which its order merely names.[22]

Right at the heart of this magnificent passage is the difficult relationship between intellect (one of the forms of consciousness) and experience, in which both parties are in motion, both dependent upon ambiguity, provisionality, opposition. I do not think it is wrong to speak of the form of this apprehension of intellect and experience as fundamentally *theoretical,* in that Blackmur's own subjectivity points away from the restraints and limitations of ego to a zone of activity not empirical or "real" but actual, that is, theoretically possible, and as he was to say in "Anni Mirabiles," "radically imperfect." Thus— here Blackmur fully anticipates that astute combination of assertive reach and deconstructive skepticism basic to twentieth-century theoretical irony from Lukacs to Derrida—"each of the modes of the mind avows imperfection by making assertions about its intentions which it neither expresses nor communicates except by convention."[23] And since conventions are recognizably conventional they cannot communicate except by the indirections of the formal, which does no more than "define" (the quotation marks of suppressed doubt are added by Blackmur himself) the indefinable.

The net effect of Blackmur's later work therefore is, I think, that of a negative dialectic, a process by which the stabilities and continuities of twentieth-century capitalism are de-defined, worn back down by a difficult, dissolving prose to the instability which the forms of art, intellect, and society had resorted to when in the first instance they tried to give permanence and shape to their apprehension. The will to explication in his late essays was regularly being displaced by the energies of writing, a disorderly tumble of rhythms unaccommodated by "points," sequential arguments, or narratable reason, morality, or purpose. Blackmur, in short, cannot easily or correctly be reclaimed for traditional humanism, as in a sense the New Critics could be, and he cannot accurately be made to serve the interests of a new institutional or bureaucratic order, as his eccentric affiliations with the academy, the foundations, and the publishing industry might suggest. Is it possible, however, more exactly to describe Blackmur's critical achievements without compromising him more than is absolutely necessary?

III

The essay form expresses discomposure and incompleteness; its meditative scope is often qualified by the essay's occasional nature (critical essays, after all, are occasioned by an outside event, a book, or a painting); most essays reach back towards the fragment, or the aphorism, rarely towards the book or the treatise. "The essay," says Adorno, "is the critical form par excellence . . . and if the essay is accused of lacking a standpoint and of tending toward relativism because it recognizes no standpoint lying outside itself, then the accusation implicitly contains the conception of truth as something 'ready made,' a hierarchy of concepts." Thus, Adorno continues, the essay is entangled in "un-truth"; moreover,

> the relevance of the essay is that of anachronism. The hour is more unfavorable to it than ever. It is being crushed between an organized

science, on the one side, in which everyone presumes to control everyone and everything else, and which excludes, with the sanctimonious
praise of "intuitive" or "stimulating," anything that does not conform
to the status quo; and, on the other side, by a philosophy that makes
do with the empty and abstract residues left aside by the scientific
apparatus, residues which then become for philosophy the objects of
second-degree operations.[24]

Denis Donoghue is absolutely right to note Blackmur's attachment to the essay's "congenial space," and then to connect that fact
with his inability ever to finish his book on Henry Adams.[25] There
was something about the definitive closure and size of books that
inhibited Blackmur's genius, kept him instead to the smaller, more
constitutively open form of the essay. Adorno's comments about the
essay form further illuminate Blackmur's quandary, I think. As he
meditated the anxious Adams he found himself face to face with the
problem of commensuration, of adequacy, synchronization, and congruence: in Henry Adams he beheld the case of a man whose attempts
at narrative raised the primal difficulty of all narrativization, which is
how to make narrative fit the material at hand, how to make the
narrative correspond with history, energy with mind, the individual
with society, temporality with sequence. Every encounter with Henry
Adams thrust the problem of congruence—of making things fit with
each other—to the fore, and this in turn highlighted the tentative
nature of Blackmur's own essay, or attempt, to grasp Adams's problem
in an adequate form. No ready-made concepts or hierarchies really
work in the essay, just as they seemed not to have worked for Adams.
And with the apparent consolidation of science and philosophy on
either side of Adams, his efforts—like Blackmur's own to understand
Adams—seemed anachronistic.

I said earlier that one of Blackmur's themes in his explications
of modernism was that necessary effort on the part of readers to
employ their "provisional imaginations" as they encountered the
often arbitrary and overworked constructs of the great modernists.
These great writers furnished the main material for Blackmur's work
as he read the contemporary iconology of a post-religious age. I also
said that we can distinguish two broad trends in Blackmur's work that
are symbolized on the one hand by the explicative and patiently
interpretive essays of *Language as Gesture,* and on the other hand by

the frankly speculative and theoretically administrative essays of *The Lion and the Honeycomb* and its later companion *A Primer of Ignorance.* (*Eleven Essays in the European Novel* is, in a sense, a synthesis of both trends.) In both instances of course Blackmur's work is congruent with and indistinguishable from the essay form. As we can now survey the whole of Blackmur's writing from the vantage point of the 1980s, after the advent and relative decline of literary theory, the slow emergence of cultural critique, the development of various comparative and contrapuntal approaches to the study of literature in society, we can see with a particular intensity how all the structures of art are either renewed and invigorated by acts of the symbolic imagination or ossified and reduced by the various executive commodifications of the administrative attitude. To have made his readers so extraordinarily aware of these possibilities is a great achievement in itself: but Blackmur did more than that, I think.

In his writing, the critical act itself was not curtained off behind the Archimedean privilege of outside or disinterested judgment. Rather, criticism itself was shown to belong to the very same class as those other activities in which various sorts of constructs, various kinds of released energy, and various brands of dogma were probable consequences of the human imagination acting in alliance with consciousness. To recognize this about Blackmur's criticism is to acknowledge a third, and possibly more elusive and difficult moment in his work, the act of self-criticism which is carefully lodged in and to some degree screened by his analyses not only of Henry Adams, but of those figures like T. E. Lawrence and Swift whom he called "the least abiding writers of magnitude in English." These figures interest Blackmur because in them, he says, "distraught endurance"—the will to go on and on—is not deflected into the positive presence of organizing structures (as in *Ulysses* or *The Magic Mountain*), but is converted by imagination "into a vice and makes stoicism, as Henry Adams called it, a form of moral suicide." How this is done is described by Blackmur in one of the great, and I would suggest, one of the central passages in his work. The following lines should be read not only as a description of T. E. Lawrence, but also as a deliberately negative foil for the massive efforts at construction and moral judgment that lie at the heart of the modernist project as it shores up art against ruin. In assessing Lawrence's "only basic" failure to mobilize conviction into "character," in identifying the man's relentless ability to let "the towers of imagination fling up . . . out of quicksand, and stand, firm in light and air," Blackmur was also characterizing that other subterranean, or at least unacknowledged, component of modernism's enormously profitable structures, a component whose service the critic, if he was really to be a critic, uniquely required. This was the dislocating faculty by which criticism "removes the acceptance" of the organizing structures of aestheticized experience, as modernism had employed them, and "leaves the predicament bare":

> In this respect—in this type of sensibility—imagination operates analogously to religion upon the world which both deny; only, if as in Lawrence, the imagination be without religion, the balance of heaven is lacking, the picture projected is incomplete and in an ultimate sense fails of responsibility. It is thus, I think, that we get from Lawrence a sense of unsatisfied excitement, inadequate despair, and the blank extreme of shock. But it is excitement, is despair, is shock; made actual, disturbing us: finding room within us in our own tiding disorder. On the imaginative level, perhaps on the moral level—or on any except the social—order is only a predicament accepted. It is the strength of an imagination like Lawrence's that it removes the acceptance and leaves the predicament bare. The weakness, which is basic only, lies in the absence of any effective anterior conviction to supply a standard of disclosure; and there, it is suggested, is the limitation, chiefly as a dislocated but dominant emotion throughout Lawrence's work.[26]

According to the terms of this description, however, Lawrence could not be transformed into a lesson, a theory, or an example to be applied elsewhere. If the absence of anterior conviction meant anything it was as criticism of the projected, completed, and responsible picture underwriting the "abiding" art of modernism, whose earlier anticipations were the monumental designs of Tolstoy, Flaubert, and Stendhal. And this more radical impulse at the degree zero of writing bore the critic along too, who makes room to speak to us "in our own tiding disorder." Yet, like Lawrence, the critic finds and re-finds the "ultimate inadequacy" that is the result, according to Blackmur, of "the everlasting effort" to write. The startlingly contemporary quality of this formulation is further intensified when we also realize that

Blackmur acquires it at exactly the same juncture from which, looking towards art, he perceives, and then refuses, the distant satisfactions of an abiding aesthetic order.

Had this ascetic vantage point been fixed by Blackmur into a position, perspective, or program we might now be reading him only for the results such a critical stance could have permitted him to deliver in one text after another. That he seems to have suspected how dry and predictable the set of readings might be that would result from a reification of his radical and essayistic critical mobility, is perhaps another extraordinary anticipation in his work that even the disciplined skepticism of post-modernist theory can be grooved like a boring train ride into the essay's brief scope and the disenchantments from which its form springs. He seems to have preferred a different regimen altogether, that of criticism as performance, responsive to shifting circumstances, uncertain of its conclusions, prepared always to be solitary and self-limiting, without influence or disciples.[27] To say of such a criticism that it displaced itself from a position of authority to a "focus of scope," is to get some sense of how wide was the horizon of Blackmur's work, and how potentially it can enlarge every critic's scope just to read and engage with his gestures.

NOTES

1. T. S. Eliot, "Ulysses, Order and Myth," *The Dial*, November 1923, 480–3.

2. R. P. Blackmur, *Language as Gesture* (New York: Harcourt, Brace & Co., 1952), 82.

3. R. P. Blackmur, *The Lion and the Honeycomb* (New York: Harcourt, Brace and Co., 1955), 303.

4. *The Lion and the Honeycomb*, 282.

5. *The Lion and the Honeycomb*, 196.

6. R. P. Blackmur, *Eleven Essays in the European Novel*, (New York: Harcourt, Brace and World, 1964), 4.

7. *The Lion and the Honeycomb*, 197.

8. *Language as Gesture*, 274.

9. *Language as Gesture*, 173.

10. Robert Fitzgerald, *Enlarging the Change: The Princeton Seminars in Literary Criticism, 1949–1951* (Boston: Northeastern University Press, 1985), 38.

11. For example, in *The Lion and the Honeycomb*, 222–3.

12. Fitzgerald, *Enlarging the Change*, 39.

13. *The Lion and the Honeycomb*, 41.

14. *The Lion and the Honeycomb*, 158.
15. *The Lion and the Honeycomb*, 187, footnote.
16. *The Lion and the Honeycomb*, 187.
17. *The Lion and the Honeycomb*, 241.
18. *The Lion and the Honeycomb*, 261.
19. *The Lion and the Honeycomb*, 272.
20. *The Lion and the Honeycomb*, 286–7.
21. *The Lion and the Honeycomb*, 178.
22. *The Lion and the Honeycomb*, 161.
23. R. P. Blackmur, *A Primer of Ignorance*, (New York: Harcourt, Brace and World, 1967), 78.
24. Theodor Adorno, "The Essay as Form," trans. Bob Hullot-Kentor and Frederic Will, *New German Critique*, 32 (Spring–Summer 1984), 166, 170.
25. Denis Donoghue, in the foreword to R. P. Blackmur, *Henry Adams*, edited and with an introduction by Veronica A. Makowsky (New York: Harcourt Brace Jovanovich, 1980), viii.
26. *The Lion and the Honeycomb*, 109.
27. See my "The Future of Criticism," *MLN*, XCIX, 4 (September 1984), 951–8.

II. Memoirs

GERALD E. BENTLEY

Blackmur and the Academy

The editors of this volume have made room for a friend of Richard Blackmur, one who is neither a poet nor a critic but who is happy to recall for Richard's admirers a few reminiscences and happy anecdotes.

Our first meeting took place at Princeton about forty years ago when he was a member of the Institute for Advanced Study and Hodder Fellow at the University. It was immediately apparent that this man did not fit into any of the familiar academic molds, and though I did, we were immediately congenial.

In faculty circles this nonconformity was often viewed with amazement and sometimes with indignation. Such amazement and indignation did not, however, constitute general antagonism, as has sometimes been asserted. Of course he had his friends and his enemies, as did I and most other faculty members. We all had moments of irritation and disillusionment and often expressed them. But Blackmur at Princeton did not work in an atmosphere of general hostility.

Of course his iconoclasm was sometimes conspicuous and to our most conservative colleagues shocking. I remember one oral examination after Richard had become a regular member of the Princeton English Department in which ten or a dozen professors were solemnly assembled to test a candidate for the degree of Doctor of Philosophy. Most of the examiners were seriously, not to say pompously probing to find the extent and accuracy of the young man's knowledge of English and American literature, but Richard's aims were different.

Early in the examination the still unsettled and terrified candidate had been led into a discussion of the versification of Spenser's *Faerie Queene*. One professor asked the tense and worried youth if he saw evidence of the influence of any other poet in a certain passage. The reply was: "Perhaps some influence of *Paradise Lost.*"

While the shocked examiners registered their scholarly horror at this anachronism, Richard broke in: "Of course you misspoke, but let's play a little game. Suppose *Paradise Lost* could be dated a century earlier. What do you think Spenser would have found admirable in it?" Relieved, the candidate joined the game, and for five or ten minutes they played with the versification and ideas of Milton which Spenser might have found congenial or antipathetic. After the game the candidate settled down and easily passed the examination. Richard had not been interested in the gaps in the boy's knowledge; he wanted to see how flexible and imaginative his mind was.

To his more reactionary colleagues Blackmur's foibles were sometimes offensive, but more often only somewhat eccentric. Each year he devoted earnest study to the annual financial report of Princeton University. Often his analysis produced interesting or at least generally unknown information. Once he greeted me with the observation: "Aha! I see you had your rent raised $20 a month."

"Well, I did, but who told you?"

"The annual financial report."

"Come off it, Richard. There is nothing about me in that report."

"Oh yes there is," replied Richard with delight at my simplicity. "That is if you read it carefully enough."

Then with obvious enjoyment he explained. Thirty or thirty-five years before, a devoted trustee of the University, concerned about the financial status of senior members of the faculty, had built twenty-five rather large houses on a tract of his land and then given the land and houses to Princeton with the stipulation that they should be rented to senior faculty members for $25 a month. With the onward march of inflation the rents had been raised, but the faculty tenants still paid rents far below the going rate. Each year the receipts from these houses were reported as University income. Said Richard, "You take these figures and compare them with those of last year. The increase you divide by 25, the number of houses, and then divide again by 12.

The result is the increase in your monthly rent. Elementary, Dr. Watson!" Of course I did not mind that Richard had discovered my rent, but I was fascinated by this new display of his taste in fun and games.

Rather less acceptable to a few of our senior colleagues was the enthusiasm of students for Blackmur as a teacher. For several years the undergraduate newspaper had conducted a poll of students about their estimates of their courses and teachers. As usual with such student polls, the count was carelessly taken, the questions were crude, and the raw figures were never analyzed. Nonetheless it was better than the customary hearsay and at that time the best available guide to undergraduate evaluation. Richard's students put him near the top of the list, sometimes replacing older colleagues whose indignation was vociferous. Many explanations of the "unfairness" of the poll were proposed by wounded egos, but the results were respected by most undergraduates.

Blackmur's brilliance as a critic was even more generally recognized in England than in America, and around 1960 he was invited to Cambridge University to serve for a year as Pitt Professor of American History and Institutions. Characteristically he concealed his pleasure, and he was really reluctant to go. By that time he was suffering from circulatory problems, had a little trouble in walking, and was susceptible to cold weather. A few of his friends were most eager for him to go because we knew he would be impressive and a delight at high tables. But there were problems. The rooms provided by most colleges for their Fellows were kept at temperatures far below the American norm and in such temperatures Richard's legs were sure to suffer, perhaps seriously. Because of the walking problem Richard's residence needed to be centrally located, not remote like Jesus with which two of us had connections. Finally, large colleges like Trinity and St. John's had too many Fellows to provide a high table of a size congenial for our friend.

Several of us with some Cambridge experience cast about and settled on Christ's, which had recently built modern centrally heated quarters for some of its Fellows near the center, and whose high table was of a congenial size. We had no trouble in getting the Master and Fellows to invite the Pitt Professor to join them for the year and not too much difficulty in persuading Richard to accept after we had outlined the advantages for him. The year, as it proved, turned out very well.

The warm room and the short distances kept the circulation problems under control; he was a brilliant success at the high table; and he was impressed by the history of the fifteenth-century college. From the stained glass oriel window near the high table in the hall former members like John Milton and Charles Darwin gazed down at him. He admired the collection of ancient college silver which had been given to Christ's over hundreds of years, and he enjoyed college ceremonies, especially college feasts, to which he was invited not only by his own college but by others as well.

College feasts are ceremonial dinners generally endowed by rich former members like the treasurer of King Charles II, and used by the Fellows to entertain visitors and friends from other colleges. All students are fed early and the entire hall is devoted to Fellows and their guests. Such feasts are surviving banquets from former days with many courses, six or eight wines, displays of college silver, and elaborate food. Like most American guests, Blackmur loved them.

When he came home to Princeton, on his first visit to the departmental mail boxes, Richard was surrounded by younger members of the department whom he was regaling with stories of British academic adventures. Inevitably college feasts were among the features of his discourse, and he was doing full justice to the many wines, the formal toasts, the elaborate displays of silver and linen, the spectacular dishes. When I joined the group he was telling of one dish which occasionally appeared, carried in on a huge platter of antique silver. This was a swan served in a natural pose, clothed in all its feathers as if alive. One enthralled youngster said "Gee, Mr. Blackmur, what does swan taste like?"

"Oh," said the nonchalant Richard, "about like peacock."

It was in 1962, I think, that Richard made a long visit to Italy, and for a few months thereafter was saturated with things Italian. One quirk in this Italian phase was demonstrated on me.

For a year or two I had been receiving much of my usual flood of advertisements from publishers, magazines, book dealers and such, addressed not to Gerald Eades Bentley, but to Gerald Apeface Bentley. As soon as I received the second piece of mail so addressed, I knew the source of the name change but I could not fathom the method by which such a widespread substitution had been managed. The source had to be a lifelong chum of my son, a merry youth who had the most fertile sense of humor I have ever encountered. Years before when we had all played outdoor games together the standard insult for any blunder—a dropped pass, a missed fly ball—had been "Oh Ape Face!" Only Jimmy had been both aware of our use of this boyish epithet and possessed of the imagination, the ingenuity and the persistence to get the hoax spread over two continents. Eventually I encountered Jimmy and persuaded him to tell all.

One summer he had achieved a lowly job at the huge Donnelly printing plant in Chicago. In those days Donnelly was said to be the biggest printing establishment in the country, after the printing house of the United States government. One of their minor lines at the Lakeside Press—after metropolitan directories, Sears Roebuck catalogues, city telephone books and such—was the sale of mailing lists. One could order from Donnelly 30,000 provincial dentists, or 50,000 hardware dealers, or 5,000 animal hospitals, or 75,000 teachers of English literature, or 20,000 podiatrists. I suppose the system has changed by now, but when Jimmy worked there the purchaser of a list printed his letter or flyer under his own letterhead, stuffed them into his company envelopes and sent the lot (unaddressed) to Donnelly. That company then took from its file the addressograph plates of 30,000 provincial dentists or such and ran the envelopes through its addressograph and sent them back to be mailed by the purchaser.

The inquiring Jimmy learned all about this system and even persuaded the operator to show him how the plates were made. The rest was simple. When the eager and charming lad was allowed to try his hand at making a plate he punched out

Professor Gerald Apeface Bentley
Department of English
Princeton University
Princeton, New Jersey

The plate was supposed to be a souvenir, but Jimmy watched for his opportunity, and just before he quit his job he stole my plate from the file of English teachers and substituted his souvenir. In the course of operations over the next few years I got scores of pieces of mail with my new name.

I thought this escapade and its longterm and widespread results one of the best practical jokes I had ever encountered and told it to Richard soon after his return from Italy.

"Well I'll be damned," quoth he, "I had been meaning to ask how you ever acquired that Italian name Appa-fa-chee!"

Richard's sponsorship of talented but difficult young writers was long lasting and widely known. Perhaps the most notorious of his protégés was John Berryman whom Blackmur rescued from unemployment at Harvard by wangling for him a post at Princeton, where he remained on one appointment after another for several years. John's paper qualifications were fine—Columbia, Cambridge, Harvard—but he was a thorny, even habitually insulting character, though brilliant and talented perhaps to the verge of genius. Sometimes his performances were only eccentric or presumptuous. When he was writing *Homage to Mistress Bradstreet* he was blocked by his need for detailed information on parturition and the pains of childbirth. This was a poet's need, and therefore he should be allowed to suffer no let or hindrance. At four o'clock in the morning John telephoned an acquaintance just returned from the hospital with her newborn infant. He badgered her for the facts he needed; he got the facts, but he enraged the woman and her husband, who did not appreciate the paramount importance of the poet's need and who broadcast the story.

John Berryman's wildness was equally notorious but often less personally offensive. One time after a drinking party he had to be rescued from his perch on the roof of a building. Since John was Richard Blackmur's protégé, Richard's name was often associated with these eccentricities, usually without justification.

When John and Eileen Berryman lived around the corner from us he and I used to play chess at night until our wives got together and discovered that both of us stayed awake most of the night after the game. They put a stop to the series; the beautiful Eileen was the only individual who could ever exercise any constraint over her husband. Of course John insulted me as he did everybody else, but I found that Richard was right: "John Berryman is a brilliant man; you just have to tolerate him."

Generally speaking, tolerance was what John Berryman did not get and seemingly did not want. He was zealous in displaying his contempt for most people: he refused to speak to most of his colleagues; he would conspicuously turn aside or cross the street to avoid them. He took every occasion to sneer at academics; he belittled Princeton whenever possible. The result, naturally enough, was that he was a generally unpopular character.

The fact that John was a poseur furnished ammunition for his belittlers. Once after I had read a laudatory review of a piece of his I encountered him in the library and offered congratulations. "I never read reviews," said John, and turned his back on me. He liked to tell people that he was really a textual scholar, which pose was greeted with hilarity by faculty members, several of whom had written at least an article or two of textual analysis. So that when John announced that he would give a public lecture on "Problems in the Text of *King Lear*" his victims gathered in gleeful throngs to jeer at his amateur flounderings.

A few days before the lecture Richard said to me, "You'd better go, I don't think this is a pose." Even before Richard's tip, I had had inklings of unsuspected knowledge; two or three times John had boasted to me of his correspondence with W. W. Greg (later Sir Walter Greg), probably the most distinguished bibliographer and textual critic of his time. I had suspected that John was lying, but one could never be sure.

The lecture was a bombshell. At meetings of learned societies I had often heard papers on the textual problems in this or that masterpiece of literature, especially Shakespeare's. As part of my ordinary scholarly chores I had read scores of articles attempting to solve problems of corruption in the early publications of Shakespeare's plays; the problems in the text of *King Lear* were among the most intricate and controversial. No wonder the academic audience had come to jeer at the presumption of Berryman.

But they sat in stunned silence as the speaker calmly elucidated with great clarity the unsolved problems and suggested a few tentative solutions. Never had I heard a cleaner exposition. A few youngsters went up to congratulate the speaker but most of the veterans departed as obscurely as possible.

Richard continued to sit in the back row—smiling.

This posture is one of those in which I still remember him—a smiling Buddha. His other favorite posture, which still recurs in my memory, is Richard talking. He would sit slightly slouched to the left; in his right hand he held a cigarette, grasped in the middle between his thumb and third finger. As he talked he would slowly rotate the cigarette, end for end, with his forefinger. How many of his juniors have burned their right hand trying to imitate this gesture!

Robert Fitzgerald:
Blackmur, Princeton, and the
Early Gauss Seminars

Edited, with a Preface,
by Edmund Keeley

In July of 1984 I wrote Robert Fitzgerald to ask if he might be willing to contribute a piece on his friend Richard Blackmur to the present collection, perhaps focusing on their shared experience in setting up what became the Princeton Gauss Seminars in Criticism, the enterprise that was the occasion for first bringing them together. Fitzgerald answered by return mail: "I haven't been well—the diagnosis is lung cancer—and the treatments have been enfeebling, so I don't feel I can undertake anything on Dick now. The report on the early Gauss Seminars will be coming out in the fall, however, and I hope this will do something to fix and honor his memory."

Fitzgerald's "report," originally submitted to the Rockefeller Foundation in the early 1950s, proved to be an extraordinary document, published under the title *Enlarging the Change* by Northeastern University Press shortly before the author's death in January, 1985. In its "Prologue" the book sets the stage for the emergence of the Gauss Seminars in October 1949, and in the eight chapters that follow it describes—with clarity, wit, and acute perception—the extended Seminar offerings of Erich Auerbach, Francis Fergusson, Mark Schorer, René Wellek, Jacques Maritain, and Fitzgerald himself. The report also comments on a series of single Seminars by various hands on Mann's *Dr. Faustus,* and it provides delicious excerpts from the heady, impassioned, and sometimes acerbic dialogue among participants in the Seminars during the "discussion periods" that followed the more formal presentations by the invited Seminar speakers.

A reviewer in the daily *New York Times*, D. J. R. Bruckner, aptly captured the novelty of Fitzgerald's Rockefeller Foundation document by calling it "the most unusual, certainly the most eloquent, report sent to sponsors in our time." And though it gives ample air to Princeton's postwar season of "frigid brilliances . . . blue-red sweeps / And gusts of great enkindlings" that Fitzgerald points to in his epigraph from Wallace Stevens, the report most likely went unread initially by the Gauss Seminars sponsors and participants alike. In any case, as Fitzgerald tells us in the preface to his book, no top copy of the report has yet been found, and it was only after R. W. B. Lewis's comment in print that the Rockefeller Foundation document was "eminently publishable" and the interest this aroused at Northeastern University Press that Fitzgerald decided to release the carbon copy he had allowed to remain buried for years in a file of his own. Fitzgerald rightly decided that the report not only recorded the unusually bright genesis of the still living Gauss Seminars but in fact had a broader interest, what he called the story "of a fresh humanistic adventure carried out in a remarkably liberal and warm center of intellectual life," where "time, place, and persons coincided in promise, justifying the élan of large ambition."

Fitzgerald goes on to say that part of the story is how that large ambition "became tempered, though not quenched, by difficulties local and general," and one catches glimpses of these difficulties in the report's account of increasing parsimony at high administrative levels and a certain cool competitiveness entering to diminish the warm expectations of shared enterprise on the part of Princeton University and the Institute for Advanced Study in Princeton, discrete institutions then and now. What Fitzgerald's report couldn't anticipate was the gradual change in the Gauss Seminars that E. D. H. Johnson's remarks reflect in his contribution to the present volume: the emergence of R. P. Blackmur as the truly distinguished performer at each of the Gauss Seminars year in, year out, however distinguished the performance of the invited speaker might prove to be. And since Fitzgerald's account of the Gauss Seminars covers only the first two years of Blackmur's fifteen-year tenure as their chief participant, Fitzgerald's image carries little hint of the satire that eventually became one lively by-product of the Seminars, especially in the late phases of Blackmur's regime, when the limited possibilities remaining in his generation or the luck of the draw could occasion a thin slate of speakers in a given year, and when the discussion periods, whether at the Seminar itself or during the sometimes boozy hours that followed in Blackmur's home, could show the strains of longevity in rather tedious ways. One remembers, for example, the supremely distinguished lady author often down from New York who was given to posing questions, in a heavy German accent, that might run as follows: "I have only one question to ask our eminent speaker. It is in three parts. The first part has to do with—how shall I put it delicately?—the basic confusion, not to say essential contradiction, obvious in the speaker's clearly absurd proposition that . . ."; and perhaps ten minutes later the speaker might be allowed to say: "If I understand you correctly, and that I can hardly be expected to believe, let me attempt to approach the third part of your question first, because, having lost much of the drift of the other two parts, it would surely not be fruitful . . . ," to which Kingsley Amis, in town to await his own "Gauss" on science fiction later in the year, might be heard to mumble: "Just like bloody Oxford."

Fitzgerald's account of the earliest "Gauss" years has a freshness, almost an innocence, that rouses nostalgia in those of us who followed the Seminars in both good and uneven years over several decades, though his account does give us a few sample instances of the harsh wit and arrogant posturing that are perhaps inevitable when some of the great and less-than-great thinkers of a given generation get together in a small space. Fitzgerald tells, for example, of John O'Hara's attitude toward literary criticism in general and Mark Schorer's Gauss Seminar in particular, expressed in the wings after one of Schorer's sessions: O'Hara "observed that The Novel was obscenity; obscenity The Novel, he advised." And in another instance, he describes John Berryman's contribution to the discussion period in terms that became all too familiar to some of us long in residence (those who eventually came to be called, with no doubt appropriate irony, "the Permanent Seminarians"): "Berryman, who had been growing red, began speaking now with overriding alarm and impatience. 'Either I do not understand this poem or there has been a series of violent misconceptions. . . . Here is my interpretation for what it is worth, though I do not see how it can be wrong: . . .' "

I have limited my excerpts from Fitzgerald's text to those moments that focus directly on Blackmur and the particular Princeton climate that he helped to define in his early years at the University. The first section is from Fitzgerald's "Prologue," and I have called it "The Scene," which I think is self-explanatory. The second section brings together two excerpts from Fitzgerald's account—in Chapters One and Two—of Erich Auerbach's Gauss Seminar, which can be taken as a model of the early Seminar mode and which inspired a written "meditation" by Blackmur, offered here as fully as Fitzgerald presented it. The third section, which I have called "Blackmur at the English Club," consists of a brief commentary by Fitazgerald (at the beginning of Chapter Six) on a lecture that Blackmur delivered before his fellow English professors in the bar room of the Nassau Club, a commentary that provides valuable reflections on Blackmur's relation to both the New Criticism of which he was considered a founding father and to the University that was his home for the last thirty years of his life. These excerpts hardly do justice to Fitzgerald's scintillating record of the intellectual feast that he and others fashioned in Princeton between 1949 and 1951, but I hope that this loose gathering of material from his text will serve to underline that expressed purpose which Robert Fitzgerald wanted his book to fulfill when he found that he wouldn't be given time to fulfill it otherwise, that is, to fix and honor his memory of his old friend R. P. B., an impulse fully shared by the editors of this collection, who also hope to fix and honor our memory of Robert Fitzgerald in this partial way.

—E. K.

From the Fitzgerald Volume:
The Scene

In 1949 the writer spent a day in Princeton at the invitation of two men whom he had known more or less well for years. Richard Blackmur he had first met in Boston in 1932 carrying a large parcel of research on the *Cantos* of Ezra Pound; it was a cold night, and Blackmur sat huddled over his parcel, saying nothing, in the backseat of an unheated car. Francis Fergusson, in the writer's earliest memory of him, sat amid a budding grove of Bennington college girls in 1935, talking about Euripides. These men were six years older than the writer, and belonged to the generation of his instructors. Each, too, belonged to a milieu, a ramification of friendships, prized by the younger man.

In neither case had these shared interests or affections ever had anything to do with Princeton. The university that the writer had in common with Blackmur and Fergusson was Harvard, and the friends they had in common were of Harvard and New York. Neither of the two men had set out to be a scholar or teacher; each had practiced an art, and conspicuously well: Blackmur the art of writing, Fergusson the art of the theater. They, like the writer, though earlier than he, and like other men of their calling, had taken to teaching presumably because it gave them a living. But what had brought them to Princeton?

Once, before the war, the writer had gone to a dinner party in Princeton at which the principal guest was H. T. Lowe-Porter, the translator of Thomas Mann. Her husband, a humanist and paleographer, had become a member of the Institute for Advanced Study. Until then the writer had thought of this foundation, established in Princeton by the Bamberger fortune of Newark, as a preserve of scientists and mathematicians of whom the most famous was Albert Einstein. He had not thought of it as attracting to Princeton people interested in the art of letters, or in any art: people with whom one might have dinner.

Such, however, was indeed the case. And the presence of the Institute, so one might think, worked a change in the atmosphere of Princeton. It was as if a garage staff devoted to the gasoline engine had received a cyclotron for Christmas. A community could scarcely be called provincial in whose midst there were the internationally great, the showy dazzlers of the world. Thomas Mann himself lived in Princeton for a time; the writer heard him lecture there on Goethe. The displacement of eminent persons from Germany began early, but it was to continue—and not only from Germany—during and after the war.

There were other causes, but the Institute appeared to be one, for the fact that the university bestirred itself to seek a fresh, and broader, distinction. At any rate, Blackmur, who had never in his life been on a class list in a college, much less the recipient of a college degree (he had attended lectures at Harvard with the consent of the professors), and who therefore had no academic standing, as it is called, had been invited to teach creative writing at Princeton in 1940. More exactly, the university invited the poet Allen Tate, and when Tate invited Blackmur the university concurred.

Up to that point Blackmur, who was thirty-five, had not only never enrolled in a university class, he had never taught one either. He was a professional and absolutely independent writer. After helping to edit the *Hound and Horn,* a quarterly started in Cambridge, and a Harvard product if there ever was one, he had composed in the thirties a number of literary studies wonderful for their verbal and formal connoisseurship and strength of attention, among them the first really good critical essays on Pound, Cummings, and Stevens. Any highbrow writer would have said that Princeton was lucky to get him; and the Princeton community continued to keep him when the creative writing course at the university was suspended during the war. From 1943 to 1946 it was the Institute that offered Blackmur hospitality, along with such other guest intellects as Bertrand Russell and Niels Bohr.

Of these facts the writer learned vaguely during a couple of casual meetings with Blackmur in 1948, both at symposia of literary people. By this time Blackmur was an associate professor at Princeton. If, at their first meeting long before, he had been impressively silent, he was now impressively articulate, self-possessed and lucid in open forum. He had the air of one who had prevailed, and he had; in what sense, and to what end, will perhaps appear in the course of this chronicle. At the second of the symposia the writer also met Francis Fergusson again. He too was, or was about to be, at Princeton as a guest of the Institute, where he intended to finish a book on dramatic art that he had been meditating for twenty years.

This was the year of the Russian blockade of West Berlin and the Berlin airlift, interpreted by some beholders as theatricals cheaply produced by the Russians to divert attention in Europe and America from the Communist conquest of China. The writer, as it happened, looked in on the United Nations meeting at the Palais de Chaillot in Paris and thought it served chiefly to make the diversion more successful. He had been in Spain and Italy, and returned to New York the next year. In late September 1949, Fergusson wrote to invite him down to Princeton for a talk about some seminars.

The impression of this visit was that the Princeton now given to the visitor for contemplation—for the first time, the university itself—had put on a new dress and faced the ominous world. In visible aspect the principal change was the lately opened library, a mass proportioned with discretion in the fine Goodhue tradition, like an architectural Carthage founded from the Tyre of West Point, but far glassier, more gracefully recessive, and faced with warmer stone. There, in a bright vacant office, listening to Blackmur and Fergusson, the writer felt that for the time being something like an open academic society existed at Princeton.

Common sense would tell him that this must be partly illusory; but his friends, at any rate, were living in a universe of possibility, and what they envisioned they were apparently in a position to bring about. The idea was to keep up, during the course of three academic years, a running discussion of literature among a small and intent group of people who were not only interested but competent, including others besides university people, and any of the highest competence who were available. T. S. Eliot, for example, had been a guest of the Institute the year before; he might return, and if he did he would take part.

The method was to organize an annual program of seminars, four series of six weekly sessions each, each series to be conducted by someone with something to say. Kenneth Burke had led a pilot series the preceding spring at the Institute, and Robert Oppenheimer, director of the Institute and an old friend of Fergusson's, was sympathetic to the program. So were the people on the Humanities side of the university, chiefly Donald Stauffer, Whitney Oates, and Ira Wade, heads respectively of the English, Classics, and Modern Languages departments. The Rockefeller Foundation had put up $10,000. Fergusson, as director of the seminars, had a university appointment as associate professor in modern languages.

The first series of seminars had already started, led by a German scholar named Erich Auerbach, one of the two or three greatest

Europeans in Romance philology; and one of the others, the renowned Ernst Robert Curtius of Bonn, under whom Auerbach had studied, was also a guest of the Institute and had attended the first meeting. Jacques Maritain, then holding a professorship in philosophy at Princeton, would be a participant. Fergusson proposed that the writer, too, give a series of seminars.

Fergusson is a quiet man with an undeluded eye. Meeting it, the visitor realized in a moment that there had been no mistake, that neither Fergusson nor Blackmur took him for a scholar, and that they wanted not only men who had mastered the Muse, in Auerbach's way or another, but occasionally one still relatively callow in her company. They also wanted a seminar in some subject out of Greek literature. The academic year in question would be 1950–1951, and Blackmur proposed that the writer come to Princeton that year as assistant in the Creative Writing Program. This job had been held after the war by the poet John Berryman; a younger poet, William Meredith, had the position now, while Berryman lived in Princeton and worked on a biographical study of Stephen Crane.

Berryman and Meredith, and the writer as well, were men for whom the making of verse was a vocation, so far as they could manage it; they were poets if they were anything, writers in general as a consequence of being poets in particular; and for any university this was rather a high concentration in that category. Serious writers in the United States had most often done their work alone; that is, at best, though alone, they had done it. But: "The best things come, as a general thing, from the talents that are members of a group," Henry James had written in 1879, with regard to Hawthorne's loneliness. How could a group be formed, or to what group could one attach oneself? In 1940, the year Blackmur went to Princeton, he had published "A Feather-Bed for Critics: Notes on the Profession of Writing" in which the following sentences appeared:

> Serious men require the institutions of society almost more than they require to change them to fit their will and imagination, require them sometimes in the offing and sometimes at hand. Serious writers are no different; for them it would seem today that the university is the only available institution, whether in the offing or at hand cannot certainly be said, except by the university itself. I think at hand.[1]

Further:

> It is not that the university, even when properly employed, furnishes
> the ideal guarantee of the writer's profession; not at all—too many
> mistaken choices, too much misled energy are certain to appear; but
> it is the thing at hand, and it is the business of the positive critic, when
> he can momentarily bring himself to exist as positive, to lead writers
> where they necessarily are going.[2]

Now, in reflecting on the Princeton tableau of 1949, the writer had
decidedly the sense that these programmatic sentences were being
enacted before his eyes. It was clear that the Princeton Creative
Writing Program and the Princeton Seminars in Literary Criticism
would together, for their all-inclusive effect in his own case, make him
for a year and possibly longer a part of the institution that was
Princeton University; and it was clear that nobody had done more
than Blackmur to bring this to pass. The writer had little of the
passion of professionalism, so marked in his friend, nor had he felt
that he precisely required, except in the sense of employment, the
institutions of which he had up to then been a part. Blackmur on the
other hand was engaged, as the phrase went in those days. Part of his
strength lay in knowing the extent to which others including the
writer were not, but might become so; and another part lay in the fact
that he was engaged on the side of the university as well as on theirs.

   If the university, a house of studies, were to become a patron of
the art of letters, as Blackmur had foreseen, it would necessarily do
so through cultivation of the study of literature. In the end, whatever
residential appointments or equivalents of research fellowships might
be imagined, this meant teaching, in some effective and acceptable
sense, of literary matters. Here was the tide-rip between the life of the
imagination and the life of scholarship. "These people think they can
tell us how to teach literature; but we know how to teach literature,"
one of Princeton's elder professors had said; how to amend either half
of the statement was a delicate question.

   Among the younger teachers by trade at Princeton there were
many of more generous mind; and there was, besides, behind Blackmur and his friends, the encouraging presence of the venerated Christian Gauss, for years professor of French and dean of the college, who
had in fact been the prime mover in the Creative Arts Program,

started in 1939 under a grant from the Carnegie Foundation. This grant, and the one lately made by the Rockefeller Foundation for the Princeton Seminars, appeared to indicate something else: the gentle pressure of assistance from thoughtful people near the central switchboard of society. How did these lofty agencies, with so much money to dispense, justify the dispensations in question? The answer would no doubt be elaborate. What the men of letters at Princeton had to offer, essentially, was a disinterested approach to mysteries, recognized as such. It may have seemed that these mysteries—having to do with the work of the human spirit in language and in imagination—were worth honoring, or at least acknowledging, in a time very low in fruitful mysteries but very high in barren ones: too close for comfort, in fact, to chaos and the void.

More general and more easily formulated was the sense that during the breaking of nations certain substructures of tradition had been laid bare for the United States to take account of. The twentieth-century fling at the purely experimental life had begun to look unnecessarily wasteful. Circumstances in the world at large appeared to demand a certain centering, grounding, and girding up—hence the new attention the universities were giving to humanistic studies on their own grounds, not as adjuncts of social or other sciences, and not as adornments of the politely educated. This, which might have been called the critical movement in the colleges, antedated the war, but the war had made it more earnest. At Princeton, undergraduates were invited to enroll in something known as the Special Program in the Humanities, an interdepartmental collaboration. One avowed and obvious purpose of the new seminars was to strengthen this program at the top.

However profoundly and almost unrealizably threatened abroad, the United States had enjoyed after the war a breathing space at home in which the citizenry might take thought, if they cared to and were capable of it, about the significance of the life of which they found themselves still in possession. They had the money and the leisure that are held propitious to the arts, and they had the incentives that have been mentioned to pull themselves together and make use of the sources of wisdom. Many others besides the writer had consciously tried to do so. So far as he was concerned, Princeton fitted in with this effort, and the seminars should instruct it . . . so, at least, ran his first speculations.

Blackmur's Meditation
on Auerbach's Flaubert

The Princeton Seminars in Literary Criticism formally began on the evening of Thursday, October 6, 1949, with Erich Auerbach's series on Pascal, Baudelaire, and Flaubert—a triptych in itself worth meditation. Thinker, poet, and novelist, the three established a certain range for the seminars at the start; all French, they established what would in fact be a recurrent if not dominant cultural sounding board or backstop of literary reference; and it would have been difficult to choose three figures with more magnetism for the modern educated world of thought and letters. In the case of Pascal there was presumably an interest that the scientific personages at the Institute could share, and in all three there were varieties of interest for those to whom the difficulties of thought and art terminate in religious difficulty—a class of persons rather augmented, at Princeton as elsewhere, during the preceding decades. Auerbach's approach to all three was in terms of "stylistics," as became the critic trained in philology. Anyone could see how appropriate this was to Baudelaire and Flaubert, who represented sheer literary power at its apogee in styles that had carried over into the twentieth century and were as influential in the English-speaking world as in continental Europe.

Auerbach's method was to devote each evening to the discussion of a text, brief enough in each case to be mimeographed on a single sheet and thus put in the hands of everyone present. This procedure had obvious advantages in tethering the random horses of discussion to a single pin, a datum for minds to meet on. It was no doubt vain to hope, and it would have seemed impertinent to the director, Fergusson, to require that all subsequent seminar leaders adopt the same technique; but several in fact did so to good effect. With Auerbach it was standard operating procedure, a convention employed throughout the series of essays in his book *Mimesis,* a work of massive learning and considerable vivacity, published at Berne in 1946 and at once a *succès d'estime* among scholars, though at the time of the seminars not yet translated into English. Auerbach's seminar papers were further essays in the same mode, put into English by himself for the Princeton occasion.

Mimesis was not published in the United States until May 1953, when it appeared from the Princeton University Press in a very good translation by Willard Trask. By that time at least two excerpts from it had been published: a long chapter on Stendhal, Balzac, and Flaubert in the *Partisan Review,* and another long chapter on Dante in an issue of the *Kenyon Review.* These essays won Auerbach a much wider reputation in the United States than he had had before. In linguistic and historical range, at any rate, he pretty clearly surpassed any literary critic writing in English with comparable scholarship. This distinction, which *Mimesis* more than confirmed, had become evident in the fall of 1949 at least to the writer and, he supposed, to most other participants in the seminars at Princeton. Only a few, however, including Fergusson, had already read *Mimesis* in German and were acquainted not only with the full range of Auerbach's work but with its guiding interest or intention. Auerbach's method of exposition—the text with commentary—tended somewhat to obscure this intention, but with the two final evenings it emerged in reasonable clarity. The study of Flaubert might well be thought crucial not only to his seminars but to his whole work. For Auerbach's effort during those years in Istanbul when he wrote *Mimesis* had been to show, by stylistic study, the forms of literary realism shifting from Homer and Petronius through the ages to Zola—shifting toward, then away from, and then again toward the serious, the "existential," treatment of everyday life.

In the century between 1848 and 1949 there were, in this line, probably but two artistic efforts of comparable temper and density, Flaubert's *Madame Bovary* (1857) and the work of James Joyce. The writer, like many of his contemporaries, had first opened his eyes in literature upon a world created by both. Existence itself, taken in by the sense of identity as well as by the direct drinking of the senses until the mind had all it could hold—this seemed to him at twenty, facing *Ulysses* (1922), the primary donnée of the artist, to be retained, however transformed, in art. When he was twenty-one he sat until he was stiff over the pages of a cheap copy of *Madame Bovary* in a yellow paper cover, Bibliothèque Charpentier, at a long window opening on the rainy odor of the rue Molière. The book was printed from broken type in gray ink rather than black, a torment to the retina. It was the only French novel the writer would ever ponder sentence by sentence, from beginning to end. His head ached from the type and the cheap wine he drank with his lunch. He was trying to learn something he might inadequately have called the art of prose. Whether he learned it or not, he felt from that April onward more respect for Flaubert's novel than he could often feel for the verse of Baudelaire. The writer held with those professionals, his predecessors, Ford and Pound, who believed that poetry should be as well written as prose, that is, as Flaubert's or Joyce's; by "well written" they would understand "ordered, concrete, intense, and economical." He had therefore an interest of long standing in what Auerbach would perform on his chosen text in this instance.

The choice was modest; a paragraph near the end of Part I, at the climax, one might almost say at the peripety, of Emma's life in Tostes—the paragraph beginning: "Mais c'était surtout aux heures des repas qu'elle n'en pouvait plus." With his usual sharp delicacy in such matters, Auerbach pointed out that the scene is presented through Emma, yet what her consciousness contains is not rendered in her terms but in Flaubert's, of which she would be incapable. If she herself could have formed the sentence, "toute l'amertume de l'existence lui semblait servie sur son assiette," she would have outgrown herself and thereby saved herself. On the shape and texture of these sentences Auerbach was excellent, up to a point. He declared that Emma's disgust with the food was in the rhythm and was thus a part of the content of the sentence, likewise that the second sentence, "Charles était long à manger . . ." introduced a new rhythm; but he did not say anything in description of these rhythms. What he wanted to make clear, in the given passage and in a later sentence quoted from Chapter 12 of Part II, was the imposition by the artist of his own hand in the choice and ordering of detail, a trait that set the work apart from anything "naturalistic."

Taking the text as typical of Flaubert in particular and nineteenth-century realism in general, Auerbach then raised the question as to how it differed from the realism of earlier periods. The material and the scene, a man and wife at table, were usual in art. In the seventeenth century the scene might have been an idyll of family life, and in an older, more grotesque art, there might have been an amusing quarrel. But the story of Emma Bovary was neither sentimental nor satirical, nor was it a love story, *au fond;* it was "a serious representation of a whole tragic existence." Yet, said Auerbach, the tragic mode of past periods would scarcely have admitted as a minor climax a scene during a regular meal at home. The scene disclosed a wrecked marriage—not, said he, the marriage of the eighteenth century wrecked by mischief after mischief with a final solution, but the wrecked marriage that is a permanent condition. There is no quarrel because there is no contact, and on Charles's part not even an awareness of this. Each of the two lives in a windowless world of his own, with no one to help, no one for company, and no genuine reality; moreover, this is true of everyone in the novel. People meet for business or by instinct, never for community, and they are hampered everywhere by their lying, silly hatreds. Their isolating *bêtise* prevents a common life. Their public officials are all like the priest who fails to see that anything is wrong with Emma. When an illusion breaks, it breaks not on truth but on another illusion—and the word *Bovarysme* has entered the French language to designate this kind of life in an unreal world.

"But what the world would really be, the world of the 'intelligent,' Flaubert never tells us," said Auerbach. "In his book the world consists of pure stupidity, which completely misses true reality, so that the latter should properly not be discoverable in it at all; yet it is there; it is in the writer's language, which unmasks the stupidity by pure statement." In this way he approached the matter of Flaubert's famous religion of art—his faith, as Auerbach put it, that every event, if one is able to express it purely and completely, interprets itself and the persons involved in it far better than any overt judgment could do. Auerbach noted that faith in the truth of language responsibly employed was a classic French tradition; Vauvenargues had said, "Il n'y aurait point d'erreurs qui ne périssent d'elles-mêmes, exprimées clairement"—"There are no errors that do not perish of themselves when clearly expressed." But Flaubert went further: he believed that the truth of the phenomenal world could also be revealed in linguistic expression. A true expression was a real happening, placed with its value clear, just as God would judge it. This "mystical-realistic" insight, as Auerbach put it, associated Flaubert with Baudelaire as a stylist, for it entailed a certain view of the mixture of styles. Since the universe was a work of art produced without any taking of sides, the realistic artist must imitate the procedures of creation, and every subject in its essence contains, in God's eyes, both the serious and the comic, both dignity and vulgarity; if rightly and surely reproduced, the level of style proper to it would be rightly and surely found.

Auerbach ended by discussing the question as to whether Emma could be considered a tragic heroine. He thought not. Neither author nor reader could ever feel sympathetic or at one with her, he said, because the style itself judged her silly as well as wretched. Balzac invested Père Goriot with tragic dignity, as Stendhal made Julien Sorel a tragic hero. Flaubert's attitude and tone were quite different and should be called, Auerbach said, quite simply "objective seriousness."

In the general talk that followed, various people seemed uneasy as they tried to match Auerbach's ever-incisive formulae with the novel as they knew it. Fergusson wanted to know if there was not something tragic in Flaubert's style itself. Curtius objected to the whole category of "realism" as applied to Flaubert, observing that Flaubert himself explicitly disavowed the intention of realism. He went on to say, even more cantankerously, that the critical study of the history of literature uses terms that won't bear examination; we should dispense with these venerable terms.

Auerbach (stung): Why question the characteristic things called realism in the textbooks?

Curtius (Olympian): Because the textbooks are all wrong.

Auerbach (fighting back): Isolated, the term has no meaning, but it is sufficiently understandable in the context—French nineteenth-century realism. No matter if Flaubert did not want to be called realist; he worked the same way whether he liked it or not.

But the mention of Flaubert's other work, especially *Salammbô* (1862), made Auerbach concede that only part of Flaubert was realist. "But," said he, no doubt putting his finger on what was, in a sense, the heart of the matter, "I was writing a book on the treatment of everyday life!"

The next relevant remarks were made by Ira Wade, and they were closely relevant. Flaubert, he recalled, once said that he wanted to fuse the tragic and the lyric—an intention that Auerbach had not mentioned, though it was clearly related to his discussion of the style of Baudelaire. Wade wanted to know how you could get along without using such terms to bring out Flaubert's transformation of reality to lyrical writing. In the passage Auerbach had discussed, he called attention to the alliteration on "s." The writer thought this a useful remark, and made use of it himself later to discover that in fact the alliteration in the passage was progressive, beginning with the explosive "p's" of impatience and ending with the "f" of disgust.

As to the matter of tragic tone, Gauss severely interposed that Emma was not tragic because the tragic are those who deserve to live, and deserve to live Emma did not. Curtius returned to the attack on the category of "realist," remarking that it was very interesting (that is, nonsense) that Stendhal, Balzac, and Flaubert should all be lumped in one category; did not Balzac and Stendhal enjoy life while on the contrary Flaubert was a prey to despair? What was important was not what novelists have in common but their differences. Auerbach mildly replied that you couldn't get at the individual in Flaubert without historical common denominators. Fergusson and Curtius tried again to slit the straightjacket in which they evidently felt that Auerbach had encased a living work of art. E. B. O. Borgerhoff [Professor of French at Princeton and Blackmur's close friend], having thought the matter over, disputed one of Auerbach's principal points; the judgment in Flaubert's presentation of Emma and Charles at table, he said, was *sympathetic* to Emma; the reader shared Emma's feeling. Moreover—and this was Borgerhoff's liberating stroke—there was other evidence of the novelist's sympathy for Emma:

"Remember how Flaubert shows her at the time of extreme unction. . . . That is sad. To me, there is a quality like the ballads: something is celebrated, and properly."

Blackmur's meditation on this session, written down afterwards, read in part as follows:

"No matter who hammers against him, Auerbach must insist on his 'realism,' his 'sublime and common' and his 'dead earnest' or 'seriousness,' these, I take it, representing mode, medium, and point of view. When he applies his method to three authors with whom he is out of sympathy, as he has here to Pascal, Baudelaire, and Flaubert, he comes out somehow narrow but penetrating. What is narrowed away is the humanity of his authors; what is penetrated is their defect: the point where their work did not reach the level of performance, for him, but turned to some form or formula or rationalization or mere method: the antithesis in Pascal, the fusion of sublime and common in Baudelaire, the contempt and seriousness in Flaubert. I think myself he gives too much credit to these formulas on the work of the authors, where they were only aids, and too little credit to the actual material that got into the work with their aid. . . . He forgets that every writer who survives is constantly wrestling with a burden of actual experience by no means amenable to anything but disposition (disponibleness) by the method. Thus he not only missed but denied the wrestling, swindling authority of life itself, apart from all categories, in the series of images that lead to the whiff of all human ill in Emma's soul—a whiff looking out its home in the smoking stove, creaking door, sweating walls, damp floor, and above all in the odor of the food; and missed, too, our chance at that whiff while Emma pecks at the hazel nuts or marks on the oil cloth—those creases that come and go—with her knife. No; for him it is *bêtise* judging *bêtise a la bête,* with a further cruel judgment in Flaubert's *style.* That was Auerbach's predilection; and it is true that he has made it present; it must be taken account of.

"The pity is that this goes along with the prejudice in favor of tragic figures—those who deserved to live; and with the worse, because human rather than artistic prejudice, that Emma could have fixed everything up if only she had been more intelligent: the prejudice, in short, that emotion is capable of maturity. There is mature thought or attitude or understanding about emotion, but maturity is not a concept which applies to emotion; a lesson one would have thought universally taught in art, and one of the signs of greatness. Maturity is the solution, not the experience of the tragedy of individuals, and the solution is commonly death.—At any rate that is the predilection I gain from my reading.

"Turning from Auerbach to Curtius, one sees the great protection from follies afforded him by his doctrine of *loci,* the common *places* of mankind's efforts to express itself, its conditions and aspirations, in the arts. Curtius is, relative to Auerbach, a deep anarch of the actual. Every blow he struck at Auerbach was meant to break down the formulas whereby we see how unlike things are like. . . . He understands why it is that the textbooks *must be wrong:* because they are designed to take care of the reading we do not do: a legitimate enterprise when provisional, fatal when permanent. . . . It seemed to me, then, that Curtius was potentially always on the verge of breaking through into Emma's life itself, or into the moving subject or locus of literature. Or—to put it the other way round, to put it critically . . . Curtius was struggling toward the development of a neutral vocabulary, good for any insights. . . . I do not say Auerbach does not see all this; that he would not concede it in any instance, as we might all of us do; but that he has not the magnitude of mind or sensibility . . . to emulate it in original practice. . . .

"Borgerhoff seemed to me to make the remarks of richest possibility, and especially when he compared the fusion of the lyric and the tragic in Emma Bovary to the kind of thing a ballad does: a celebration of the beautiful and the strange and the true, where the meaning is in the celebration, and the celebration is a mystery, with many voices. . . . Note well that, for the moment, in Borgerhoff's use of it, the word 'ballad' is neutral: and, so to speak, here engineers a whole human vocabulary—though one that conspicuously would not last. . . .

"[One might put] the question whether the members of the seminar find it part of the common enterprise of culture. If they do, it is at a lower level both of collaboration and of individualism than the level anyone would name as optimum. The enterprise is there, is common, and the commonalty is of individuals; but the members tend mostly to run off into the artificializing formulas which make problems easy to discuss and easier to escape in discussion. It seems to me . . . that there are two ways in which we can promote both greater collaboration and greater individualism. One: when 'history' is at issue, in any sense of the term, it is certain that literature provides us with . . . documents in the *experience* of ideas or thought or the mind; literature is the history of the experience of the mind. It is also the history of the experience with which the mind has been coping or—more important—what it must now cope with—and—most important—the experience with which the mind has never yet been able to cope. The other line is this: that it is a probable rule in literature, that whatever can be wholly subsumed under categories or formulas of any kind represents the work that the writer either could not do or was not interested in doing or refused to do. . . . Applied to criticism it means that categories, sets, formulas, slogans, and so on have constantly to be refreshed by the direct look: by the individual look in company with the collaborative look. These two lines, boiled down and made almost habitual, should provide the right questions and the living questions. They provide means for the reaccession to the experience *in* literature—of which the experience *of* literature is only a part."

Blackmur at the English Club

Some of Blackmur's personal and literary quality came of being saturated in the noblest English styles of modern times; James, Adams, Yeats. The title of the paper that he gave, in the fall of 1950, before the English Club of Princeton, was taken from Isaiah by way of Yeats's poem to Von Hügel, and the writer found this paper, "The Lion and the Honeycomb," relevant to the seminars, to the Princeton group, and to what he himself thought of offering for discussion. The *organon,* in Schiller's words, that would mediate between philosophy and art: this was still to seek, and Blackmur seemed to propose that it be sought on the critic's side. He proposed at any rate that literary criticism construe itself afresh for a new effort and a larger growth.

The "New Criticism," which had meant, in the hands of Eliot, Tate, Empson, Yvor Winters, John Crowe Ransom, and Blackmur himself—to mention stars principal only—loving and expert attention to the formal and verbal characteristics of poems, had so decisively won its point that by the time it was named, in a book by Ransom in 1941, its proponents were tasting the ashes of success. The title, of course, rather bored them all. And they had almost all, even by that time, escaped the category of New Critics by other means than by growing *older.* But Blackmur was thinking of them and of the fashion that had followed upon their zeal; of Miss [Rosemond] Tuve's instruction [that is—as Fitzgerald mentions earlier—her having shown, during a published exchange with Empson, that some of Empson's ingenuities on the text of George Herbert's poem, *The Sacrifice*, were possible only to ignorance], and of his own capacious and recently intensified interests; he was thinking of the next phase, and he wanted it original and fruitful, as before. He could see it grinding into a self-centered methodology in Ransom, in Empson, and particularly in the "grammars" of Kenneth Burke, and an analogy from ancient times served him: "Rhetoric," he said, threatened to absorb the other "modes of the mind," as it had done in the centuries between Plato and Quintilian. His paper was a plea for the restoration of "dialectic" and "poetic" as such to the repertoire of the professional writer, the complete literary man.

One had seen how Blackmur affected the university; here perhaps was an instance of how the university, and the idea of a university, had affected Blackmur. A certain pollen for his bloom of discourse could be traced to the physical and friendly proximity, at Princeton, of the Classics department and its energetic chairman Whitney Oates, who worked down the hall and around the corner. The writer had now seen how this worked; it worked by joint recourse to coffee in mid-morning at the little library cafeteria two floors above. In these conversations as in those at the Nassau Club, one noted Blackmur's versatility of interest; he had a mind "of large general powers," in Johnson's phrase. Oates was a Platonist whose finest recent work had been done in prefacing and editing the big *Basic Writings of St. Augustine* for Random House. He had noted the kinship of Plato and Augustine in what he called, on Plato's part, the "intense desire to keep his philosophical inquiry alive and not permit it to crystallize into a series of verbal formulae," and this "openness" of "dialectic" was evidently part of what Blackmur, too, understood in that term.

"The Lion and the Honeycomb" also clearly owed something to the example of Dante, as Fergusson had interpreted him, and to the *Poetics* of Aristotle, reviewed likewise in the light of Fergusson's work. Blackmur even suggested that as I. A. Richards had written his most vivid book *On Coleridge and the Imagination* (1934), he might take in a further range in a book called *On Aristotle and Imitation*. He recommended, indeed, to all concerned that they inhale the air of these large worlds in Aristotle and Coleridge, getting into relation with other than literary objects—with theology, history, politics, and personal experience.

After hearing this essay read to a roomful of teachers, each with his glass, in the Nassau Club barroom, the writer's exhilaration outlasted the evening. Not that he failed to appreciate his friend's delivery, and in some turns of phrase, that touch of the proconsular—the calm of the small compact silver head—that, as he realized by this time, had kept Blackmur's popularity decently incomplete among the professors.

The writer was not a New Critic nor indeed a critic of any title at all, though he had for some years put his mind on books and written about them for a living. He disliked specialization and liked the various employments of being alive. He could not see any such magic rings around accurate study, reasonable discourse, or the making of verse as should deny a human being serious occupation with all three. He took Blackmur's essay as a statement on his side—only the latest and most deliberate, indeed, for Blackmur had extolled the amateur before.

NOTES

1. R. P. Blackmur, *Language as Gesture* (New York: Harcourt, Brace and Co., 1952), 408.
2. *Language as Gesture*, 406–407.

E. D. H. JOHNSON

Seminars under
R. P. Blackmur

It was the seminar, especially as conceived and practised at Princeton, which elicited Richard Blackmur's unique gifts as a teacher. While often brilliant, he was apt to be self-indulgent in conversation to the point of pontificating. At such times the flow of his thoughts resembled a series of finger exercises, usually playful, sometimes outrageous and calculated to shock, a display carried on as much for his own entertainment as that of his audience, although apparently chance remarks often foreshadowed critical opinions still in the germinal state.

On the other hand, Blackmur was never completely at home on the lecture platform. He lacked presence, speaking in a monotone without much inflection or carrying power. And this fact, combined with the intricate structure and mannered style of the prepared texts from which he read, made it difficult to grasp his meaning except in fragments. At the opposite extreme from his conversational virtuosity, Blackmur's lectures approximated the finish of his published essays, calling for leisurely perusal in printed form.

As a pedagogic device, the seminar may be said to occupy a middle ground between the sprightly improvisation of social intercourse and the more authoritative tone of public utterance. The conduct of small selected gatherings convened to discuss set topics Blackmur found particularly congenial to his temperament; and it was through this means that he undoubtedly exercised his widest influence

152

on the university community at Princeton. To his leadership, for example, must be attributed the success of the Gauss Seminars in their heyday.

These seminars yearly brought to Princeton outstanding figures from the world of letters, who were expected on four or five successive weekly evenings to give to an invited audience readings from their works then in progress. Yet, distinguished as these performances often were, it was not they, but the ensuing periods with Blackmur in the role of interlocutor which remain most memorable to those of us privileged to attend. With skill which defies analysis, so urbanely unobtrusive it was, he evoked an atmosphere of shared enquiry into which all members of the gathering felt drawn. Following a regular procedure, Blackmur would begin by engaging the speaker in a dialogue designed to explore further implications of the latter's presentation. Before long, however, this interchange would have become the launching pad for more general discussion, with one after another of the auditors competing for attention. Yet, one was always conscious of Blackmur's hand on the reins, quietly restraining any individual from monopolizing more than his due share of time and guiding the discourse back to the issues appointed for consideration when it threatened to stray too far afield. Whatever the benefit to the principal speaker from the critical barrage to which his work was thus subjected, there can be no doubt that for the rest of us these seminars under Blackmur's aegis left in their wake an exhilarating sense of having had a creative share in the evening's proceedings.

Although I was a fairly regular attendant at the Gauss seminars, my most vivid recollections are of the concurrent series which Blackmur conducted on his own initiative around the middle years of the century. They were for him clearly a labor of love; and I am under the impression that they were offered gratuitously without teaching credit. For me, whose training had been largely in the fields of historical scholarship, they constituted nothing less than a postgraduate course in literary criticism.

Again, the format of these seminars followed a pattern especially congenial to Blackmur's habits of mind. The series of meetings, one or two each term, took place on a weekly basis in Firestone Library and occupied a full evening of three hours. The participants, about a dozen in number, were largely drawn from academic colleagues representing all of the departments of the humanities, with a sprinkling of graduate students. Each seminar was devoted to a single major literary work, usually fiction. The books considered in the seminars at which I was present included Mann's *The Magic Mountain,* James's *The Wings of the Dove,* Dostoevsky's *The Brothers Karamazov,* and Gide's *The Counterfeiters,* as well as Eliot's *Four Quartets.* In a period before the establishment of the Department of Comparative Literature these seminars thus did much to foster an interest in interdepartmental studies at Princeton.

Blackmur reserved the first half of the evening for his own exposition of the assigned reading. This he pursued in a consecutive and seemingly impromptu manner from the text open before him, apparently taking the cues for his remarks from the heavily scrawled margins of the pages as he turned them. From time to time he would also refer to an accompanying notebook in which he had apparently outlined more general headings for his discussion. How one would have liked the opportunity to inspect these jottings, but they were rigorously guarded from prying eyes!

It was, however, a measure of how scrupulously he had prepared his performance in advance that, in contrast to the lectures, he never gave the impression of being tied down to his working notes. His approach to his material, delivered in a casual, almost offhand way, was unfailingly oblique, tentative, exploratory, anything but dogmatic. As he spoke, he smoked incessantly, cigarette held stiffly between tobacco-stained index and second fingers; and his gaze traveled alertly from one to another of his auditors, as if seeking for our mute confirmation of views provisionally set forth. Yet, this seeming randomness of method was at the service of a densely integrated argument, calling for the closest attention, but then constantly productive of fresh and compelling insights into familiar works.

The proof of the success of the Blackmurian seminar came in the invariable liveliness of the discussion which dominated the latter half of the weekly gatherings. In retrospect the give-and-take of those evenings remains among the high points of my thirty-five years as a member of the Princeton faculty. The excitement communicated by Blackmur's initial remarks made each of us eager to contribute his own thoughts, which were, I fear, less original than they seemed in the intoxication of the moment, and more often than not derivative from ideas implanted by the foregoing exposition. But what matter if sober reflection on the following morning failed to sustain the complacence born of the spirit of intellectual rivalry in which we had matched wits, competing for our leader's approbation?

Indeed, despite or perhaps because of the intensity of one's involvement, it was always difficult to reconstruct in any detail the particulars of these seminars. This was especially true of Blackmur's own presentation, the nuances of which were at once arresting and fugitive in their subtlety. He had a gift for encapsulating his perceptions in aphoristic form; one copied these sayings down only to find that they had become wholly enigmatic when divorced from their original context. Here from the endpapers of my copy of *The Brothers Karamazov* are some examples of Blackmurian dicta which have continued to tantalize me down the years with their half-glimpses of lost meaning:

> This book is the fable of how the conscience creates itself.

> Smerdyakov the impure form, the Devil the pure form of Ivan's flunkeyism.

> Fyodor, the unmotivated out of which motives are made.

> Ivan and Katya love each other like enemies;
> Mitya and Katya hate each other like lovers.

What one took away from these ever-memorable evenings, however, is not to be weighed in terms of the remembered joy of active participation, great as that is, so much as of the manifold ways in which one's imaginative response to supreme works of literature has been nourished by the opportunity provided through the seminars for intimate association with Richard Blackmur. I never return to the novels which we discussed in those meetings without grateful awareness of all I owe to one whose teaching of yesteryear continues to enhance each rereading.

ROBERT V. KEELEY

An All-Purpose Mentor

In the beginning I knew Richard Blackmur as a teacher of creative writing. At the suggestion of John Hite, a popular and controversial instructor in the English Department at Princeton during the years immediately following World War II, I applied for admission to the Creative Writing course at the end of my freshman year. Bill Meredith, Blackmur's assistant, accepted me on the basis of a story entitled "god" about a young man's loss of religious faith over the failure of his prayers to God to prevent him from contracting a venereal disease from an encounter with a prostitute financed by his roommate (this may sound silly, but any humor was unintentional). Meredith termed the story "powerful stuff" with what I suspect was irony which I didn't recognize at the time.

On starting the course in the fall I found I had been assigned to Blackmur rather than Meredith. We had to submit some written work every two weeks. I scrambled through most of the fall term by ladling out small portions of poetry I had accumulated over the summer. Blackmur didn't much like my poetry, which I deduced from the fact he practically never talked about it during our biweekly conferences. I don't recall ever having revised a poem as a result of his criticism or suggestions. From early on I had the impression he was more interested in me than in my writing.

What he found interesting was the campus gossip I would pass on to him, bits of scandal and controversy that I acquired working for the *Daily Princetonian* and authoring a weekly gossip column for the paper. For example, through our conversations Blackmur was always privy to the latest development in the John Hite case—the popular Hite was being let go because he had failed to complete the requirements for his Ph.D. degree, and the students were up in arms over his imminent departure. Blackmur couldn't help being interested in this case since he lacked even Hite's inadequate academic credentials, and he liked to be one up on his faculty colleagues with inside information.

After I had graduated Blackmur frankly told me he hadn't liked my poetry. It was too "obscure." I laughed, because coming from him that ought to have been a compliment. But of course that was wrong; he never thought he was obscure, though nearly everyone else did. Blackmur never said anything negative about my poetry while I was in his course because he avoided saying anything that would discourage a student or dent what self-confidence he had.

He liked my prose a good deal better, and I wisely shifted my writing in that direction. One piece he particularly liked was a group of connected stories called "Three Loves and an Epiphany." Blackmur insisted on changing the title to "Three Loves in Four Acts," a take-off on Gertrude Stein's *Four Saints in Three Acts*. I cannot say I learned much from Blackmur that improved my writing. Occasionally he would hit me with a memorable hortatory axiom such as: "If you are writing about love, love is the one word you should never use."

But that would be in the final five minutes of our session, after he had pumped me dry of campus news and gossip and had reciprocated with a long monologue filled with fascinating reminiscences, literary and personal, and critical analyses of great literature that were often incomprehensible to me. I believe he thought I might in time make a competent journalist, because the imaginative writing I submitted to him usually didn't "fully engage my sensibilities," as he put it.

Invariably Blackmur would greet me as "Herr Doctor Professor" when I arrived at his office in Firestone for a conference. I doubt this was exclusive with me; it was his way of mocking the academy, but also of kidding me about my vague intention to become a teacher. He thought I should rather seek a career in the "real world," a job involving writing perhaps but one far distant from any academy: journalism, politics, diplomacy, something not purely intellectual wherein the use of the mind was linked to action.

Our relationship began as teacher-student, but of a closeness that is one of the virtues of the Princeton system, and over time he became my guide and adviser, an all-purpose mentor, and eventually a friend whom I called "Richard." In a real sense he shaped my academic career, with assists from other leading lights of the English Department such as Donald Stauffer, Dudley Johnson, Willard Thorp, Carlos Baker, Alba Warren, Tom Riggs, and Lawrance Thompson. Blackmur liked to encourage rebellion—more precisely, to nurture the existence of rebels—in the academic community. He had himself been the supreme rebel, for at a young age he had refused to return to school after a disagreement with his teacher. His mother, an unusual type, had backed him up fully. His father was a different sort: for two years they did not exchange a word. Richard had called him a liar; he told me that in retrospect he thought he should have accused his father of "departing from the truth."

In an academic community Blackmur was the anomaly—without a secondary school diploma, a factor which had prevented him from matriculating at Harvard. By 1948 he was on the faculty at Princeton and he could no longer rebel. Yet he still personified rebellion against the academy. Though he could not be an active rebel, in his heart he hadn't changed, and he could continue rebelling through surrogates—willing ones.

Late in junior year I deplored, in one of my last creative writing conferences with him, my inability to settle on a senior thesis topic. Under the Special Program in the Humanities which was my major, one devoted almost the entire senior year to what was supposed to be a grand and glorious thesis. I had nearly decided on James Joyce and had read everything available by or about him—this was 1950, before Joyce had become an academic industry. But I also wanted to write a novel during my senior year. With the nearly nonexistent course load of an SPH senior I thought I could manage both a thesis and a novel. Blackmur doubted I was that "smart." Frederick Buechner, who was smart, had written *A Long Day's Dying,* his first novel, during his senior year and had also dashed off a short thesis on the metaphysical poets.

Blackmur declined to comment on Buechner's novel since it was by an ex-student (he never reviewed the *Nassau Lit* or the rival magazine I edited, *MSS.*, because they were both filled with the work of his students) but he said Buechner's thesis was not all it should have been. So, he said to me, why not combine the two? Why not submit a novel as a thesis? It had not been done before, but there had to be a first time.

I will pass over the conspiratorial work that got this thesis project approved by the SPH. The toughest nut to crack was the conservative English Department, but its Chairman, Donald Stauffer, was my thesis adviser and he was sympathetic to my proposal. Blackmur was of course central to the process, in fact he was the key as well as the secret instigator. The committee which granted approval instructed me to produce one-third of the first draft by September 15 and to turn it in to Blackmur, who would judge whether this one-third showed sufficient promise to warrant final departmental approval. All summer I worked as a reporter for the *Vineyard Gazette* newspaper in Edgartown, on Martha's Vineyard, thought about the novel, and continued reading Joyce in case I didn't pass muster. An intense, abortive summer romance provided the material and motivation for the novel, some hundred pages of which I dashed off in the first two weeks of September. What else could Blackmur say but that it "showed promise"?

Someone talked me into taking Professor Albert Friend's renowned course in Northern Renaissance art as an elective. I was apparently the only person who ever took it who thought it was a lot of mush about very little. I admit I didn't understand most of what Friend was up to. Among other things, he had us stare at three brightly illuminated white billiard balls on a billiard table for an hour and then record our reactions. Mine was nullity. I wrote the required paper for the course, killing two birds by handing in a chapter of my novel in which Professor Friend was a thinly disguised priest whose task was to defend the practice by painters throughout history of using whores and other women of easy virtue as models for their paintings of the Madonna. Friend thought my paper had very little relevance to the course. He was right.

At the end of the fall term the exam in Friend's course was the only one I had to take. I decided to skip it, to give myself three full weeks off-campus during which I could concentrate on my novel. It was not a matter of trying to avoid a low or failing grade. SPH majors had no course grades recorded during their senior year. I slipped a note under Professor Friend's office door apologizing for skipping the exam.

While I was away from Princeton all hell broke loose. A special faculty meeting was called, for I had committed a grievous violation of academic probity and Friend was angry. His point was that his exam was an integral part of his course, was really its *raison d'être*. So I had heard, which was an additional reason for wanting to skip the exam.

Once again Blackmur and Stauffer had to come to my rescue, obtaining a suspended sentence and limiting my punishment to the requirement that I take the exam in one of the two courses I had signed up to audit in the spring term. That was a bother, but since no grade was recorded it didn't matter whether I passed it or not. The choice was not difficult; I had signed up for Blackmur's course in Criticism and Stauffer's course in Poetics. I agreed to take the exam in Blackmur's Criticism. Privately Blackmur was immensely pleased that someone—at least one undergraduate—had found Bert Friend's course less than enchanting. Any sort of unanimity went against his nature.

The novel had to be accompanied by a preface which was just about as demanding to write as a regular English Department thesis, though more fun. My preface was a very idiosyncratic polemic projecting all my literary likes and dislikes, with the heaviest artillery directed against Henry James, a writer who was one of Blackmur's favorites but for whom I had not then acquired a taste. Blackmur got his revenge through my final exams, which he helped prepare. One six-hour exam consisted in its entirety of three quotations from Henry James, as critic, with the usual formulation: "Comment, with appropriate illustrations from your reading." Two hours on each James quotation! There was a second daylong exam made up of three quotations from my preface, again chosen by Blackmur. I remember only one, which Blackmur relished as having been aimed at him personally: " 'The critical mode of mind destroys the creative, and vice versa.' Comment, with appropriate illustrations. (2 hours)" That was one fun exam.

I competed for a Rhodes Scholarship my senior year and, given the makeup of the selection committee, I should have been an easy winner. The committee for the New Jersey region consisted of three of my English professors—Donald Stauffer, Courtney Smith, and Alba Warren—a professor from Rutgers, and George Gallup as Chairman, who dozed off from time to time as the second round of interviews stretched past midnight. All three of my professors were former Rhodes Scholars, and they had all written letters supporting my application. How could I lose? I managed to throw it all away by getting annoyed with their rule against Rhodes Scholars getting married (I was planning to do so shortly), and with Cecil Rhodes's reputation as a racist imperialist, and finally by making the outrageous statement that I might actually prefer the English Department at Cambridge, which I had heard was superior to Oxford's. Even a committee stacked three to two in my favor couldn't swallow that, and I lost out in the finals. Blackmur, who had also supported my application, though half-heartedly, was vastly amused by this turn of events, and thought it served the Rhodes people right for being so stuffy and superior. He told me I probably wouldn't have liked it at Oxford anyway.

In the spring I heard there was something called the Manners Prize in Creative Writing, which consisted of a 14-carat gold medallion of a tiger but also a good deal of cash. Blackmur chaired the selection committee. I asked him if I should submit my novel for the Manners Prize. He said that would be unfair to the committee, to ask them to read something that long. He suggested I submit my "Three Loves in Four Acts." Naturally I took his advice. Somehow I doubt that the committee ever met. At graduation it was announced I had won the Manners Prize, and a short time later, while in Mexico on my honeymoon, I received a letter from Blackmur enclosing a fat check which financed an extension of the honeymoon into September.

When I asked Blackmur's advice about accepting a fellowship to study English at the Princeton Graduate School, taking into account that I didn't really want to study what was taught there—which was how to write boring scholarly papers on subjects no alert human being could be interested in—my mentor suggested that I ignore the Graduate School's "requirements." He had examined the catalogue and nowhere in it had he found any statement that an enrolled student had to take any courses. Why not just study on my own, or write full-time? I followed this rather unrealistic advice only partially and therefore cannot blame my entirely undistinguished record during three terms at the Graduate School on him. The advice was of course consistent with Blackmur's own "academic" temperament.

I gave as much time and attention to Blackmur's evening Gauss Seminars as I did to my course work at the Graduate School. It was far more interesting to listen to lectures by Randall Jarrell on Auden, Edmund Wilson on the Civil War, and Leon Edel on Henry James than to pore over *Beowulf.* Blackmur invited my wife Louise to attend the seminars as well. We were mostly spectators at these academically prestigious gatherings; they were an intellectual pressure cooker that intimidated all but the bravest and most egotistical gladiators in the academy.

In those days survival was uppermost on our agenda. Louise worked in the Firestone Library and then for the Educational Testing Service, and I was a public-opinion poll interviewer for Ken Fink's New Jersey Poll and a truck driver for Applegate's Floral Shop on Palmer Square. When Edmund Wilson needed a part-time "research assistant" to chase down books in the Firestone stacks to help him find quotations he needed for his *Patriotic Gore* Blackmur threw the job to me, as I needed the extra money. We lived an interesting life in genteel poverty. Blackmur often dropped around unannounced to our slum-like dwelling on Linden Lane to share our dinner, go to a movie, and end the evening with the inevitable nightcaps of undiluted bourbon-on-the-rocks.

During my first term in Graduate School I failed Old English, the first student to do so in a generation, I believe, and there was a huge fuss, which resulted in the professor who taught the course being relieved of that duty, and a second chance being offered to me, which I declined to take. As usual, Blackmur was amused by my antics. The following year he was allowed to teach a graduate course for the first time, a major concession to a man lacking a high school diploma. I took his course—it was in literary criticism—maintained my pro-creative, anti-critical animus, and received a grade of "pass," one small notch above failure, from Blackmur. It was what I deserved, despite having, at his insistence, plowed through I don't know how many volumes of Flaubert's letters in French looking for a few *bons mots*.

I abandoned graduate school, finally, to do my military service in the Coast Guard and redeemed my academic reputation by graduating first in the class from Officer Candidate School at the Academy in New London. The motivation for seeking that ranking was to have first shot at a desirable assignment, which turned out to be Cape May, New Jersey. On visits to Princeton I consulted Blackmur about a choice of career, admitting a temptation to stay in the Coast Guard. I liked the sea, was commanding officer of a small patrol boat, and it was a secure living that left time to write on the side. Blackmur liked the idea, for he was a sea person himself, and had at one time thought of attending the Naval Academy.

But he was even more pleased when I joined the Foreign Service and became a career diplomat. That was the kind of life which he had yearned for but which he had had to forego for a variety of reasons. I naturally used him as a reference when I applied to take the exams. He was asked to comment on my intellectual ability, personality, temperament, loyalty, and weaknesses and defects. His answer on "temperament" was written in characteristic Blackmurese: "As to temperament, insofar as I can distinguish it from personality, his temperament is half sanguine, to use the old term, and half vivacious." That was the first, and last, time anyone has called me vivacious—even half so.

When I informed Blackmur that I'd passed the exams and had been accepted into the Foreign Service, he said: "You'll do all right as a diplomat, but you'll have your problems. I expect one of these days we'll hear that you've undertaken to set our misguided Secretary of State straight by saying to him, 'Mr. Secretary, you unfortunately have your facts all wrong. That policy simply won't work.'" He chuckled to himself at the thought. The Secretary at the time was John Foster Dulles. Given my very junior rank it is not surprising that I not only had no opportunity to set Mr. Dulles straight but I never met the man. I have had some problems in my career, and it may be that some of them resulted from a subconscious effort to live up to Blackmur's expectations of me.

The November before Richard's death I mentioned that I was hoping to arrange a year's sabbatical from the Foreign Service to learn something about economics and to do some writing. His final gesture toward me was characteristic: he phoned the Associate Dean of the Graduate School and asked him to help in any way he could to get me admitted to Princeton for my year off.

It is strange, but true, that I owe so much to someone who said so many things to me that I so little understood.

W. S. MERWIN

Affable Irregular

How old we all were! It is harder to believe than to remember, even when I cast around, one more time, for reasons, explanations, and manage to persuade myself that I have spotted a few. They don't add up, and they explain nothing. John Berryman's cadaverous features and vaulted intonation—he was in his early thirties—still the young man of the Cornelia Walcott drawing in the 1946 edition of Oscar Williams's *Little Treasury of Modern Poetry*—but he enacted an imperious need to be one of his elders. He talked as though he were a contemporary of Allen Tate's, at least. And Blackmur, only ten years his senior, seemed already older than he would ever, on the calendar, live to be. He had the gravity, the voice, the deliberation, the walk, even the smile, of a man far into his sixties. Fortunately I could not know, when I met him, that earlier in the same year he had concluded that his life was really over. Russell Fraser's exemplary study, *A Mingled Yarn*, reveals that on January 14, 1946, Blackmur, then a week short of turning forty-two, had written, in his notebook, "the days or years that remain after this date I consider posthumous." What he anticipated was merely a "pre-mortem interlude." The actual semblance of age, whatever it told of his own will, must have been his for a long time. He had always been precocious. Fourteen years before I first saw him, his friend Sherry Mangan described him as "that artificially aged dodo, our old friend Dick Blackmur." When he wrote that, Blackmur was not yet thirty.

There was some corresponding assumption, a little ahead of time, of the unspeakable burden of years, among those of us—there were really very few, in that era—who considered ourselves to be, whether formally or not, students of Berryman or Blackmur, or of

them both. Some of the false ripe manner may have been nothing but
a perennial phase of the student role, a donning of impressive earnestness and the long face of the acolyte. And some of it was noted and
considered special even at the time, and was praised as a new seriousness, attributed to the ending of the war and the return of veterans
who were said to have grown to appreciate the real importance of
getting an education, and who wanted to make up for lost time. Some
of them really were several years older than was usual for undergraduates, and some were married, which in an exclusively "men's" school
gave them enviable privileges and a distinction usually associated with
later years. For the aspiring literati among the students, as for Berryman and Blackmur themselves, one of the looming figures of the
period was Eliot—at forty, and perhaps long before that, the aged
eagle. But it was not a matter of a solitary imposing model. It was only
twenty years since the legendary 1920s and F. Scott Fitzgerald's
Princeton, and the cult of novelty and youth that supposedly had
characterized that time. It all seemed as remote as the Civil War, and
Blackmur and those he spoke of as colleagues clearly hailed from an
authority that was at once more immediate and more ancient. More
honorable, in our eyes, and more interesting. More profoundly uncon-
ventional, and more mysterious.

Money—the lack of it—no doubt contributed to the loyalties
and preferences that evolved among those of us who liked to see
ourselves as already writers. Students were still not allowed to have
cars on campus, nor, I believe, in town, but many alumni and undergraduates, and some among the faculty, continued to cherish the
reputation of Princeton as the country club among universities, a view
which, after all, antedated Gatsby and roadsters. On the other hand,
many of those who then wanted, or imagined they wanted to write,
represented a kind of unorganized and unacknowledged dissenting
minority not peculiar to Princeton and the times, yet the more conspicuous for appearing in what was traditionally a rich man's college.
Some even then surely cherished a lively regard for money, and some
went on to acquire substantial quantities of it. But a number of them,
as students, had and were used to having very little of it. Some were
there on scholarships, or eked out GI Bill checks from month to
month, or both. The image of the bohemian artist helped somewhat—or I imagined it did. It provided a model drawn from other

ages and situations, of dedication and behavior that mocked, and affected to mock, not only the conventions and pieties in which most of us had grown up, but also the presumptions of the young sports with Princeton banners or Confederate flags above the rows of steins on their mantelpieces. Neither Blackmur nor Berryman, as we knew, had been students at Princeton, and we were sure that, in respects we could not even guess, they were out of all that. Blackmur had been moneyless all his life, and even when I knew him his salary, as rumor soon told us, was pinched and its continuation uncertain. He and most of the following that gathered around him and Berryman tended, or were forced, to be outsiders. A kind of necessary privation which both of them built into the basis not only of a virtue but of an ethic of fierce devotion to an art in a philistine society. To art itself, and a view of life in which its importance was beyond question, preeminent and predominant.

I had finished two school years at Princeton before I met either of them, and for most of that time I had not even heard their names, though I imagined that I was determined to be a writer, indeed a poet, of a vague, variable, but feverish variety. I owe the meeting, as it came about, to Anne and Keene Fleck, who ran the Parnassus Bookshop in a small, pretty, old, yellow-painted (at one time) house on Nassau Street. I was led there first by a friend, Don Cook, and I took to haunting the shop, alone or with a crony or two, though I had no money at all to buy books. The pair of downstairs rooms off the hall were lined with old and new volumes, and there was often someone in a corner chair, or sitting on a low stool—a round green velvet stool with three legs made of steer horns held together by a chain—reading, and someone also browsing in library-reading-room quiet that began at the front door. Anne, or more rarely, Keene, might be deep in hushed conversation, repeating what seemed to be esoteric gossip with an intimate, and once I came to know them, Anne would tell me, after they had gone, who *that* was. I was in my third semester there, and was busy being Shelley, mostly, and a bit of Beethoven, in ill-fitting pieces of discarded army uniform passed on to me by my father, who was a chaplain and whose sizes were different from mine. If I was alone, I walked everywhere reading—Shelley or Milton, Keats or Spenser. I was, in important respects, a rather retarded seventeen.

It was Anne, with her gaunt gypsy face and smoker's laugh, who suggested that I meet Blackmur—Blackmur in particular. Berryman certainly occupied a conspicuous place in her pantheon, but she may have been somewhat afraid of him. Of the two, he was more obviously aloof, unpredictable, savage, whereas Blackmur's manner, at least, was usually benign, formal, courtly. She spoke of them both with evident awe, showed me their books, and also a small anthology called *Bred in the Bone* by poets who had been students at Princeton in the years just before I had arrived, at which I glanced from too great a height to make it out distinctly. She told me of Blackmur's perspicacity with a poem of her own which she had shown him. He had pointed out, almost at first sight, the very passage from which she had just cut two lines, in the previous version. She extolled Blackmur's kindness, his humor, his wisdom, the range of his learning, and his love for Maine, where he then was. She and Keene suggested that I send him, in his summer retreat, some poems of mine. It must be said at once that this was apparently a normal procedure in applying for admission to the still quite recently formed writing program at Princeton. And from my point of view, the suggestion came at the right moment. I wanted to know for sure how you could tell whether a poem you read, or (a little shifty) one you wrote yourself, was really good or not. Some of the professors pronounced upon specific poems and poets in categorical fashion, but when asked how the judgment had been reached their answers had not contented me. I suspected that they did not really know. And I thought it possible that this Professor Blackmur, who had no degree and was not a professor, might. Heaven knows what I sent him.

After all the buildup, my memory of the first actual meeting is hazy. One rainy autumn afternoon in a small office in McCosh Hall, I stood in a dripping crowd of students, the whole assembly steaming and smelling of wet rubber. On foot in one corner a severe, bony, superior figure all in browns managed to whirl, flash papers, snap answers, ignore most of the callow hopefuls. I learned that that was Berryman. By now I see him there in his brown porkpie hat, which is likely enough. But the long maroon-and-yellow striped knitted scarf, insignia of high days at Oxford, and the gabardine, may have formed on him later, though it is true that for a while he seemed always to be wearing them. And was it not Blackmur, sitting behind a desk, smiling up in answer to questions, all but inaudible, and eclipsed, much of the time, by the students who had come to register for courses? I think I saw him without meeting him, and was out of the room before I knew it was he—if it was. Such an encounter would have been typical of the man and the relation to him: the low-voiced benevolence on the one hand, and the remoteness on the other.

I never formally took a course with him, nor did I visit him with any designated regularity. Our acquaintance, then our friendship, accumulated imperceptibly through chance encounters, often with mutual friends, on the campus, on the street, or in that echoing cafeteria with its shower-room decor, across Nassau Street from the campus gates: the Balt. Occasionally, after a while, at his house on a Sunday afternoon—visits to which my shyness and his own reticence lent a stammering awkwardness on my part, at first. Gradually we circled a bit nearer to each other. The will was there. What I recall of Blackmur's speech during those years survives from such conversations, from the weekly talks on Joyce, Dostoevsky, Flaubert, and Mann that he gave regularly in the evenings in Clio Hall—one of the neoclassic temples in the middle of the campus—which were attended by a small fervent band of aficionados, and from a graduate course or series of seminars on the history of criticism which I sat in on toward the end of my time at Princeton, after the dean of the graduate school and I had agreed—mutually, if somewhat precipitately—that I was no longer a graduate student.

My abrupt break with the graduate school was something that Richard regretted, at least in the form of it, which he felt had been quite unnecessary—a misunderstanding on both sides. Dean Taylor, he assured me, if properly acquainted with the circumstances, would have been sympathetic to my situation. He reproached himself, he told me later, for not having made things clear to the dean in time. I am not sure just what in my situation Richard supposed would have elicited the dean's forbearance. I can hardly imagine that anything more enthusiastic could have been expected, even by Richard. I learned in roundabout ways, over a long time, of some of Richard's efforts, before that fateful conversation, to make it possible for me to continue as a graduate student. As he understood matters, according to the letter of the law if someone attended classes for one year as a registered graduate student, and read the books on the relevant department's reading list, that student was entitled to sit for the examination which, if successfully completed, entailed the conferring of the master's degree. At the time of the rift I had finished a year of graduate courses in the Department of Modern Languages, and was working my way through the reading list in French. I was spending my days in the library and living in Morrisville, across the river from Trenton. Yet I had never been entirely certain whether I wanted to take the examination for the degree even if I was allowed to do so. Richard's own lack of degrees was more to my taste, and continued to claim my admiration. I had considered ignoring the bachelor's degree that I had earned, or at least skipping the graduation cere-mony, and had bowed finally to various persuasions, notably those of my parents. Richard seemed no more eager for me to acquire graduate degrees than I was, myself. Once, in a rapidly passing mood, I men-tioned the possibility of working toward a doctorate, and he asked me what on earth I wanted a doctorate for, if I wanted to be a writer. It was my own question as well as his, but at that point, whatever I may have said, I was perhaps less ambivalent about the answer than he was. On the other hand, it seemed to him a good idea for me to stay on in Princeton for a while after graduating, unless some remark-able alternative offered. I would be able to use the library, and as for the graduate school itself, a good education, as he put it, would do me no harm.

But I had done my undergraduate work in English, and if I stayed on I wanted to read, and try to translate, the poetry of other languages. I had barely met the entrance requirements for the gradu-ate school in the Department of Modern Languages, and my admis-sion put me in a position roughly analogous to his own, on the faculty, where the allies, known or unknown, regarded the very irregularity of his presence, with no degree and no academic background, as some-thing of an adventure, a welcome exception, while the more conven-tional among them ground their teeth and waited for the chance to set things straight again. I was an erratic graduate student from the start, impatient with what I considered the duller stretches of the canon of French literature, and eager to indulge instead discoveries and enthusiasms of my own. I was being Ezra Pound, by then, in the same seedy bits of old uniform, but with a ratty pointed beard which Bill Arrowsmith referred to, not altogether accurately (with respect to the shape), as an armpit. Pound's criticism, which I was avidly ingesting along with the required French literature, did not help my tact or my status as a student there on sufferance. Blackmur's arguments in my defense (which were needed sooner than I knew) did not have to do with scholarship, of course, but with that far more debatable presence, talent, and the university's role in recognizing, encouraging, and making exceptions in order to harbor it. His urging on my behalf may not always have been much more tactful than my own conduct as a student. I was told recently that once, when the subject of my continuing in the graduate school came under review, Blackmur asked one of the deans, "What do you know about so-and-so?" "Never heard of him," was the answer. "Well," Blackmur is supposed to have said, "that's not surprising. He's only remembered because he was the don who expelled Shelley from Oxford."

Whatever the relation of the story to what really was said, it is interesting as an example of a continuous campaign of Blackmur's, not, of course, merely on my own behalf. During his teaching life, Richard repeatedly displayed a patience, generosity, and kindness that have become legendary, toward certain of his students whose talent he seemed to take on faith, for there was little enough evidence of it, and whose academic conduct stood in need of apologies. His personal writings make it plain that he was far gentler to us than he was to himself. In defending us, obviously, he was speaking out for the Richard whom he wished, or thought he wished, with a great part of himself, that he had been, or that he might have become. The faithful, unswerving outsider, rather than the salaried teacher however untenured, underpaid, and uncertain. The unpredictable, the insecure, the risky, the unrespectable. The writer in him, or his image of the writer in him, which he went on feeling that he had betrayed by committing himself to the university life. Whatever its general truth, the conflict represented a dichotomy of his own and was relevant to him first of all. Others have managed to combine writing and teaching more or less happily. And others have suffered from something like his guilt, self-hate, and disappointment without transmuting those poisons into generosity toward the young.

And it is also worth remembering his own history of unbroken poverty, the years of living on pittances earned from reviewing, the unpublished and unfulfilling novels. And that the time when he started his defense of such inconvenient students of his was the 1940s.

For another fifteen years, respectability and a steady careerism would be the dominant mode in most quarters, even among the young, quite as though there was no alternative. Richard was speaking for alternatives. To be discovered, invented, made. He was insisting that the artist—and by extension, the individual life—can have no formula for survival.

At least occasionally his influence in favor of finding one's own way corresponded with a half-formed, ill-articulated, floundering (he would have said "inchoate") urge that was integral to a particular student. I think it was so in my case. My friends there almost without exception were older than I was, and most of those with literary leanings took it for granted that they would teach. I took it for granted that I did not know what I would do for a living, and even more strangely I took it for granted that I would not know for a while. My friends spoke of their own assumptions as proofs of maturity, in contrast to my own unrealistic childishness. I learned, to my surprise, that Richard abetted my improvidence, and although he was generally chary about what he saw as direct meddling in other people's vital decisions, he discouraged me from considering a university career. More than a decade after I had left Princeton, on a visit to Boston, where I was living, he prefaced an invitation to give a series of lectures at Princeton by saying that he hoped I would not teach, but that if I was thinking of it he would like me to consider, first, a proposal that he had come to make. His reluctance echoed my own.

By the time I sat in on his graduate seminars on the history of criticism I was no longer a graduate student, and the irregularity of my presence in the course clearly pleased Richard. A university was there for the students who could use it, in his view. As for the institution itself, an order, as he would put it in his ponderous but muffled diction, was strong and rich precisely in proportion to its ability to contain within itself the seeds of its own destruction. I could not quite see myself as anything so ominous, looking out the window, watching spring unfold in the trees above Nassau Street, listening to the revolving talk about *Antony and Cleopatra,* Longinus, Aristotle, Croce. Blackmur had set up the course taking *Antony and Cleopatra* as the single central text, to be read afresh each week, along with the work of a different critic whose theories were then to be exercised in relation to the familiar play, to see where they led us. They led us, as I recall, nowhere very definite, and certainly not to any fixed, dogmatic notion of the real function of criticism or of one absolutely right methodology, in the way of Babbitt or Winters or Leavis. Blackmur thought of a good critic as a house waiting to be haunted. Which was fine with me: I loved the play, loved reconsidering it regularly, was fascinated by the form of the course and above all by listening to Blackmur on the subject before us, or on any other. Yet something in the course, no doubt, wound down, lost not only impetus but form as the weeks passed and the days grew longer and the windows opened onto days nearer and nearer to summer and the end of the school year. Blackmur held the talk, spun it, handed it back, wandered off from it into his own meandering improvisations which veered from startling insight to mumbled incomprehensibility, and I suspect that some of the graduate students who had taken the course for orthodox reasons may have been disappointed. I remained more interested in the teacher than in the course—and I was leaving. Some of the Blackmurisms promised to be inexhaustible. One heard them and missed the next five minutes, or one went on listening and lost them. Some may have been scribbled down in notebooks, and Richard himself may have used some of them again elsewhere. But most of them, by the nature of the talk itself, were probably lost.

For some of us the course was simply an extension, employing a certain amount of dialogue, of those evening sessions at Clio Hall that Blackmur had been giving during the time I had known him. They were the most heady, suggestive, illuminating, and bewildering lectures that I had ever heard, and in the years since then, nothing has replaced them in my mind. They were monologues, lasting several hours each evening, and in considerable part they were improvisations from notes and from annotated texts and marginal jottings. They were not transcribed. The click of the cassette box was not yet with us. Some of the faithful—most of the faithful—came equipped with hardback notebooks and tried, session by session, to take down the substance and the phrasing, but I think no one managed to keep up the practice consistently, or in reliable detail. Some of the material, in Blackmur's own decoction, saw the light in later essays of his, particularly in those on the European novel. But much of the real body of it, its character and force of suggestion and evocation, its humor and its intimation of discovery, survived only in the recollection of those who were present. And the fact that most of us have so few nuggets of language and perception to show for the hours spent listening to that unpredictable voice must be as maddening, or as gratifying, to Blackmur's detractors—who for years I could scarcely believe were serious—as the opacities and infelicities occurring in his written work.

The novels on which I most distinctly remember him expatiating were *Ulysses, The Magic Mountain,* and *The Brothers Karamazov, The Idiot,* and *The Possessed.* Each of them, read and re-read with his massive, rumbling commentary, took on the nature of an initiatory process—a situation, certainly, with built-in dangers. But those lectures fostered and deepened, in a number of us who had the luck to hear them, a veneration for the human imagination as it makes and finds and moves in language. It is ironic, and altogether consistent with Blackmur's nature, that the two fragments I remember most clearly from those hours of monologue are what they are. One has to do with character, and arose in reference to *The Brothers Karamazov.* In Blackmur's judgment, at that time, at least, Dostoevsky had characterized more profoundly than any other novelist. His characters were founded so deeply, in fact, that they acquired what Blackmur termed "potential reversibility." However he used the idea later, at the time of those sessions this meant that Dostoevsky's personages were able to act in ways inconsistent with what one had thought of, until then, as their true characters, without the reader's ceasing to believe in them. It was a statement of Blackmur's own vision of the bewildering intricacy, and beneath that the unseizable depth of human individuality. The other shard was not even commentary—or not in its intent. I am not sure, either, what led him to bring it up, though I believe it arose in the course of his chapter-by-chapter perusal of *Ulysses.* It was simply Blackmur's quotation, in his doughy Italian, of Virgil's line to Dante (Inf. III, 18) explaining that the tenants of Hell are those *"ch'hanno perduto il ben dello intelletto"*— "who have lost the *good* of the intellect." He rolled the word "good" with his remarkably small mouth. The quotation emerged from his own most intimate, familiar, and continuing perception, and for me, at least, it leapt from the context of the talk. Neither his own personality and upbringing nor, it must be said, the time and company, would have tolerated any suspicion of private plaintiveness in the delivery;

but, whether or not I was immediately aware of it, I came to realize that the line spoke to him of what he thought, much of the time, of himself.

Part of the quality of those talks, their richness, and their freedom, arose from the fact that they did not represent a course, were not part of any curriculum, and that no one attended them for university credit. They too were irregularities; and I recall, as clearly as the Dante, Blackmur's smiling relish in repeating Yeats's line "an affable irregular"—another, and happier, image of himself. In the tradition, as he saw it, of Flaubert and Yeats and Pound, he believed, or said he did, in the work that was formed out of the life *as against* the life itself, whatever that was or is. For decades, he insisted on the distinction between them, and on something like the autonomy, or at least the sufficiency, of the latter. But despite my admiration for his written work, it was the man who impressed me, first and last, whom I am happy to have known and to remember, and toward whom I have felt, since those years, a continuing debt and affection. When I met him, as I see now, I was in search of some kind of absolute touchstone, and I saw both him and Berryman through the lens of my own expectation. Neither then nor since have I doubted the authenticity of either of them.

And with Blackmur, as with Berryman, most of what I remember, and remember with deepest gratitude, survives from private conversations. Axioms. Blackmur telling a student who complained of not having enough time to write that "you always have as much time as you need." Or remarking about a possession, "in order to keep it you have to use it, and in order to use it you have to add to it." Helen Blackmur's story of his sitting up in bed suddenly, one night, and mumbling, "a good sinner makes mighty good eating," and then lying back and going on sleeping. (He said that he dreamed of Coleridge often at that time.) His confiding, while talking of something I had written, that he had wanted for years to get the word "inchoate" into a poem—a glimpse, when he said it, of his own humility. His walking down Nassau Street in a Harris tweed overcoat that he mentioned buying years before in Filene's basement, talking of his own coming birthday, of the late starters such as Conrad, or of Titian saying that at forty-seven he was just beginning to learn to paint, and going on from there, somehow, to discourse on the theme of Molly Bloom's fart, which he described as "the spiritual extension of the animal soul."

At times I felt that, even in his talk, and often in that of students around him, nodes of experience, literary or non-literary, got involved in intolerable cocoons of abstraction, where they seemed to perish, and sometimes he revealed a similar impatience. He helped some of us not to take ourselves as seriously as we imagined was necessary. "Stop talking to me about Aristotle," he said one day to one of the Balt habitués, "I don't sit on his pot." When I mentioned, some months before I left, that I was thinking of applying for a grant offered for the study of diplomacy he smiled and said, "You're incapable of diplomacy." The first translation that I published happened to be of a poem by Richard Coeur de Lion. When I showed it to him, or told him about it, he quoted with pleasure, *"O Richard, o mon roi, l'univers t'abandonne."* I was slightly disappointed because it came from a nineteenth-century opera. He thought, finally, as I did, that it was important for me to get away from the university, to live in some other milieu, and without constant reference to literary criticism. Shortly before leaving Princeton I told him that I was reading through his essays again. "Oh, you shouldn't do that," he said. And he went on to urge me to avoid criticism entirely, for a few years at least.

I wrote to him a few times, but we did not correspond. Over the years there were happy reunions. In Princeton, and at his favorite Greek restaurant in Boston. One afternoon, we went together to the Boston Museum of Fine Arts, and in the Asian collection he talked of the concept of the Bodhisattva. That afternoon he seemed inexplicably yet unmistakably like a father. A father to me. Particularly when he was turned away, was looking elsewhere. But the meetings were rare. Years after leaving Princeton, when I finally had a book of poems that I wanted to show him, I dedicated it to him. I wrote to him beforehand, but by then it was no longer his approval that I wanted so much as a way to thank him. For what, it is still impossible to say. For confirmations that have survived him, among them a tenacious esteem not for the human alone but for the inchoate in humanity, as it struggles inexplicably to complete itself through language. In the purity of impure human language, in language as a vehicle for the unsayable. A faith in empty words. I still send him my poems.

III. Texts

JOSEPH FRANK

Blackmur's Texts:
An Introduction

R. P. Blackmur chose very carefully, when he came to compose his
volumes of essays, among the considerable corpus of writings that he
turned out over the years with unremitting regularity. The books now
tend to give the impression of a sovereign judge who, from time to
time, sat down to write a definitive and magisterial essay; but the
presence of Blackmur as a critic as felt in his own time was certainly
quite different. As the variety of his early uncollected articles and
reviews makes clear, he was an active participant in the literary life,
who served with distinction in the journeyman ranks of regular reviewers and whose name kept cropping up in the journals. Beginning
in 1927, when he was twenty-three years old, there is not a year in
which anyone reading the magazines of the time would not have come
across one or two items by Blackmur (in some years, many more). He
wrote not only in the *Hound and Horn,* which he helped to edit in
its first years, and which quickly earned a rightful prestige as the
American equivalent of T. S. Eliot's *The Criterion,* but also in the
New Freeman, the *New Republic,* and particularly in *Poetry.* Most
of this small-scale production remains buried in the pages of these
periodicals; and in republishing here some of the more interesting
ones, we hope both to fill out the historical record and also to provide
a more faithful image of Blackmur's activity as a practicing critic. The
present selection includes longer late essays as well and spans the
entire period of Blackmur's literary career; but it is the abundant
early work, of which only a meagre sample can unfortunately be

included here, that offers the most new insight into the foundations of Blackmur's achievement as a literary critic.

It was, of course, by his longer essays, first collected in *The Double Agent* (1935), that Blackmur made his major impact—if one can use the word "major" without overstating the case. He was read and appreciated by the small group of people seriously interested in the contemporary poetry then being written; and the book was published by an obscure avant-garde press called Arrow Editions, which expired a few years later after issuing Blackmur's second volume, *The Expense of Greatness* (1940). All the same, the steady stream of reviews were also having their effect and in some cases introduced Blackmur to those who would soon become his fervent admirers. There is a touching testimony to how they inspired the best young talent of the time in "Olympus," from John Berryman's *Love and Fame:*

> In my serpentine researches
> I came on the book review in *Poetry*
> which began, with sublime assurance,
> a comprehensive air of majesty,
>
> "The art of poetry
> is amply distinguished from the manufacture of verse
> by the animating presence in the poetry
> of fresh idiom: language
>
> so twisted & posed in a form
> that it not only expresses the matter in hand
> but adds to the stock of available reality."
> I was never the same after *that.*
>
> I found this new Law-giver all unknown
> except in the back numbers of a Cambridge quarterly
> *Hound and Horn*, just defunct . . .

These lines illustrate both the easy adaptability of Blackmur's prose to Berryman's colloquial verse-style, and also the importance of these shorter reviews as an independent voice in the animated literary give-and-take of the time. I do not know if any zealous student of Berryman has tracked down the source of this quotation; but it will now be readily available. It is the first sentence of a review of a book by Norman Macleod, *Horizons of Death,* published in *Poetry* (May

1935), and it continues with the equally impressive and highly significant assertion: "Since we no longer live at the stage where the creation of idiom is the natural consequence of the use of language, many of our best practitioners have necessarily to manufacture a good deal of mere competent verse in order to produce a few good poems." Whether a time ever existed in which "the creation of idiom" (in the sense meant by Blackmur) was simply "a natural consequence of the use of language" may well be doubted; but it illustrates his literal acceptance of T. S. Eliot's idea that a Golden Age of poetry had existed before the "dissociation of sensibility" in the mid-seventeenth century.

Norman Macleod, though his name was not unknown to those who, like John Berryman, spent their time in "serpentine researches" among the periodicals of the mid-1930s, was hardly an important literary figure. It is all the more striking, then, that Blackmur should have prefaced his review by the statement of his credo as a critic that so much struck Berryman; and this fact illustrates one of his characteristics as a reviewer. Each of the writers he attends to receives his undivided, sharply focused attention; there is no slackening or tightening of scrutiny according to rank or importance, as when a host will shade greetings to various levels of invited guests; all are deemed worthy of requiring the same intensity and integrity of critical response. Norman Macleod is read with the same care and scrupulosity as Wallace Stevens, Ezra Pound, or Hart Crane; this is why Blackmur feels it necessary to establish in advance the high and exemplary critical standard by which the poetry will be judged.

There is also another quality of Blackmur's reviewing that is exemplarily illustrated in the Macleod piece. Precisely because his critical standards were so high, and because he knew how difficult it was to fulfill their requirements (since the "creation of idiom" was no longer "natural"), he resisted being merely dismissive. In the midst of his most negative judgments, he would always search for signs of artistic seriousness and of achievement, even if on lower levels than the one he would recognize as culminating in a genuine work of art. So far as Macleod is concerned, Blackmur writes: "Of the forty-two short poems Mr. Macleod has here collected, six seem to me of fresh idiom and good within their magnitude, nine good but for various reasons incomplete, and the rest of indifferent manufacture." Whatever his reaction to these words, Norman Macleod could hardly claim that he was not being read with great care. There is also the further statement that "the feelings are profoundly entertained and are full of implication, and the phrasing is often lovely with affection and discrimination; and there is no question but that the poet is genuinely at home with a genuine subject which he has felt as poetry." But, Blackmur maintains, in the bulk of the book Macleod did not *realize* his subject sufficiently to turn it into poetry, for lack of an "imposed form." He concludes, however, with the consoling remark that "the problems of poetry cannot be discussed except in the work of those who, like Mr. Macleod, actually write it."

It is worth further illustrating this charitable quality of Blackmur in the case of writers whom he values much less highly than he evidently does Norman Macleod. Take, for example, the review of Sacheverell Sitwell's *Doctor Donne and Gargantua: The First Six Cantos* (1931). This is one of his most severe pieces; the second sentence declares that "hardly a superficial fault of texture, hardly an essential weakness of conception, but appears egregiously and flourishes at length in these eighty pages." Then, after calling the poem "traditional," Blackmur writes that it "goes a long way toward preserving out of the past and presenting in all baldness the principal maladies of English poetry." One might think that, after all this, Blackmur would continue to show no mercy; but after a few paragraphs containing a brilliant improvisation on the various causes of sentimentality in poetry, he ends on a note of regret. "The saddest thing," he writes, "is that the essential weakness and cloudiness of the poem destroys the pleasure that ought to be taken in the fine things there are in it, the occasional rich sonorities of line and sweet delicacies of association. For Mr. Sitwell is actually a poet, as may be seen by this as well as by past performances." Some incidental felicities in the text, and the memory of others in the body of Sitwell's work, thus help to redeem this otherwise unrelieved failure, and the condemnation is mitigated.

Blackmur is merciless, however, when pretentiousness is allied with incompetence and vulgarity. The most cutting review is devoted to a now forgotten poet, Leonard Bacon (did he not write some light verse à la Ogden Nash?), who made the mistake of devoting a narrative poem to "the life and death of the legendary Arthur Rimbaud."

The snippets that Blackmur quotes from this opus are unbelievable in their coarseness of sensibility, and he calls the work "an active poem, full of waste-motion, din, conventional cleverness, verbal fireworks, and dullness around the corner, just like Life. It has a Kiplingese virility, tinged with the Y.M.C.A., which equals Robert W. Service." Such a sentence gives some of the flavor of Blackmur's conversation, and of the satirical verve that he usually kept in check when it came to the printed page. But here he was so clearly outraged, and with such good reason, that he allowed his temperament a freer rein. What particularly aroused his indignation was the blurbs the book had received from reviewers in the newspapers and weeklies, and he felt called upon to urge them to defend their *own* standards (not Blackmur's) a little more discriminatingly. "Mr. Bacon is one of those who carry the burden of our academic poetry, which is a serious and honorable burden to bear; and it has been the sole intention of this review to point out that he carries it a little too jauntily, with the ease and itch of a journalist."

Besides enriching our image of Blackmur as a critic, these early pieces provide valuable glimpses into his intellectual formation, which he tended, if not to conceal, then at least to take for granted in the later work. There is, for instance, his notable sympathy with the attack on what he calls, in his review of Wyndham Lewis's *Time and Western Man*, "the romantic-scientific, sensational, and naturalistic habit of soul," and there is his obvious preference for the position of such writers as Lewis himself, Irving Babbitt, and Ramon Fernandez (not to mention Eliot), who were "concerned to restore the intelligence and the sensibility by adverse criticism of any such misapplications of science." These lead him to agree with Herbert Read that Proust and Joyce lack "a sense of values," and that, as a result, there is an "absence of orderly intelligence, of discipline, in the major works of these writers." Such judgments will later be considerably modified; but they show the strong influence of a neoclassical bent on the early Blackmur—who yet, all the same, already has some qualms about basing aesthetic evaluation primarily on such implicitly moral criteria. For while seeming to agree in one passage with Lewis's negative view of most of modern writing, he remarks later that "as to Lewis' judgments on James Joyce, Ezra Pound and company, they are valid only from Mr. Lewis' attitude." Moreover, Lewis "is not, in this essay, primarily interested in the works themselves." When it come to *these*, Blackmur leaves open the possibility of another standard.

As can be seen from the second section of his two-part essay on T. S. Eliot in the *Hound and Horn,* Blackmur is greatly concerned with this problem of art and morality (or of "values," to stick to his terms); and this early Eliot essay is of great help in clarifying the road he took towards its resolution. His later statements of doctrine, such as "A Critic's Job of Work," rather illustrate than attempt to explain Blackmur's position; but the Eliot essay shows him grappling with the issue, and finding a solution by extending some of Eliot's remarks. Incidentally, it also shows that the same dilemmas tend to recur, and that Blackmur's concerns have lost little in relevance despite all the fuss currently being made about literary criticism and critical theory—which has now, presumably, passed far beyond the primitive standpoints of the recent past.

Any observer of the contemporary scene knows that literary theory is at present moving from a phase of Structuralist Formalism to one in which the *values* expressed in the works have become once again a focus of attention. In other words, critics are again worrying over the perennial question (perennial at least since Plato ejected from his ideal Republic those poets who refused to confine themselves to sacred songs) of whether works of art should be considered exclusively as autonomous aesthetic objects, as assemblages of certain formal properties or structures, or whether their value depends on the manner in which they interact with other areas of human life. It has become commonplace to consider Blackmur an unconditional partisan of the first alternative, and in his informative but annoyingly patronizing biography Russell Fraser simply perpetuates the myth that Blackmur thought that the study of what he called "executive techniques" was enough; "he left the matter of content to shift for itself."[1] But this is a gross oversimplification of the complex synthesis that Blackmur tried to achieve, and whose theoretical underpinning he lays out at length in the Eliot essay.

Way back then, in those dark ages before even the antediluvian New Criticism had been born, Eliot was making the same shift so evident today in the contemporary post-Structuralists. Beginning roughly with Formalism, or Art-for-Art's sake as it was then called, Eliot had announced a new turn in 1926. Blackmur noted that in a review of then-recent books by Herbert Read and Ramon Fernandez, Eliot had pointed out that "both, instead of taking for granted the place and function of literature—and therefore taking for granted a whole universe—are occupied with the inquiry into this function, and therefore with the inquiry into the whole moral world, fundamentally, with entities and values." This marked the moment when Eliot's return to (or public assumption of) religion began significantly to affect his criticism; and Blackmur, far from rejecting such a development, welcomes it as an enrichment. But he attempts to reinterpret it in a way that will widen the critical horizon while, at the same time, preserving the benefits that have accrued from Eliot's earlier work with its intense scrutiny of the language of the poetic text.

Blackmur uses Eliot's essay on Massinger as his example, and shows how the criticism of Massinger's language, which Eliot saw as more rhetorical than suffused with genuine feeling, is also linked to a *moral* criticism not so much of the playwright as of the period. "What may be considered corrupt or decadent in the morals of Massinger," Eliot wrote, "is not an alteration or diminution in morals; it is simply the disappearance of all the personal and real emotions which this morality supported and into which it introduced a kind of order." The quality of personal emotion in language thus becomes the basis, not only for an aesthetic, but also for a *moral* evaluation of the writer; and Blackmur tries to generalize this remark into a method of criticism "whose approach shall be technical, in the terms and in the interests of literature as an art" but through which we shall "reach the moral values where our last interest lies."

Blackmur's strenuous attempt to define such a method can be read in the essay itself; there is no reason to expound it any further in these prefatory remarks. But it would seem to imply that a successful work of art is the true locus of morality because only there is individual moral experience grasped in a complexity that transcends the ordinary application of moral rules. Such appears to be the sense of Blackmur's observation that "the failure of ordinary systematic moralities could be shown in their inadequacy to judge such works as *King Lear;* where it is the intensity of the fusion of the emotional elements that makes the play intelligible and *valuable.* " To return to the present for a moment, one is reminded here of Wolfgang Iser's notion that art invariably points to the "gaps" in the systematic moralities of its time; it is only through the concrete experiences of the work that such deficiencies are revealed. Blackmur is saying much the same thing in his remark that art possesses moral value "because it represents the most concrete fate and character in an ideal form in itself ultimate."

Further, if we are to understand Blackmur's point of view, it is necessary to pay heed to his idiosyncratic definition of "technique." "Byron's misanthrophy," he writes, "was part of his technique, not of his 'philosophy' so far as we are concerned. Similarly with Keats' view of the Greeks, or Swinburne's sweets of sin. Swift's Houyhnhnms and Yahoos increase their savage contrast if they be considered as *technical* devices for the definition of emotion. In Shakespeare certain of the characters exist as part of the technique, as witness the character of Enobarbus and the astonishing emotion defined with it." What this means is that "content" will be handled, not as something extraneous to "technique," but as receiving its *full* expression only through its artistic realization.

As a result, one never finds "content" discussed by Blackmur in isolation from the technique by which it is given expression; and this means that he never speaks in terms of conventional and easily recognizable "ideas." But anyone reading his reviews can see how Blackmur invariably communicates the underlying sense of life that he discerns operating through the work and seeking expression, more or less successfully, in its language. This is the case as well with some of his most famous early essays, which are usually considered examples of his exclusively linguistic approach to literature. Take, for instance, the pioneer study of Wallace Stevens, which has lost none of its pertinence and value in the intervening fifty years. After quoting some lines from "Sunday Morning," Blackmur remarks that "the full weight of the lines is not felt until the conviction of the poet that the sun is origin and ending for all life is shared by the reader. That is why the god might be naked among them." A bit later, after citing the use of various color-words in Stevens's poems, he comments: "Mr. Stevens has a notion often intimated that the sky is the only permanent background for thought and knowledge; he would see things against the sky as a Christian would see them against the cross. The blue of the sky is the prevailing substance of the sky, and to Mr. Stevens it seems only necessary to look at the sky to share and be shared in its blueness."[2] If these remarks do not contain a discussion of "content," then the English language has lost its meaning; but the poet's views are suggested rather than stated, and seen in terms of a clarification of the full weight of poetic imagery.

This is the balance that Blackmur tried to achieve in his criticism, and which, in combination with his piercing insight, literary flair, and brilliant gift of phrasing, made everything he wrote so unusual and striking. "Some critics make a new work of art; some are psychologists; some mystics; some politicians and reformers; a few philosophers and a few literary critics altogether. It is possible to write about art from all of these attitudes," Blackmur remarks in his essay on Eliot, "but only the last two produce anything properly called criticism; criticism, that is, without a vitiating bias away from the subject in hand." All these types of criticism are still with us, and, just as in Blackmur's day, those who practice the first four kinds are far more prominent and vociferous than the sort of critic Blackmur was himself—"a literary critic altogether."

Few of the others from Blackmur's day, however, now have more than a historical interest, while Blackmur's work retains its freshness, vivacity, and power to stimulate and enlighten; perhaps there is a moral here whose lesson should be pondered. And in reply to a likely outcry from the post-Structuralist young that all this concern with "literature" is terribly out-of-date, one has only to open the November 7, 1985 issue of the *New York Review of Books* to find Helen Vendler reminding her readers that "naturally, all kinds of ethical and civic topics turn up in poetry, as do trees and flowers and ladies' eyes; but they all are material for the transformation into green" (or, as Blackmur said of Stevens, into blue). In other words, they enter "into the dynamic system of relations in the poem, and their allegiance is reordered in that magnetic field, which extends outward to the entire *oeuvre* of the poet, and thence to the culture itself."[3] Or to put it somewhat more familiarly—Blackmur rides again!

Blackmur's exclusive focus on "literature" is derived from a deeply rooted system of convictions that he rarely spoke about abstractly, but which is continually present in his work. One sees him constantly fending off the attempts of both philosophy and theology (in their incarnations as American Humanism and the then-current version of Marxism, as well as Eliot's Anglo-Catholicism) to exercise any hegemony over literature. He believed, as we have already said, that these forms of thought (and *any* theories that professed to define a final and ultimate truth about life) were a grosser type of response to experience than literature. And since he regarded all such statements of truths about life to be nothing but poems of thought, there was no reason why they should arrogate to themselves the right to judge poems that sprang more directly from the specific occasions and conjunctures of human existence. It was this belief, it seems to me, that ultimately inspired Blackmur's love of literature, and lay behind his refusal to accord ultimate seriousness to any sort of doctrinal declaration, while always remaining willing to acknowledge and value the human emotion that such declarations might embody.

The attitude inspiring his criticism is the same with which he approached the larger issues of life itself; and no better statement of this attitude can be found than in the concluding words of his review of Santayana's *Obiter Scripta.* It is appropriate that so illuminating a passage should appear in such a context because so much of his own philosophic stance was molded by Santayana's influence.

Our age, full of conflict and aggressive social needs, is, being without it, frantic for faith as a guide and stabilizer of action; and we suffer everywhere from single insights and formal expressions of single aggressive needs—what we call "ideologies"—set up with absolute authority. Such heresies, like private passions, are perhaps inevitable for immediate action. If Aristotle himself was a heretic—in that he ignored physics, and "cast the universe in the molds of grammar and ethics"—there seems no likelihood any of us can escape, in persuading ourselves to action, a worse if different heresy.

Yet, as we are critics of action, valuers of experience, as we are philosophers in the old, wisdom-loving sense—and not mere advocates—we ought at least to sample the remedy for heresy which Mr. Santayana proposes, and which his philosophy attempts to enact. That is, to confess the notorious truth that "a system of philosophy is a personal work of art which gives a specious unity to some chance vista in the cosmic labyrinth." So confessing, our heresies become graphic and legitimate myths. If opinion is chastened and action is less, there is also less tragic waste in either realm, and a better chance for the "plain deliverance of a long and general experience" upon which the arts of action and philosophy ought both to be founded.

These words are more than just a statement of philosophic preferences; for those who knew Richard Blackmur, they also express an essential quality of the personality they were familiar with. It was this quality which, whatever the disorders and frustrations of his private life, shone through in him and accounts for the influence he exercised and the loyalty he inspired. It also accounts for the reverence he evoked among generations of Princeton students, who may not always have grasped some of his more sybilline pronouncements but who sensed very well the breadth of human understanding they conveyed all the same.

NOTES

1. Russell Fraser, *A Mingled Yarn* (New York and London: Harcourt Brace Jovanovich, 1981), 272.

2. R. P. Blackmur, *Language as Gesture* (New York: Harcourt, Brace and Co., 1952), 240.

3. Helen Vendler, "Looking for Poetry in America," *The New York Review of Books* 32:17 (7 November 1985), 60.

T. S. Eliot

(1928)
(Part II of a two-part essay)

"Eriger en lois ses impressions personnelles, c'est le grand effort d'un homme s'il est sincère."—So runs the epigraph to the first essay in *The Sacred Wood*, which is called, very much to our present purpose, "The Perfect Critic." If we knew what laws were, and could all agree as to their validity and application—or if our ignorance of these matters was total—we might describe the criticism of Mr. Eliot or of any other critic in a paragraph, add a period of commendation, and have done. But our knowledge is only interrupted by our ignorance; and there is no set of theories more contentious, no principles existing in such wayward isolation, as those of literary criticism. With the result that if the critic does not jade us he supplies us with stimulation and excitement, with almost anything, surely, but criticism. We have thus a necessity beyond the criticism of literature; we are ramified entirely in the criticism of critics, and end, each of us, where we began—in kissing, without zest, our favourite cow. We can show no more contempt—or possibly, sympathy—for the judgment of others than by repeating Mr. Beerbohm's Greek: ὅστις τοῖα ἔχει ἐν ἡδονῇ ἔχει ἐν ἡδονῇ τοῖα.*—each looking, meanwhile, at his neighbor's heifer.

No critic but confesses somewhere to his impotence in this respect. Even Mr. Eliot can step aside in mid-career and say, with an air of incorrigible seriousness, "Our valuation of poetry, in short,

*"For people who like that sort of thing, that is the sort of thing they like."

190

depends upon several considerations, upon the permanent and upon the mutable and upon the transitory. When we try to isolate the essentially poetic, we bring our pursuit in the end to something insignificant; our standards vary with every poet whom we consider. All we can hope to do, in the attempt to introduce some order into our preferences, is to clarify our reasons for finding pleasure in the poetry that we like."

Mr. Eliot indicates, I think, the only exit when four pages further in the same essay (that on Dryden) he discloses these observations. "The poet who attempts to achieve a play by the single force of the word provokes comparison, however strictly he confine himself to his capacity, with poets of other gifts. Corneille and Racine do not attain their triumphs by magnificence of this sort; they have concentration also, and, in the midst of their phrases, an undisturbed attention to the human soul as they knew it." This resolution consists in, or at least involves, the discovery of morals, of representative significance, in the values assignable to literature.

Art is ethics in action and has all the intimacy of going off to sleep; it is the action of the soul. . . . It is enough here to indicate the existence of this idea; later, it will furnish the main dish of this essay.

The quality which makes Mr. Eliot almost unique as a critic is the purity of his interest in literature as literature—as art autonomous and complete. Hence the power and penetration of his essays—the fullness of his point of view—the disciplined (and thus limited) fertility of his ideas. Personal taste has its influence but is not paramount. He may or may not suffer from a romantic morality; may adhere to the tory principle in politics, and the catholic regimen in religion—or be both whig and protestant: these connexions are private and cannot much prejudice his business as a critic. This separation of interests is accomplished not by an arbitrary divorce of forms but by an honest recognition of limits. Mr. Eliot's purity of interest has been the chief taint on his reputation as both critic and poet; the accusation of sterility is common, and his very lively, even agonised mind is sometimes described as without interest in human life; whereas the right indictment will be more technical, that his choice of limits has been a little imprudent, that his essential virtue has been pushed a little beyond the extreme verge of the appropriate. Literature the most sophisticated, the most refined is yet very much in the raw: the most intimate because the most controlled contact with the feelings and emotions other than those personal to us: and every critic, in his criticism, must needs save himself from submersion. Some critics make a new work of art; some are psychologists; some mystics; some politicians and reformers; a few philosophers and a few literary critics altogether. It is possible to write about art from all these attitudes, but only the last two produce anything properly called criticism; criticism, that is, without a vitiating bias away from the subject in hand. The bastard kinds of criticism can have only a morphological and statistical relation to literature: as the chemistry of ivory to a game of chess.

Mr. Eliot has chosen to be a critic, and because the profession is unpopular and scantily membered, has used much of his time in emphasizing the limits of his task and in setting up a handful of principles and definitions suitable to the control of his material. Naturally, everything depends on the general problem of order and structure. Most of his principles are ideals of form (and a given form is only a manifest order). Most of his definitions are of distinctions and contrasts of the modifications of form. The approach is invariably technical; I mean the matters touched on are always to some degree generalised characteristics of the work in hand. No overt attack is made on the "contents" of the work directly; the marvel and permanent value of the technical method is that, when prudently and fully applied, it results in a criticism which, if its implications are taken up, provides a real and often immaculate judgment on those "contents."

Possibly a special sense of the word "technique" is here understood. A little has already been said on the subject in the earlier section of this essay. The real technique of an art is in the modes of registering feelings and creating emotions. It is not the possession of any one man but the affect of a more or less general sensibility. We judge a poet by the intensity with which he expresses the emotions cognate to the sensibility of his time—not the intensity of the emotions, which matters only to the individual, but the intensity of the artistic process. Upon which M. Ramon Fernandez comments: "It follows that the parts of a work should not be related to such or such feeling of the author's, but to the totality of the work, and the work itself to the totality of works in its order." M. Fernandez further comments apropos Eliot's general ideas on the method of the poet that he has an "anxiety to transpose the integral experience of man," and a "conception of the hierarchy which brings him to instaurate what others suppress or forget."

Again if the following phrases taken from Eliot's paper on Marvell are considered as an attempt to expand the theory of technique, they will have an explicit force and use denied to them in their capacity as mere general observations. "We can say that wit is not erudition; it is something stifled by erudition, as in much of Milton. It is not cynicism, though it has a kind of toughness which may be confused with cynicism by the tender-minded. It is confused with erudition because it belongs to an educated mind, rich in generations of experience; and it is confused with cynicism because it implies a constant inspection and criticism of experience. It involves, probably, a recognition, implicit in the expression of every experience, of other kinds of experience which are possible."

Byron's misanthropy was part of his technique, not of his "philosophy" so far as we are concerned. Similarly with Keats' view of the Greeks, or Swinburne's sweets of sin. Swift's Houyhnhnms and Yahoos increase their savage contrast if they be considered as *technical* devices for the definition of emotion. In Shakespeare certain of the characters exist as part of the technique, as witness the character of Enobarbus and the astonishing emotion defined with it.

On another plane, such things as the dying speeches in Elizabethan drama, the nature-effects in poets such as Cowley or Gray or Rossetti, the five-o'clock feeling in Mr. Cummings and certain of the Georgians, are conventions of the most technically useful order. What cannot be conventional (and allow the appearance of poetry) are the feelings which warrant the particular instance of the convention: and this is the sure test for false feeling in poetry.

Another sort of technique lies in the state of language at a given time and the relation of language to the feelings which it denotes, and its equivalence or disproportion as the case may be to the sensibility then current. Hence Mr. Eliot observes the great importance of the fact that in the year 1600 French prose was already mature—an exact equivalence had been obtained; and that English prose was not. Montaigne could not have written in English, but he could be translated.

Music and painting are ordinarily free of "ideas" and the correlations of science; and these matters can be more firmly established in those arts by a little inspection. It is easy to see, to take an obvious example, how the paintings of G. F. Watts fail by the substitution of a literary idea for the original feeling which that artist never possessed. It is not so easy to compare Thackeray and Flaubert and to prove that Thackeray's lesser stature is due to an analogous failure. Flaubert possessed what Thackeray to a large extent did not, a fresh feeling for language—a feeling at once for the precision and the indefinable suggestive qualities of words as they take hold of and signify things. It is the difference between conventions which are inspired continuously and with each use by a particular experience, and conventions which, inspired only by themselves, become empty simulacra, effective only by the fictions of intercourse. Art is not much concerned with intercourse but with intelligence; it is prone to no exigence but that of the facts. And as for proof of the artist's allegiance we do not need Sterne's letters to show his agonised fidelity to his feelings, nor Eliot's essays to show his: we need only read the *Sentimental Journey* and *The Waste Land.*

It will be observed that technical criticism of this order has the merit of being altogether literary. Every other consideration is subordinated; and being subordinated takes its appropriate place. It does not cheapen intelligence, it heightens it, to limit its field; its penetration is increased by the diminution of opportunities. The essays on Jonson, Marlowe, Blake, and Dante in *The Sacred Wood* are essays of this order. But a full estimate of Marlowe is implied, is even logically articulated, by the consideration of the tone and tempo of the blank verse of *Tamburlaine* and *The Jew of Malta.* Some of this estimate is worked out by the introduction of a theory of ferocious farce and the isolation of the quality of feeling, the quality of distortion, belonging to it. Some of the estimate is left *in parvo,* for the imagination of the reader familiar with Marlowe to supply; but the imagination is directed.

Mr. Eliot's essays are never without point to present problems in style or feeling; which is always the mark of the good critic, that the past is alive as it bears on and exists in the present. This quality arises only from the critic whose angle is technical and whose material is the facts in the work under consideration as they are relevant to literature as such—and not the same facts or others contorted to the interests of psychology, philosophy, or general good will.

Mr. Eliot has made his choice as a literary critic out of what one supposes were the necessities of his mind, of any well ordered mind. Yet he is practically alone not only today but in the past. A fragment of Arnold, a little Coleridge, a little Dryden, and now and then Dr. Johnson; and of these perhaps only Dryden's interest was serene and whole. From the rest, as they are valuable in this connexion, we have less than fragments. Hence the occasional superstition that Mr. Eliot is essentially sterile, that he is out of touch with human life.

Mr. Francis Fergusson, in an essay published in *The American Caravan* dealing with Eliot's impersonal theory of art, makes the accusation very plain. I extract a few sentences from their context. "The only significant thing in the world for Mr. Eliot is art; no wonder his theme can only be the struggle to create, and that he presents the spectacle of a man doomed by sterility in the effort to make art out of art . . . The kernel of Mr. Eliot's position is his inability to see man the free being which is in all humanly significant figures . . . By preferring a literary tradition to a human background he has limited himself to form . . . Deprived of any sympathetic connection with the world outside poetry, he can only mount to an ever narrower and less significant field of thought."

So far as this is metaphysics, one sits somewhat in another corner; so far as it describes Mr. Eliot, it is, if one thinks of it, impossible in a literal sense and can be a valid description only of intentions and emphases in Eliot's mind.

What is a "literary tradition" but a more definite "human background"? As for "man the free being" there are those who believe that the only freedom consists in the recognition of necessities and the submission to control. And so on. But the general indictment while not found true has yet a taint of cause. It is not, however, a cause which Mr. Fergusson mentions. It is this, that just as Eliot attacks literature proper from a technical angle, so the frame of his theory is made as abstract as possible; and for the same reason—to make it more supple, to make it *inherently* imply more. Interest in and connexion with human life were thereby increased, granted, even, something of the purity of the abstractions themselves.

Take for example the essay to which Mr. Fergusson resorts, "Tradition and the Individual Talent." Eliot is a classicist and this essay is simply his own most abstract statement of the classical dogma.

Recourse to dogma, when the dogma is critically held, is not the sign of an opinionated or sterile mind but of an active intelligence in need of a principle of control; it may be the sign of a realistic mind, a mind interested in its object without wishing to be lost in it, a mind which neither identifies the universe with the self nor the self with the universe, but distinguishes the difference as well as the connexion between the two.

The inveterate tightness and concision of the style of Mr. Eliot's essay make it almost necessary—to give the cogent strength of its argument—to quote it entire. I leave the burden of cogency to the individual reader and detach a few ideas and phrases.

If we approach a poet without prejudice for what is individual to him, "we shall often find that not only the best, but the most individual parts of his work may be those in which the dead poets, his ancestors, assert their immortality most vigorously." This suggests the sort of tradition in which Mr. Eliot is interested. But tradition "cannot be inherited, and if you want it you must obtain it by great labour." It involves the historical sense, which "compels a man to write not merely with his own generation in his bones, but with a feeling that the whole of the literature of Europe . . . has a simultaneous existence and composes a simultaneous order. This historical sense, which is a sense of the timeless as well as of the temporal and of the timeless and of the temporal together, is what makes a writer traditional. And it is at the same time what makes a writer most acutely conscious of his place in time, of his contemporaneity." The necessity that the poet "shall conform, that he shall cohere, is not one-sided. . . . The existing monuments form an ideal order among themselves, which is modified by the introduction of the new (the really new) work of art among them . . . For order to persist after the supervention of novelty, the *whole* existing order must be, if ever so slightly, altered; and so the relations, proportions, values of each work of art toward the whole are readjusted; and this is conformity between the old and the new."

This is a fragmentary formulation of Mr. Eliot's dogma of tradition. The relation of the individual poet to such a tradition is a necessary result and concomitant of the attitude which recognizes the tradition. The main principle is this: that art demands more from the artist than the artist, *as an individual*, exacts from his art. Precisely as the poem is not able to exist aside from its connexion with other poetry, so the poet must continually surrender himself "as he is at the moment to something which is more valuable . . . The poet has, not a 'personality' to express, but a particular medium, which is only a medium and not a personality, in which impressions and experience combine in peculiar and unexpected ways. . . . It is not in his personal emotions, the emotions provoked by particular events in his life, that the poet is in any way remarkable or interesting. His particular emotions may be simple, or crude, or flat. The emotion in his poetry will be a very complex thing, but not with the complexity of the emotions of the people who have very complex or unusual emotions in life. . . . The business of the poet is not to find new emotions, but to use the ordinary ones and, in working them into poetry, to express feelings which are not in actual emotions at all. . . . Poetry is not a turning loose of emotion, but an escape from emotion; it is not the expression of personality, but an escape from personality." We wish to find expressions of "*significant* emotion, emotion which has its life in the poet and not in the history of the poet." And, if I may quote again what so many have quoted before me, "It is not the 'greatness,' the intensity, of the emotions, the components, but the intensity of the artistic process, the pressure, so to speak, under which the fusion takes place that counts. . . . The difference between art and the event is always absolute."

Properly understood, these dogmas of an impersonal and traditional art, far from divorcing poetry and life, ought rather permanently to establish the only connexion possible between them; —to make both in a high sense more germane to the mind—which is not, after all, except diminutively and pejoratively, either poetry or life.

Other dogmas might permit mature poetry; but these guarantee to exclude the immature. By the adoption of such dogmas we lose the right, as we think it, to a great deal of loose "self-expression." We lose our natural talent for being ravished by every stray emotion and each successive dream. But we permit ourselves these great losses only because of the depth and delicacy of our interest in emotions. We discover that our poetry has, because we do not leave it in the anarchy of the flux, a far more direct contact with the emotions, the passions, and the person. If we look for the individual in any field, we shall not find it in the specious alone; what is specious is undefined and incoherent, is inchoate by necessity; to discern the individual requires the presence of an order, a direction, something very like a purpose, to which all the data subscribe, and in relation to which they shall be defined. In art this is an emotional unity for the given work; and is an intellectual unity, a tradition, for the body of works of a given kind. The business of the critic will be to preserve contact between the emotional unity of the individual poem or picture and the sum of the tradition. Whatever dogmas he may erect will be in the interest of these unities. If he is a philosopher also, he will take the matter of "self-expression" for granted and apply himself to the consideration of art as a measure, a judgment, and a definition of experience.

When we wish to define we do not wish (except ideally) an exact tautology, an entire identity; because we should then possess a duplication which in the degree of its success would leave us where we began. We wish a symbol, some sort of general formulation of significance. An apple does not define an apple except to itself. In art, the definition of an apple would be an arrangement of its qualities as they entered our feelings and were adjusted by already existing feelings of a relevant variety: what we would end with would be an emotion about that apple, of a highly qualified order, which yet did not inhere in the apple itself. It would be an emotion appropriate to art and not to produce-dealers. But it is originally and incorrigibly important that the particular apple should have been directly felt, perceived; not as free sensation, which is impossible, nor with an idea of action, which is irrelevant, but for the sake of its being and meaning. The artist's native talent will be for perceiving apples, and everything else, in this way: his equipment will be the technique of transmuting his perceptions, his feelings, his experience, into a kind of objective emotion. Only in this sense does art create the object it contemplates. Otherwise, in every rhetoric of reality, the eye is on the object *in the beginning.* The object may not be recognisable as such when it comes out in a poem or a picture; but it will be something much more important—a definition, in the terms of art (of feeling and emotion) of that object. Your romanticist thinks he can do without objects, or use only strange objects, and persist on novelty alone. Or to the contrary he believes that the objects can take care of themselves, and his poem will be comfortable and prosperous if he stuffs it up with the first objects that come to hand. He is an adept at sensation and intuition but he knows nothing about experience. Your mature artist is distinguished by his adherence to experience, as it is conceived apart from its flux and seen in perspective and in order.

To quote the last sentences of Santayana's essay on Goethe's *Faust:* "To be miscellaneous, to be indefinite, to be unfinished, is essential to the romantic life. May we not say that it is essential to all life, in its immediacy; and that only in reference to what is not life—to objects, ideals and unanimities that cannot be experienced but may only be conceived—can life become rational and truly progressive? Herein we may see the radical and inalienable excellence of romanticism; its sincerity, freedom, richness, and infinity. Herein, too, we may see its limitations, in that it cannot fix or trust any of its ideals, and blindly believes the universe to be as wayward as itself, so that nature and art are always slipping through its fingers. It is obstinately empirical, and will never learn anything from experience."

Mr. Eliot's great deficiency, according to Mr. Fergusson, is that, in his present position, "he can only mount to an ever narrower and less significant field of thought." He is "deprived from any sympathetic connection with the world outside poetry." And so on. If the interpretation I have made of Mr. Eliot's dogmas is correct the essence of Fergusson's indictment is false. Those dogmas rather insist on a connexion, whether sympathetic or not, with the world, a connexion all the more thorough for refusing to be lost in it. Only by insisting that art is not life can art express life.

The difficulty with Mr. Eliot's ideas is that they have been put rather one-sidedly. We have on one side a rigid and exquisitely formulated doctrine of method. We have a thoroughly satisfactory conception of the artist as a responsible technician, and we are told what that technique should control. But the account is always on the technical aspect of the feelings and emotions of which art is made; very little is said directly as to standards for the judgment of these feelings and emotions. "Art for Art's sake" seems just around the corner, an awkward ghost. Awkward because inherently out of place in this regimen. But if the present examination of Mr. Eliot's dogmas bears up I think they will be found to have stated, though indirectly, a very satisfactory scheme of values. A talent for significant experience is a prime prerequisite for any intensity in the process of expression. The earlier part of this essay attempted to show Mr. Eliot as a poet putting his sensibility to work and to establish as a working principle for the construction and judgment of poetry the standard of the intelligence. Such a standard involves the closest possible contact with experience consonant with significance and value.

But what is important here is to show that Mr. Eliot's critical work in some measure sets up and supports such a standard. Mr. Eliot has, in other words—and this is what some of his critics deny— aligned his method of technical approach with the moral world. The effort in this direction has been more articulate since than previous to the publication of *The Sacred Wood,* but it was to be found even in that volume, and especially in the essay on Massinger, which will be employed as my chief example. Only, a recent shift of emphasis makes the effort easier to distinguish.

The general position of a critic, or of any mind aware of its responsibilities, is liable to change when the impetus of thought is altered in mode or intensity; but the change, in an interested mind, will usually occur along a line the chart of which only ignorance prevents us from predicting. The past will not be destroyed nor its sense often confuted; but understood with a different emphasis, reproportioned by the present interest so as to maintain its usefulness. If the change turns out well we call it growth, and say it represents an increase in the depths of personality, the dimensions of sensibility.

In a review of Herbert Read's *Reason and Romanticism* and Ramon Fernandez' *Messages,* published in the *Criterion* for October, 1926, Mr. Eliot articulated such a change of position. The articulation was accomplished with an energy so dense that it has not yet been exhausted; when it began a controversy even now intermittently proceeding, which has included Fernandez, Middleton Murry, Father D'Arcy, Charles Mauron, and T. Sturge Moore as participants. The matter in dispute is the opposition of intelligence and intuition; Mr. Eliot being, as against Mr. Murry, on the side of the intelligence. Mr. Eliot makes these observations of his two authors. "Both, instead of taking for granted the place and function of literature—and therefore taking for granted a whole universe—are occupied with the inquiry into this function, and therefore with the inquiry into the whole moral world, fundamentally, with entities and values." Mr. Read and M. Fernandez reject in consequence of this inquiry the work of Marcel Proust because of *l'absence de l'élément moral chez Proust.* Such a

judgment, says Mr. Eliot, is "a point of demarcation between a generation for whom the dissolution of value had in itself a positive value,
and the generation for which the recognition of value is of utmost
importance, a generation which is beginning to turn its attention to
an athleticism, a *training*, of the soul as severe and ascetic as the
training of the body of a runner." Mr. Eliot then proceeds to distinguish between the generation (our own) "which accepts moral problems and that which accepted only aesthetic or economic or psychological problems," and outlines the divergent attitudes towards moral
problems expressed by Mr. Read, the metaphysician, and M. Fernandez, the ontological psychologist. The reader is referred to the
works of these gentlemen.

We are not here interested in Mr. Eliot's dialectic; but in the
assertion of an ideal, and in the connexion of that ideal to the body
of literary criticism. Hence the sentences quoted require an alignment, which the author does not make, with other essays. They
require even an interpretation.

In an earlier essay on "The Function of Criticism" these sentences occur: "I do not deny that art may be affirmed to serve ends
beyond itself; but art is not required to be aware of these ends, and
indeed performs its function, whatever that may be, according to
various theories of value, much better by indifference to them. Criticism, on the other hand, must always profess an end in view, which,
roughly speaking, appears to be the elucidation of works of art and
the correction of taste."

To perform the complete transition between the ideas embedded in these last sentences with the idea that this generation accepts
moral (as opposed to *merely* aesthetic or psychological) problems
would be to confront the chief dilemma of the artist and his critics
with something very like a solution. This is the dilemma variously
construed as the relation of art to morals, of the individual experience
to the total judgment, of the content of art to that which in "reality"
it does (or does not) represent. It is also the question of the possibility
of a dogma of external authority which the artist is so much concerned, not to obey, but to discover; and to which he everlastingly
feels the necessity to adhere—and feels, as a rule, and at this time,
in vain.

Mr. Eliot is in the process of making such a transition and is perfectly competent to distinguish the implications of his own thought. But he does not always aid his readers, and of late he tends rather to take up his implications outside the field of literature altogether and lingers rather in religion. But it is not difficult to re-import such of his ideas as we need into the realm of our own interest.

Thus, the semblance of an attitude, at least a tentative solution for our dilemma, will be provided if we place beside the sentences quoted above a third set chosen from the essay on "Shakespeare and the Stoicism of Seneca." Mr. Eliot is quarreling with Wyndham Lewis over that gentleman's statement that Chapman and Shakespeare are the only *thinkers* among the Elizabethan dramatists. "It is this general notion of 'thinking' that I would challenge. . . . We say, in a vague way, that Shakespeare, or Dante, or Lucretius, is a poet who thinks, and that Swinburne is a poet who does not think, even that Tennyson is a poet who does not think. But what we really mean is not a difference in quality of thought, but a difference in quality of emotion. The poet who 'thinks' is merely the poet who can express the emotional equivalent of thought. But he is not interested in the thought itself. We talk as if thought was precise and emotion was vague. In reality there is precise emotion and there is vague emotion. To express precise emotion requires as great intellectual power as to express precise thought." To which should be added this from the essay in *The Sacred Wood* on Dante: "Dante's is the most comprehensive, and the most *ordered* presentation of emotions that has ever been made."

The distinctions expressed in these quotations and the ideal of practice implied in the last, form Mr. Eliot's most important contribution to literary criticism. Their literal truth need not concern us— though I think it could be provisionally established. What is the pressing *energy* here is the attitude towards the nature of poetry and its responsibilities.

It is an attitude (and a theory emerging from the attitude) which attacks chiefly the facts about the contents of art in their most concrete terms. For Mr. Eliot this array of facts has evidently generalized itself, and has enabled him to perform judgment as to the *moral value* of Massinger's plays, for example; and to determine, besides, for his private self, precisely what constitutes moral value in a work of art.

If we examine the essay on Massinger with such of the ideas

quoted above as can be kept in mind, we may be able to account for his judgment and discover the principles on which that judgment can be formulated.

Mr. Eliot's essay was evidently prompted by the appearance of a scholarly work on Massinger by Cruickshank. He quotes Mr. Cruickshank to the effect that Massinger was "typical of an age which had much culture, but which, without being exactly corrupt, lacked moral fibre," and announces this quotation as his text: and sets out to find cogent reasons, or facts, to support the judgment.

The facts which Mr. Eliot presents almost all have to do with the use and abuse of sensibility—with the modes of perception, the modes of expressing perception, and the substitution, by Massinger, of something other than his own perception.

"One of the surest tests," says Mr. Eliot, "is the way in which a poet borrows. Immature poets imitate; mature poets steal; bad poets deface what they take, and good poets make it into something better, or at least something different. The good poet welds his thefts into a whole of feeling which is unique, utterly different from that from which it was torn; the bad poet throws it into something which has no cohesion." Mr. Eliot then places next one another passages from Massinger and their "originals" in Shakespeare and Webster. As a result of these comparisons he finds cause for observations such as the following: "Massinger's is a general rhetorical question. Shakespeare's has a particular significance. . . . A condensation of meaning frequent in Shakespeare, but rare in Massinger . . . Massinger gives the general statement, Shakespeare the particular image . . . Massinger's phrase only the ghost of a metaphor." And so on. "We may conclude directly from these quotations," he adds, "that Massinger's feeling for language had outstripped his feelings for things." The language of Middleton, Webster, Tourneur, had a talent "for combining, for fusing into a single phrase two or more diverse impressions" where "the metaphor identifies itself with what suggests it. . . . With the end of Chapman, Middleton, Webster, Tourneur, Donne, we end a period when the intellect was immediately at the tips of the senses. Sensation became word and the word was sensation. . . . It is not that the word becomes less exact. The decay of the senses is not inconsistent with a greater sophistication of language. But every vital development in language is a development of feeling as well." Massinger's verse "is not a development based on, or resulting from, a new way of feeling. On the contrary, it seems to lead us away from feeling altogether." So much for the "technical" defects of Massinger.

The judgment of Massinger's moral fibre is similar, in fact the analogue is startling. "What may be considered corrupt or decadent in the morals of Massinger is not an alteration or diminution in morals; it is simply the disappearance of all the personal and real emotions which this morality supported and into which it introduced a kind of order. As soon as the emotions disappear the morality which ordered it appears hideous . . . Massinger dealt not with emotions so much as with the social abstractions of emotions, more generalized and therefore more quickly and easily interchangeable within the confines of a single action. He was not guided by direct communications through the nerves . . . Marlowe's and Jonson's comedies were a view of life; they were, as great literature is, the transformation of a personality into a personal work of art. Massinger is not simply a smaller personality; his personality hardly exists." . . . He "looked at life through the eyes of his predecessors, and only at manners through his own."

Comparisons are indeed odious. Consider Mr. Galsworthy's latest novels and plays under the light of these observations on Massinger. Compare the *language* of, say, Herman Melville and George Eliot with an eye to discovering in which was "the intellect immediately at the tips of the senses." Apply the whole judgment to the works of W. D. Howells, Edith Wharton, and Henry James: James increases his eminence, and his extraordinary moral value, precisely because his talent for *feeling* was so thoroughly developed; Howells and Mrs. Wharton sink just because their moral codes very often prohibited feeling, made whole classes of feeling impossible. In making these observations you have performed moral judgments on literature on grounds which are altogether literary. A great confusion is gotten rid of: in the arts, moral values have nothing to do with the preoccupations of professional moralists, but concern, first, a technique of language, and, second, a technique of feelings which combine in a sensibility adequate to a view of life.

Whether Mr. Eliot's observations on Massinger can be made to contain the basis of a general theory supplemental to and modifying the theory of tradition and the individual talent, is at least highly interesting. Consider again with these observations the quotations drawn from the essay on Shakespeare and the review of Read and Fernandez.

These notes present themselves very tentatively as being in the direction of such a general formulation. We are looking for a method of criticism whose approach shall be technical, in the terms and in the interests of literature as an art—not as an exercise in science or dialectic. Only so shall we be free of preoccupation and prejudices. Only so shall we reach the moral values where our last interest lies.

We take Mr. Eliot's distinction between thought and feeling in poetry. We do not wish "thought" in poetry unless it is "felt" thought, unless it is not thought at all. The distinction is arbitrary. Thought defines relationships as formulae and makes a shorthand, a blueprint of its subject matter. The definition of an emotion establishes a very different sort of unity; it places or condenses perceptions of quality (including the *quality* of thought) together so as to form an emotion. Both have a unity of structure. The structure of thought is schematic, dialectic; the structure of an emotion is felt; is organic. The definition of an emotion, for the purpose of art, will have nothing to do with its origins in the glands but will concern its origins in associated feelings. The definition will be in the most concrete form possible to the medium—which is language when words are taken as surds of feeling.

Interest does not lie in free sensations, but in perceptions, in feelings which have been adjusted to other feelings and made intelligible. Here the problem of representation enters. What is represented is not the object in physical reality (if any) but the object in the imagination; the object as conceived for its qualities and significance and moulded with other objects. The object is emotion. Emotions in art are never reproductions of experience, but its result. Art judges as well as expresses its field. Representation is ideal, but the ideal must have a "real" reference; must be *of* something.

Art is itself experience. It is a transmutation of ordinary experience into so precise a form that it cannot be redefined qualitatively, and must be understood as the expression of sensibility. An adequate sensibility conforms to ordinary experience as its only original source and inspiration. But it modifies ordinary experience in so far as it is conventional (that is, makes general symbols), traditional, and impersonal. Its particular experience is individual but the general frame is the result of collaboration. Emotions continue under the same names and specious characters, but the feelings which produce their specific instances are unique. Else convention substitutes for emotion instead of being filled by it. In poetry the difficulty is to maintain the proper equivalence between the feeling for words and the feeling for things; when the unity of emotion will take care of itself. To establish such an equivalence implies an adequate sensibility.

Sensibility makes all that is intelligible to it germane to the spirit in the sense that it forces its own terms on experience and gives it a concrete and significant character.

Moral value in art will then depend on the degree in which the sensibility is truly adequate to its subject, and, precisely as much, on the degree in which the sensibility is kept fully on the stretch to dispose the material which experience supplies to it. Poverty of experience would prohibit value and ensure sterility after the first initiation; as in love. Sensibility, if it is to establish values, must not exceed its object. Any object is appropriate to art provided only it is made sufficiently intelligible; —if it is sufficiently allied to the intelligence to give it actual significance. It is at this point that the "intensity of the artistic process" (as that is differentiated from the mere intensity of the emotional object) becomes important. Technical superiority when real, and directed upon the real world, involves moral judgment, because it establishes value upon the object of necessity.

The failure of ordinary systematic moralities could be shown in their inadequacy to judge such works as *King Lear;* where it is the intensity of the fusion of the emotional elements that makes the play intelligible and *valuable.* It follows, almost logically, that any conflict, any triumph, defeat, despair, or glory, any *movement* of man as he is conscious of himself and his environment is a good subject for art; and if that chosen movement is made intelligible in the terms of art it will possess moral value—because it represents the most concrete fate and character in an ideal form in itself ultimate.

The necessity for great art is the necessity of completeness, the necessity of a complete attitude towards life. A philosophy is not necessary—as in Shakespeare; or if present is not used as a philosophy—as in Dante. But a view of life cannot be absent. It will depend, in the artist, on the presence of real emotions and a unity between them. Every system of morality is equally excellent, if it is alive; if all feelings are permitted under it, and all are valid to their objects. Hence the necessity of change; for moralities are the briefest of conventions and live at the ends of the nerves. The intellect must be kept always "at the tips of the senses." In art all values are eternal for their time; but the times are always way ahead of our thoughts.

There is no more a *stare decisis* in the judging of literature than in judgments at law. The learned court is, presumably, in possession of all the facts as they concern the case under consideration; whereby he is enabled to apply, and modify to the necessity of the moment, the full body of precedent. He sees the case before him as isolated, but to be fitted into an existing system. On the other hand, the critic of literature, no matter how learned, is never in possession of all the facts; because those facts are such as to be insusceptible to a frame of logic—they concern the feelings and amount to an emotion, and can be seized only by the imagination. The case exists not only isolated but in a sense complete; and the problem is not to fit the case into a rigid body of precedent, but to mould the already existing *corpus* and the individual case together, so as to form a fluid and coherent whole. It is a problem of order. Law tempers its formal excesses with mercy and sometimes wisdom; literary criticism can only depend upon insight to govern the rigidities of its prejudice and the extravagance of its rules. All this difficulty comes because the critic cannot temporise, must aim at the facts, and is compelled to a thorough-going honesty. With *insight* the mode of first contact as well as last resort, and with only the principles of taste between, how can a literary judgment be anything but the most daring—the judgment of a soul? and the most uncertain—the judgment of a moment? We should say, perhaps, that literature is its own judge; that we have, as critics, only to recognize and to elucidate—to expose and arrange; and so let judgment come of itself. But to judge is a necessity of the spirit as it touches the world, and one of its finest triumphs; and it is better, surely, since judge we must, to educate and bring thoroughly into consciousness the insights with which we judge. This is to make a structure of the intelligence, to acquaint our intuitions with their neighbors and predecessors, and to instruct the absentminded intellect, on every occasion, in the doings of the senses. We shall need great genius—that incalculable constant, intelligence at its utmost.

Hence most great criticism occurs in the mind of the artist at the moment of creation; hence the merit of Mr. Eliot's remark to the effect that Shakespeare had a very extraordinary *critical* mind; and hence the fact that there is almost no *permanent* judgment to be found in any criticism other than that embedded in works of art. For the rest we can make statements about works of art and invent theories to govern their arrangement; and if the critic has a good eye for facts, has the insight to connect them, and the intellect to arrange them, the kind of judgment we desiderate will sometimes be implied, as it were, under his words, if not expressed. Something very like ideal law would then be articulate in the back of the mind; a kind of consensus of, and prophetic instinct for experience; so that if we could not make eternal judgments, still we should know what they would be like if they did appear.

Mr. Eliot is, on his own plane, very much such a critic; both as a practising poet and in his consideration of other poets. He has a very highly developed sense for the facts pertinent to his obligations. A talent which would have made him an admirable scholar, had he not also been given the rarer faculty for finding his facts taking their place in a scheme much more important than the sum of those facts. His most remarkable criticism and his most trivial equally carry that mysterious weight of authority—which is really only the weight of intelligence. For the intelligence is powerful just to the extent that it discerns and submits to the authority of facts, and its work is permanent just to the extent that it is able to conceive an authority beyond the facts and independent of the self. Such a discipline may prevent an easy tranquillity and certainly increases the labour of the mind; but it has this advantage, that the criticism which it produces assigns values other than the personal, and gives the reader, not the experience alone of sharing Mr. Eliot's experience of poetry, but of examining the poetry itself. The rarity of such a mind will be observed in the degree that the reader is familiar with English and American criticism. Mr. Eliot's labours in the restoration of interest in literature as opposed to the interest in opinion and psychology deserve all our gratitude; his work on the theory of literature requires all our collaboration; his criticism of individual poets makes some of us feel that criticism had hardly ever been consistently written before.

It might be advanced as one of the strongest proofs of the

validity of the doctrine that the whole of poetry has a simultaneous existence, that Mr. Eliot's criticism of the poetry of the sixteenth and seventeenth centuries has had a wide and notable influence on the poetry of many men writing today. It is also notable that with the exception of an early pamphlet and a late review on Ezra Pound, a paper on Henry James, and a note on Paul Valéry, Eliot has made nothing but the slightest remarks on contemporary poets. His investigations have been limited to the Elizabethans and their successors with the addition of Dante, Blake and Swinburne. Whenever this interest becomes modern it turns to the works of other critics, which is excellent; or to the ramifications of the Thomist movement and its analogues—and these are not, as M. Fernandez points out, quite to the spiritual baking of our generation. Yet, says Mr. Eliot himself, we criticize the past only in order to understand the present. So far, he has performed only half his job; he has made a present possible, but he has not yet put it in order.

To conclude this essentially random discussion with even a provisionally formal estimate of Eliot as a critic would be both unnecessary and ridiculous. It is easy, and no doubt irrelevant, to say that his chief contribution so far has been the nebula of doctrine around his concrete observations. To define those doctrines closely would be another matter, not as easy; there are the essays themselves. I have accented the purity of his interest in literature; I have perhaps distorted his idea of the definition of emotion and its imputation of value; I have made intelligence the criterion of possibly much more than there is warrant for in his assertion that he "is on the side of intelligence." All this because I feel that at the moment these are the most important parts of his work. Other views are possible. No attention, for example, has been given to the validity of his express judgments of *Hamlet*, of *The Jew of Malta*, etc., or of his implied judgment of Milton or of the nineteenth century. The skill of the technical approach, the insertion of the small wedge, the fertility of the compressed observations, have hardly been indicated. Nor has much been said of the excessive limitations of this particular method of criticism—of which the most considerable is that through its use it is almost impossible to touch what we call the *content* of a work of art except by implication, or indirectly and as if with an ulterior purpose. Mr. Eliot has been very careful to *imply* as much as possible; the method is inexhaustible, and it represents an extreme mode of criticism, but it is not the only mode. The other extreme, from a similar point of view, is in the essays of Ramon Fernandez. Herbert Read occupies an intermediary position—where the attitude is accented more on the dogmatic side. The general point of view, which is what is important, is that of this generation—which accepts moral problems and judges them by the intelligence. A consultation of the various books of these gentlemen should present opportunities to the collaborator, even to the disciple, but none to the sectary.

Notes on the Criticism
of Herbert Read

(1928)

I

Experience provides few footholds in the upper reaches of the mind, and there the beginning of a new thought is always rash, always a leap in the dark. There is something giddy and supremely difficult in the movement; a sense of existence as vertiginous and as arbitrary as God. But there is also the balance—however momentary it is yet eternal —of achieved rightness: the solidity is recorded and the vapor blown away. Something is certain. Something is true.

Such is the occasional result of the application of reason and insight to experience and the problems the arrangement of its knowledge suggest. It is a metaphysic; it is dogma. It is faithful and courageous: acting as much on instinct and the knowledge of the heart as your ready-made savage—only with more order, more discipline.

This escape from confusion to order, from lively but loose and inconsequent appreciation to disciplined criticism is as important, and as difficult, among the arts as in politics or mathematics; and the main difference in the problems to be attacked is in their application. We deal in any case with creatures of the mind. Politics tends to control our sense of experience so as to shape it towards our chosen ends. The arts transfigure experience while it is yet alive: the arts tend to control our sense of the meaning of experience, to name the risen ghost. Control is law. And if there are laws governing our faculties in these moods they will be as valid and of the same intrinsic force as those governing the moods of science; they will be laws relating to our apprehension of the forms of knowledge. Laws may not ever control substance, but they will always regulate our sense of its order. And the absence or the denial of law, which for many reasons must often happen, only controls us without our consent and beyond our intelligence: as we are strangers in death's house and are moved there willy-nilly.

There are today certain critics of literature whose attitudes and whose aims bring them at least enough together to be classed as philosophical critics. These are men bent on discovering true forms for knowledge in the field of literature: but forms having relation to the whole body of experience. The excitement of discovering such forms is the supreme adventure of the mind, and I may best begin a brief discussion of one of these critics, Mr. Herbert Read, by saying that his work provokes an almost ubiquitous sense of just such an excitement.

II

At the outset of his one volume of collected essays, *Reason and Romanticism* (Faber, 1926), he shows himself very definitely as a metaphysical critic; and his main interest is in the assertion and criticism of dogma, in the creation and clarification of concepts.

He is a little rigid in his primary assertion. "The fear that dogmas infringe liberty should not deter us for a moment, for the final object of criticism is the criticism of dogma, and only those dogmas which express values above and beyond liberty need or will survive the assaults of the critical spirit."

This sentence is the text of his whole labour. The belief that there are dogmas "which express values above and beyond liberty" is at once a major note of faith and a commonplace of ordinary experience, and there is an imaginative identity between them. The act of faith has to do with the complete acceptance of the authority of reason where reason is relevant—namely, in that class of idea or dogma whose truth is so nearly coincident with the existence of the mind that without it there is no mind at all. For instance, the dogma that the ideas in the mind refer to their objects and may be true of them, and that these ideas are not themselves the objects; or for another example, the dogma that art is a translation of experience and not experience itself: these are acts of faith and commonplaces without which the mind could not exist.

In connection with this I quote another phrase from the same essay: "For an opinion or judgment is never uttered except as the offspring of a total attitude." He adds that this belief involves not merely the science of writing but also the philosophy of being.

Mr. Read is an example of what I should call if he himself had not somewhat spurned the phrase, the classical spirit. He is on the side of experience subjected in all its constituents to reason, to intelligence. He desiderates direct apprehension of the object by and in relation to the whole mind, but without that false vivification of emotionalised thought or conventionalised feeling. Some of the constituents of this direct apprehension are expressed in a sympathy for the new physics, the new mathematics, the new psychology. I do not mean that he thinks in mathematics or in terms of it, but that there is in his mind a feeling for the beauty and daring of this method of thinking. He would perhaps translate something of the miraculous equipoise of the quantum theory into the consideration of the arts and morals. He would at least bear it in mind; for the more things borne in mind at a given moment the better for the unity of thought. The idea of unity is necessary not only for a mental frame of things but also in order that experience itself should have a sense beyond its spectacle. And it may be that the most intelligent form of unity will be precisely of the kind that mathematical physics suggests: a perfect equilibration and interrelation of concepts consistent with a single logic or a total attitude.

The unity desired is that unity to which all experience can adhere. It is a unity which is a myth of time, space, and thought, which will remain essentially the same while its incidents change with the seasons of the imagination. It is the myth of the universal mind.

A universal mind is a mind which is intelligent to any data in which instructed: a mind of which the very structure is foreign to prejudice in the acquisition of experience, but which is full of courageous prejudice in assigning meaning and order to that experience. This may be an "ideal" mind; and perhaps it may not ever be the property of one body; perhaps it is the property of the sum of articulate minds at a given time, and is in the individual no more than a sense, a feeling, a deeply faithful attitude towards experience. It is the bottomless honesty, liable to many failures but yet the chief vehicle of success, of the wakened mind.

A mind of this order, or a mind trying to reach this order at all consciously, will have the remarkable double advantage of an agile versatility upon the basis of a positive attitude. We will find, in such a mind, a definite feeling for values, for facts, for reason, and for the concepts of all these. The errors of such a mind, *within its system, its order,* will lie in mistaken apprehension. The system itself will not be prone to correction but only to disposition among possible systems; and there is no immitigable cause why some one system might not be finally right. It is a question of limits, of skill, of imagination and insight. In a sense the mind is but the cumulation of all the attitudes of the body to the field of its experience; so that within the limits of this attitude, which are the furthest limits we know, the mind may have true knowledge, and may issue true judgment.

III

The essay on the nature of metaphysical poetry begins with a distinction between "the concrete character of the lyric" and the abstract character of metaphysical poetry. The distinction is made in the two words "perception" and "concept." A second distinction is made between emotional thought and the "mental process in which emotion is the product of thought." The two distinctions are related and upon them are based the important parts of the essay.

The content of metaphysical poetry will not necessarily have the emotional unity of the "lyric" but a unity of conception; it is the poetry of universals and is the arrangement of emotions understood and translated to symbols—or I should say translated to that plane of the mind where the meaning of things is established symbolically. Mr. Read defines poetry on this plane as "the emotional apprehension of thought." The original thinking of the poem, that is, will be metaphysical in the ordinary sense; but that same thinking must be fused in poetry—"there exists at one and the same time abstract thought and feeling for that thought, expressed in poetry." To describe the process the following figure is employed. "We might represent thought and emotion as two separately revolving pulleys: one, emotion, has a revolution a thousand times greater than the other; but by the operation of a lever the two pulleys are connected, and immediately thought is accelerated to the speed or intensity of emotion." Poetry is that lever. With this last it is possible to agree; and in fact one can do little but recommend the reader to so much of the essay as is concerned with the relation between thought and emotion. But to the other distinction there are perhaps certain exceptions; and exceptions exactly in the light of his own observations. He says, truly indeed, that Cavalcanti, Dante, and their company, were able by the metaphysic foundations of their poetry to make abstract concepts as near and real and personal to them as their loves for particular women. But when he implies, as I think—perhaps mistakenly—that he does, that the lyric which is based on a simple perception and has to do only with phenomena, will not have the peculiar merits of metaphysical poetry, I think he is wrong in principle. I mean to attack the opposition of perception and concept as Mr. Read appears to make it. I can see no reason why such poetry need be limited to concepts or submitted to the reign of universals—either mediæval or platonic. Or put in another way, it may be paradoxically, it seems to me that one of the chief aptitudes of metaphysical poetry ought to be the seizure into the mind of simple perceptions *as* concepts. Such concepts could not be named or catalogued; but I think they might be "universal" even so in a reasonably technical sense. Just as most of the experience we communicate trembles and clings around the words we use to express it and is alive without definition—so it may be in the realm of essence, which includes the realm of concepts. I think Mr. Read does very much of this same thing in his best poetry. There is a double quality in his verse, and in Donne, Chapman, and Dante—and in others more modern: I mean there is by turns, and some times at once, evidence that the mind has felt an abstract idea with all the shock and nervous devastation of a cold shower, and again evidence that the same mind has reversed its position and felt the immediate sensation with all the implacable clarity and logical force of the abstract idea. It will be remembered that Eliot distinguishes in his paper on Dante between feeling and emotion: to the end, as I interpreted it, that a feeling was particular and essential and an emotion general and conventional; so that, to be very valuable in poetry, an emotion had to be "felt" anew if it was old and habitual, by the force of the imagination, or else had to be constructed out of feelings. The process of such construction would depend wholly on the arrangement of feelings; would emerge but at no particular point. (I do not wish to accuse Mr. Eliot of saying all this; only that to my mind it seemed implicit in a certain paragraph.) In other words, although new conventions, or new concepts, would be continually established—at no time would any of them take nameable form; except of course such as were but modified shapes of those already named. The bulk of experience known is only hinted at in our articulate expression; and one frequent cause for failure in articulation is surely the attempt to force foreign material into our trivial collection of misfit frames—concepts and conventions already existing and limited. That this attempt is necessary cannot be denied; but I think it ought to be made more flexibly, from the point of view of a more flexible attitude: to make the vague particular precise by aligning it with the existing concept rather than by identifying or merging it. Poetry as much as science ought never to obfuscate any chance for experience; ought rather to maintain itself ready for any experience. Limits will refer only to the *mode* of translation applied to that experience, not to the datum itself. The one type of convention which is immitigable is the principle of structure; which once known is final—as in mathematics the details of structure are irrevocable because always possible. The structure of things and events in the mind is only less so; we have created that much completely: it is an *order*. What I have to quarrel with in Mr. Read's opposition of perception and concept is that he seems so to limit the order (or structure) of metaphysical poetry as to interfere with the substance. What he says might be true of all the metaphysical poetry ever written (which it is not) and yet predicate nothing for the future. I am content to insist that to the mind properly keyed, and with an appropriate intellectual habit, no item of experience *must* fall outside of metaphysical poetry. It is a question of aptitude and attitude. And I think Mr. Read and I have only said the same thing in a different way. He is more rigid and clear; I would also be rigid and I am afraid I have been vague beyond the necessities.

Near the end of his essay Mr. Read proposes an attitude towards and a task for metaphysical poetry. "Science and poetry have but one ideal, which is the satisfaction of the reason. Aesthetic satisfaction is not, as is too often assumed, the satisfaction of the senses (the senses are never satisfied), but *is* the satisfaction of the co-ordinating judgment of the intellect—in symmetry, in rhythm, and in all the properties of universal truth." He concludes the essay with these sentences. "Science has established a large number of 'phenomena'; but these phenomena remain discrete. They lack harmonic unity. Perhaps mathematical philosophy is working in one direction to establish this unity; metaphysical poetry, working in a different direction, can, without presumption, aim to the same end." Before commenting I should like to quote a definition of reason made in another place. "Reason should rather connote the widest evidence of the senses, and of all processes and instincts developed in the long history of man. It is the sum total of awareness ordained and ordered to some specific end or object of attention." This is religious; a dogma of the soul, to which one assents with the soul and by an act of faith. It is one of those dogmas beyond and above liberty of which Mr. Read speaks in his introductory essay; one of those essential dogmas of the mind which assert and define the capacity of the mind for knowledge— whereby ordered knowledge, judged knowledge, alone is meant.

I think the ideal is plain and a good one; to which an unconditioned assent can be given by individuals. Whether interpretations of such an ideal fail to agree in concrete instances is not nearly so important as the authority of the ideal itself. Authorities, for the mind, are in the end always ideal and subject to choice and assent; the choice once made and the assent finally granted, a whole body of ideas, a whole skeleton of experience, issues complete. The question of the ideal named is provisioned by temperament as well as wisdom, and in defending the choice Mr. Read makes we are forced to summon in all those who agree with us in the character of their minds, in the leanings of their blood: we choose their company, and their collaboration, with the ideal. And perhaps we shall satisfy the reason, if but momentarily and on the run: the reason which none possesses wholly, but in which all assume joint title.

But, coming back to poetry; "the senses are never satisfied," says Mr. Read. Now it seems to me that a correction is in order here. So far as the senses in their connexion with the mind can be separated from the mind, we can say that the experience of the senses does not ever include a capacity for satisfaction. It is in their nature to be always alert, moving, ravenously in flux. Yet from a different but entirely respectable point of view, is not poetry of the kind we here consider, and by our own definition, an activity of the mind working through the senses? And is not just what we are aiming at a satisfaction of this total awareness which is reason in the medium of the senses? Is not the process of intuition (which is a considerable part of the *process* of metaphysical poetry) an act of the reason *in*, so to speak, the senses? The separation of the faculties is a fiction; and a good one only when employed to accent a *kind* of feeling: so that I think Mr. Read's distinction appropriate only insofar as it distinguishes the senses, the reason, the whole mind in the act of seizing abstract objects from the mind directed on the concrete or perceptual. So we have returned to the distinction with which I presumed to quarrel first—between perception and the concept as they have to do with metaphysical poetry. I have every reason to recommend the discipline he proposes as relevant and salutary, and I have objected to this point so strongly only because my endorsement is otherwise so hearty.

The poetry which harmonises our abstract concepts, and dramatises our ideals, giving them vivid form in the imagination, so that the remotest reality attacks the senses with the insistence of the specious phantom—is metaphysical poetry. And I can think of nothing more interesting today in our own peculiar intellectual predicament; where the parts of the mind at all instructed are imaginatively at the ends of the earth; for nothing can so satisfy this predicament—which is really a hunger of the soul—as metaphysical poetry.

IV

The kinds of reality assault us, or seduce us, differently; though each is true in its own kind and for itself, the significance, the virtue peculiar to the meaning of each, is unique and in its class; and nowhere is there more confusion than in the classifications we commonly make among them. For instance, in literature, the idea of realism applies, for various critics, to such disparate works as *Main Street* and *King Lear, Bouvard and Pécuchet* and *Faust*—to choose pairs opposing each other for very different reasons. Now it is plain that the reality of art differs from that of science, not in its subject matter, which may be the same, but in the mode of feeling that subject. Ramon Fernandez insists that art qualifies, individualizes, where science schematizes and collects relations. Seizing the individual from the flux, the valid from the specious, is an act of imagination. Any qualification, any evaluation, whether in morals or art, is imaginative.

In the course of his essay on Charlotte and Emily Brontë, Mr. Read finds suddenly that he has referred to the "fundamental experience upon which she (Charlotte Brontë) built her whole conception of imaginative reality." He is worried lest he may have used a word, *imaginative,* to cloak a lack of thought; so he is compelled to define the word for literature specifically. "True imagination is a kind of logic; it is the capacity to deduce from the nature of an experienced reality, the nature of other unexperienced realities. And upon the depth and totality of the original experience will depend the reach and validity of the imaginative process. And if the process is kept to a quasi-logical rigidity, it may be observed that merely one kind of experience, sufficiently realized, will suffice for an almost unlimited progression of imaginative analogies: the one experience will be ballast enough to carry the author through any fictive evocation of feelings and actions."

It is possible to construct an idea of imagination, parallel to the one here expressed, equally logical but after a different fashion; an excellent idea to bear in mind while considering Mr. Read's own idea. On a psychological plane the imagination—that is, the flux of images in the consciousness—may be said to move logically, in that one feeling-state produces another; a process of which the best evidence is in ordinary day-dreaming. The use of the word logical is there possible because the connections between a sequence of images are, so far as we can observe, like those implied in a sequence of numbers; where the sequence 1, 2, 3, . . . implies infinity.

Mr. Read's idea of logic is here of course very far in intention from either mathematical infinity or day-dreaming; but it has an implicit relation with *both*. Not one, or either one, but both.

But the important part of Mr. Read's definition is the sentence: "And upon the depth and totality of the original experience will depend the reach and validity of the imaginative process." A statement insusceptible of proof except by example and common observation. T. S. Eliot says somewhere, speaking on the same matter, that a poet will do as well or better to write on an experience which he has never had than to limit himself to experience with which he is most familiar. It comes back to the notion that art understands its subject matter without losing itself in it, without any loss of its own identity. The difficulty is that the artist must have a disciplined aptitude for imagining the whole of an experience where his actual perception of it has been in the merest suggestion. Such a disciplined aptitude is gained only through a previously complete experience. It is as if we asserted that an hour of a man's life is a microcosm, is all life; which is what the church, in different terms, has always taught. And this suggests the idea that very few have the genius to understand even a moment; it takes a universal mind—spoken of elsewhere in these notes—a mind having been so thoroughly intelligent to one set of data, that it cannot help, logically, being equally intelligent to any other set with which it may become acquainted.

Different orders of mind will express appropriate realities, and if we insist that the artist's reality is imaginative in the way that we have been defining imaginative, it is not to injure the truth of that reality but rather to perfect it.

V

In the essay on psycho-analysis and criticism Mr. Read notes down several instances whereby psychology is useful in the consideration of literature, where psychology helps to construct a basis for reasoning. It is hardly at all a question of applying the tests of psychology to finished works. The significance of a novel as psychological material is only the significance of its origins; its origins are the flux of the artist's mind, conscious and unconscious, the nature of the particular symbolic process he employs, etc. It has very little to do with the significance of the novel as literature, as a translation of reality to a plane more germane to the understanding. Psychology and literature are interested in two different sets of conventions. Literature employs the first to further the second, which is permissible. Psychology has sometimes judged the second in terms of the first, which is unwarrantable and irrelevant *in so far as it is literature* that is being judged.

As critics what we wish to do with psychology is very simple—to relate the body of its relevant doctrines to the appropriate body of critical ideas upon which we construct our concept of the *nature* of literature or art. And this will be, as you choose to look at it, a very large or a very small affair. The physiology of thought must underlie equally the concept of god and the idea of breakfast. But it is also true that the physiology of the two ideas has very little to do with the validity in a moral or intellectual sense of either. Keeping this in mind it will be seen that in most cases the relation between psychology and criticism will not be very precise or very direct; it will be rather by analogue and intuition. Sometimes the *possibility* of a relationship is more fertile than any actual relationship could be in producing thought.

A single exception on which Mr. Read lights is the problem of Classicism and Romanticism. He takes the theory of types as expounded by Jung—namely the classification of all minds into degrees of the Extravert and the Introvert—and suggests that if we substitute the terms of Jung a good part of the problem solves itself. "You will find, for example, that the romantic artist always expresses some function of the extraverted attitude, whilst the classic artist always expresses some function of the introverted attitude. . . . He (the critic) must see the romantic and classic elements in literature as the natural expression of a biological opposition in human nature. It is not sufficient to treat the matter one way or the other as a question of intellectual fallacy; it is a question, for the individual, of natural necessity; and criticism must finally, for its general basis, resort to some criterion above the individual." Earlier in the essay is a passage from M. André Gide, from which I quote a part, as in a measure corrective of Mr. Read's own remarks. "The classic work of art relates the triumph of order and measure over an inner romanticism. And the wilder the riot to be tamed the more beautiful your work will be. If the thing is orderly in its inception, the work will be cold and without interest."

I do not see why, in the light of both quotations taken together, whatever the decision may be upon individuals, the judgment from any possible criterion would not be against the romantic, or extraverted work. If we employ the type of perfect art as criterion, and surely there is none other even relevant, then only the "classic" or introverted artist could produce work to satisfy that criterion. A possibility exists that the artist's mind might be so complex, so properly variegated, as to have a talent for arranging the experiences of an extraverted character in the orderly forms of the "classic" mind; which is just what M. Gide says; and perhaps that is just the "type" of the artist's mind. The difficulty is to establish a balance, says Mr. Read, between the two types. The idea of balance is essentially classical; it is also a *conscious* idea. Insofar as an over-extraverted artist was aware of his condition, there would be a possibility for him *consciously* to remedy it. In which sense Romanticism is a fallacy, which may be judged, and corrected.

Another point brought up by Mr. Read. "The artist is initially by tendency a neurotic, but in becoming an artist he as it were escapes the ultimate fate of his tendency and through art finds his way back to reality . . . Psycho-analysis finds in art a system of symbols, representing a hidden reality, and by analysis it can testify to the purposive genuineness of the symbols; it can also testify to the faithfulness, the richness, and the range of the mind behind the symbol." With the first part of this quotation I agree, as a statement of fact. But the second part seems to me largely untrue, and I think Mr. Read himself partly disagrees with it. If the qualities of genuineness, faithfulness, etc., mentioned, are not demonstrable to "general critical principles" (Mr. Read's own phrase, and in this reference) then they are not true of the work as literature. The supplementary testimony of psychoanalysis *cannot* affect the work as literature, as we began by saying; it can only affect the validity or dubiety of origins. The qualities mentioned belong to another realm than psycho-analysis altogether— the realm of morals, which is imaginative.

VI

This same opposition of extraversion and introversion may be applied to the discussion of wit and humour. The use of new words for old things accents the advantage, the latent power of precision; in that words long used lose their original shape and accrue to themselves much irrelevant colour and connotation: so when the outline is obliterated, the meaning also passes or loses altogether its denoting limits. Thus many thanks should be given to Mr. Read for the following sentences.

"Humour differs from wit in the degree of action implied; or, to express the same idea psychologically, in the degree of introversion or extraversion expressed. The more the comic spirit resorts to activity or accident to gain its point, the more it tends to humour; and, in the contrary direction, the more the comic spirit seeks to achieve its effect in abstract or intellectual play, the better it merits the term wit. This distinction implies a no-man's-land where the categories overlap; and as a matter of fact it is in such a no-man's-land that some of the best English comedies, such as Wycherley's *Country Wife* and *Plain Dealer,* have their peculiar existence."

To make this idea more useful I would set it by the side of an idea outlined in one of George Santayana's *Soliloquies.* Santayana suggests that everything in existence is comic when seen in its flux as it passes in immediacy, tragic in conception or perspective, and lyric in its essence considered simply for itself detached equally from the hurly burly of its surroundings and its position in the fatal order. Here the interest is in the comic; and we might say, I am not sure how truly, that the comic spirit will attempt to set its subject, seen just as it *appears,* against the ideal or general view involved, but without in any way merging or identifying it with that ideal. The criterion and the impulse of comedy is the same as the substance of tragedy; hence the essential gravity of good comedy.

VII

Because in the nature of things it is a problem less subject to the criticism of fact, the problem of the relation between morals and art has been aggravated more than any other. As in most questions based on prejudice and feeling deep in the soul and on facts only skin-deep, the points usually raised are artificial and are settled only by the contest of vehemence and the spring-board of fanaticism. Yet how simple the question really is, what an easy probity and good will are required to envisage it. Art deciphers all sensible things and grants them almost the only meaning they may ever have for man. To perform this task the artist must be possessed of a deep-lying honesty and a true conception of the values of things. It is almost an instinct the buried presence or absence of which makes or unmakes the artist; for only when this instinct is at work can the sensible world take form or assume a unity. Aestheticism withers the vital roots as much as another fanaticism, and the arguments of the bigot of any school ignore the principle that art is meant to understand rather than to display profitable examples to imitate.

"We no longer expect (or even condone)," says Mr. Read, "the direct moral purpose in art, but, if we have any critical principles of adequate reach, we demand a quality in the mind of the artist which works out, in the end, as the moral equivalent of this purpose." And Mr. Read quotes from Henry James: "There is one point at which the moral sense and the artistic sense lie very near together; that is in the light of the very obvious truth that the deepest quality of a work of art will always be the quality of the mind of the producer." And if I may be forgiven for quoting from Charlotte Brontë something where the rhetoric a little overwhelms the statement, the artist has to do with "what throbs fast and full, though hidden, what the blood rushes through, what is the unseen seat of life and the sentient target of death."

Mr. Read finds, and I think justly, that Marcel Proust and James Joyce lack such a sense of values. The lack is illustrated by the absence of orderly intelligence, of discipline, in the major works of these writers. He adds in reference to Joyce "But *Ulysses* does not altogether lack a sense of moral values; it is even dictated by such a sense. But it does lack a sense of intellectual progress. . . . It is an art deficient in aspiration; an art of the used and rejected remnants of life, a mortuary art."

Perhaps, most simply, morals in art are but the demeanour of the soul before life, and imply an intelligent conception, upon whatever prejudice, of life such as to produce a unity either of action or form.

VIII

Mr. Read never leaves aside his principles; rather they enliven and direct his thought. Which I do not mean as something obvious or a custom on general practice. There is a rare interrelation, in these essays, between principle and object such that the process of applying a principle to a particular field sharpens, or clarifies the principle itself. As a result the reader is supplied with a weapon for war and an attitude for contemplation in a very general sense, no less than a solution for a particular problem. That is, Mr. Read sets up and *grounds* an activity in the mind which will persist as useful so long as the problem it was meant to meet remains awake and important. This is the difference, or the chief one, between personal thought which can at best come to wayward insight, and disciplined abstract thought—that the latter, having the qualities just indicated, is susceptible to both correction and collaboration. The question of originality need never appear, but only the question of rightness. That part of Mr. Read's thought as a critic or a philosopher which we discount or explain away as personal will not much diminish the whole thought; only pare it cleaner, only make it the more ready for examination and judgment.

Mr. Read would have us begin with a critical attitude, fixed in character, which involves an attitude towards life itself. The tool of this attitude is the intelligence, the reason (the "widest evidence of the senses")—in short, the universal mind. Besides this, there must be a number of dogmas, articles of faith, applying to every form of experience, but construed in respect to literature. That is a moral and imaginative theory setting up a criterion of life as definite as possible:

this based upon science and with a gesture towards St. Thomas which remains unilluminating.

"That is the final test of criticism: that its methods are perfected in science, but that the motives are spontaneous, impulsive—aspects of courage, constancy, and devotion. The real act is instantaneous, and the course of history is directed not so much by foresight as by insight."

The ideal is so august!

The Enemy

Review of *Time and Western Man,*
by Wyndham Lewis
(1928)

Mr. Lewis is an artist in two kinds—painting and literature—and we might make a fable that the circuit of our times caught him up and tangled his talents in a hard knot from which he has been trying to extricate himself, and incidentally the rest of us, for the last ten years. Hence there is a prophetic earnestness and a prophetic confusion and hurry about much of his critical writings. In this book he displays with great fervour and seriousness, with an almost self-foundering weight of knowledge and thought, the full intricacy and essential nature of the knot.

This book is such a tumult of doctrine, observation, insight and aside, that anything like a fair resolution of its contents would swell a volume and baulk the reader's appetite. Mr. Lewis has ransacked so much disorder and confusion for his subject-matter, it is no wonder the critical order he attempts sometimes strains and gasps, often overtakes and hides itself in an avalanche, and on occasion obfuscates itself entirely in polemic and distortion. But—and this is a very important but—nothing in the book, whether true or untrue, apt or irrelevant, lacks interest. Mr. Lewis has superlatively the talent for starting hares in the reader's mind; and some of them run in otherwise trackless warrens. That is, as a philosopher, he is a new type; the type of the artist; with a sensibility, a method of intelligence largely his own. But he is thus individual not from a love of self (which would have made him common) but from the necessities of the problems which strike him. These, though I think he would deny it, are the problems

227

of ethics as they strike the artist (not as they strike the moralist); and the problems of quality as they are raised by the confusion of science and common sense.

His main thesis has to do with the concepts of time and space, the oppositions which current ideas round these concepts furnish, and particularly with the contemporary misapplications of the concept of time in literature and art. He points out with veracity and much detail that many of our most important attitudes towards experience have been radically altered by what he calls the time-philosophy. And Mr. Lewis' contention is that the resulting shift of emphasis destroys the validity of these attitudes themselves; especially attitudes towards art and common sense.

What the time-philosophy is Mr. Lewis does not wholly define, but, among others, the names of Spengler, Whitehead, Russell, Alexander, and Bergson are intended to be representative. And the element in the various philosophies of these gentlemen to which Mr. Lewis most objects is the faculty for construing ordinary experience as bits, events, relations in the flux of time *only,* at the expense of concreteness and qualification. He does not object, I think, to the application of such a structure, however mathematical, to the realm of physical, in the scientific sense, matter, but only opposes its conversion to other fields. Or perhaps the real objection is still further away: to the results of such a false conversion in the minds of "Popular" thinkers. For instance, the new type of romanticism in literature, which has been inspired by a misinterpretation of the value of Freudian psychology and by the recent physiology of the nerves and glands: where the accent is all on bits of sensation and their almost technical relations between point and isolated point; and where the qualifying whole is supplied by an adulterated convention at best, and sometimes not supplied at all. Mr. James Joyce's *Ulysses* is partly an example; and his so far only serially published work is more of one. And Miss Stein's labours wholly so. *The Travel Diaries of a Philosopher* may be considered in this connection.

What has happened, roughly, is this. There are two main ways of considering experience. One is in its scheme of relations, which is the way of science, and tends at its extreme to a mathematics. The other is in terms of its qualities, which employs the intelligence to register wholes, and ends in art or poetry. One is the abstract or intellectual habit; the other the concrete or intelligent. One defines or indicates structure and assists manipulation; the other defines feelings and is a free activity. In practice the two are peradventure confused. What Mr. Lewis complains of is an ill-arranged junction.

In the last century biology, psychology, and physics provided for the first time a fairly complete structure for the world and for the mind: complete from the standpoint of science, that is. The most casual inspection of that structure makes clear its cognitive limits. But lately those limits have been denied and a philosophy has sprung up which would substitute uncritical analogues of science for the faculty of concrete intelligence in the fields of common sense. Naturally, this substitution has been made largely in theory; and sensibility has been not so much replaced as vitiated. Hence we at once successfully manipulate matter with science and totally misunderstand its individual instances by applying the analogues of science to them—producing a wholly specious world of points and relations, of introspection and solipsism. The paradigm might be risked that the distortion of one faculty into another always issues in romanticism. In philosophy the movement begins with the once discredited Bergson, whose ideas have now been restored to great honour, as Mr. Lewis points out, by relativity in its literary or non-scientific capacity.

This movement had considerable impetus in that the growth of science demolished, in its process, much of the intellectual structure in which our emotional attitudes were poised. So that we are at present either without a scaffolding or jerry-built.

Mr. Lewis calls this philosophy one of time and opposes to it the "spatialising instincts of man." He shows "time" in the hands of Spengler, for example, become a great mystical hocus-pocus, or *élan vital* for the world. And he comments justly that its presence continually causes the substitution of the personal for the impersonal, the private for the public; with the odd consequence that the individual tends to disappear in the solipsism of hot sensation.

Lewis is an individualist of the Aristotelian order. Hence his feeling against the time-philosophy amounts to the drive of terror; as if his own mind suffered under it constant irreparable injury. The time-philosophers become villains, bugaboos and nightmares; and the amazing insight into life of any sort offered by the current concept of space-time, when disciplined to relevance, is ignored.

The problem may be otherwise stated. Inspection of both Mr. Lewis and his antagonists shows that the object of his terror is only a form of dialectic. Dialectic is susceptible of disposition and alignment, not of destruction. The dialectic in question is an excellent technique for physics and mathematics—for the world as a series of relations; and has issued in a way of thinking amounting to an elaborate faculty. This faculty postures as a philosophy, whereas it is only one element of a philosophy; and that is what frightens Mr. Lewis—the success of its posture. It has been used as a philosophy where the kinds of measurement it affords are either insignificant or give a grossly false emphasis—as in history, politics, art, religion, and commonsense.

If, as many think, science has erased many of our intellectual convictions, and if, as I. A. Richards asserts, beliefs are hardly possible, it is only because either our convictions were skin-deep and not worth holding, or else we have allowed science to upset matters with which it can have no legitimate contact. Mr. Lewis is concerned to restore the intelligence and the sensibility by adverse criticism of any such misapplications of science; and all that he objects to as the result of time-philosophy may be laid to the practice of an insufficient dialectic. Which does not diminish the difficulty but makes it easier to handle.

As to Mr. Lewis' judgments on James Joyce, Ezra Pound and company, they are valid only from Mr. Lewis' attitude; are reversible from even a slightly different attitude. But that is no matter; good art sometimes exists in spite of the artist and what he thinks about it; and it doesn't follow that imitation be recommended. What Mr. Lewis is judging is the *kind* of literature, the *kind* of idea, and the *kind* of technique. He is not, in this essay, primarily interested in the works themselves. What the reader has to decide is whether he can accept the total attitude which makes these criticisms possible; when he will make his own minor corrections.

Mr. Lewis is interested in making art possible and in making good society possible from the point of view of the artist. The attitude which he attacks—the romantic-scientific, sensational, and naturalistic habit of soul—is also suffering adverse inspection in other quarters. Notably by the neo-thomist group in France; by Mr. Babbitt in this country, by Ramon Fernandez, and Henri Massis, whose *Defense of the West* has just been translated—by these last gentlemen from a somewhat different angle than that of either the neo-thomists or Mr. Lewis. *Time and Western Man* may be correlated with the work of these authors: with the result that a very definitely "intelligent" attitude emerges, at least tentatively, upon which to erect a thorough-going critical structure.

Technique in Criticism

Review of *Practical Criticism: A Study in Literary Judgment,*
by I. A. Richards
(1930)

In this volume, Mr. Richards gives us a great many facts about thirteen poems in relation to a much larger number of students; he then proceeds to make his facts available for discussion by inventing and defining the terms of discussion. The labour is the greater because he has to use words already horribly vague, full of dead presences, from the flatulence of casual custom. How far this is contrary to ordinary practice should be made plain. He does not begin by telling us what poetry is about or what it is or what it must be or even what it has been. He shows us what kind of response people actually make to poetry, how as a rule that response is inadequate and why, and how that response may be improved. It is a question of getting at a poem in terms of itself rather than in the terms of a reader's self. It is a question of learning to read English. For the rest, after you have read a poem, actually known it, you must then learn how either to discard it as bad or choose it to be a part of yourself as good. You have only to remember, before the act of choice, that the reading of a good poem is a discipline only less arduous than its writing.

Now all of us are interested in what happens to us when we read poetry, and most of us are willing to talk about it. The common tone of such conversation is either frustration or superficiality. We either do not understand one another's terms or we do not understand the substance of discussion. We commonly take our disparity tacitly for granted and go on talking as if we were unanimous—in the hope that by deceiving ourselves we should instruct our interlocutors. We should do better if in the beginning we avowed and limited our disparity. Terms would of necessity become common, unanimity approximate; because we should discover what we were disagreeing about and so find ground for agreement. Such a beginning would be mainly occupied with the collection of data and the discussion of words. We should make each of us small dictionaries of our own, where definition was knowledge achieved; and we should try to use the same words as our friends.

In the particular field of poetry, Mr. Richards is making such a dictionary, and it is in this sense that his notions of criticism are practical. We can all use his words; and many of them we could not use nearly so well until he defined them—for example, there is the four-fold definition of the word "meaning." The purpose of his special dictionary is to aid the understanding of the larger dictionary of words as used in poetry. Mr. Richards puts the matter concisely. "The understanding of speech is an art which we are supposed to acquire chiefly by the light of nature—through the operation of sundry instincts—and to perfect by the dint of practice. . . . That in most cases it remains very imperfect indeed is the principal contention of this book. . . . All we can say is that the masters of life—the greater poets—sometimes seem to show such an understanding and control of language that we cannot imagine a further perfection." He goes on to say that our understanding of language can be improved, and that it must be improved if we are to have any understanding of life itself. Elsewhere, he says: "There is no gap between our everyday emotional life and the material of poetry. The verbal expression of this life, at its finest, is forced to use the technique of poetry; that is the only essential difference. We cannot avoid the material of poetry. If we do not live in consonance with good poetry, we must live in consonance with bad poetry. And, in fact, the idle hours of most lives are filled with reveries that are simply bad poetry."

The documentary parts of Mr. Richards' work, which cannot be rehearsed in brief, amply prove his point. The categories of terms and concepts with which he supplements his data have an extraordinary importance to the critic, the plain reader, and the educator. We are here concerned with the critic and must neglect the other aspects. Even if we object to the definitions Mr. Richards advances, still, such is their importance, that our objections, to be valid, must take the form of collaboration. We may wish to modify, to rearrange. We may discern more in a term or less than Mr. Richards makes explicit. At least we must admit that Mr. Richards has made the terms freshly and definitely available to contemporary material. We can use the terms on any poetry we choose, and we will know in what sense we are using each term. No term is restricted by Mr. Richards to any poem or to any particular class of poem: that is, while his observations spring from particulars, they are invariably so expressed as to command general use.

We may admit the argument, advanced, for example, by Allen Tate that Mr. Richards is no literary critic in the traditional sense. We do not come from him stuffed with judgment and caricature upon Shakespeare and Dante; but we are better prepared to make our own judgments. Mr. Richards' works are a preparatory school to good criticism, just as the dictionary is to good writing. Though Mr. Tate reprehend it, nevertheless a sound laboratory technique is an excellent aid to the understanding of poetry and its criticism. Whether such a technique can be taught is another matter; that may be Mr. Richards' vainglory. But some may be tempted to teach themselves by the ideal he envisages.

Dirty Hands:
A Federal Customs Officer
Looks at Art

(1930)

He was a small man, not running much over five feet five, but I was physically very much aware of him. He gave off a confusion of qualities which would have put a dog in ecstasies but which can only puzzle a man. His hair was of that slick black kind—combed like a boy's on the side and a little ragged at the extremities—that strongly suggests baldness underneath. Forehead and chin were vertically cleft along the line of a rather flat nose and contrasted with a wide, tight, succulently red mouth. A floppy black windsor tie dragged on his chest. He wore no coat. A vest buttoned once at the bottom enclosed a yellow and green plaid shirt and supported a mildly straining belly. The pants were dark, wrinkled at the crotch and baggy at the knees. I did not much notice his hands at the time, but I recall that they were muscular and very hairy, and that the left one incongruously exposed a large signet ring. Altogether, I could not keep my eyes off him.

Nor could I have done so in any wise while I remembered his office. He was, this small man, censor of printed matter for an eastern port. As I had had the most excellent reasons to know during my years in the book business, his authority was practically supreme, his opinions irreversible, and his taste above impeachment. It was this authority which had brought me to his office. He was representing, for me, the benevolent side of bureaucracy, for he had agreed to return a certain book to England instead of confiscating it. I was representing my old employer, who was too busy that morning to come in himself.

I had brought with me, by the censor's instructions, string, paper, corrugated cardboard, and an addressed label: these the government does not furnish those it favors.

Our initial contact was pleasant. He had the book on his desk, all ready for me, and very agreeably got me some sealing wax and glue. While I was doing up the bundle and burning my fingers on the melting wax, I reflected on the innocuous character of the book in question. It was a volume in a series called "The Art of Eastern Love." The series was mostly composed of translation and paraphrase of various Indian texts, and circulated, I knew, freely enough in England. I wondered if perhaps it had not been banned largely on account of its inflammatory title; so I asked him what he found wrong with it. He was eager to talk.

"It's too blasé," he said; and for the rest of the time I was there I had nothing to do but prompt him occasionally. He had the great merit of believing, in his own way, in the dignity of his job and in his own qualifications therefor. "It's too blasé," he repeated. "It's not as bad as some; it's not nearly so bad as a good many. I thought it was dull, myself. But it treats a sacred subject in a blasé way, and nothing like that can get by me. You ought to see the stuff that comes in here. You ought to have the opportunity to see the vile, filthy stuff that comes in here. There's no doubt about it, it's filthy. I read it all and I know. But," he said, drawing himself up a little and raising his voice, "none of it gets by me. The kind of books you fellows get, I mean the ones you don't get, are sweet and virtuous beside the ones I'm thinking of. You can't imagine the vile stuff they try and get in."

I said I thought I could imagine very well, and asked him if he had ever felt that so much contact with filth had not perhaps injured him a little. Had he ever felt the beginning of corruption? He looked at me sharply, then spoke softly. "Listen," he said. "I'm speaking in my official capacity. As a human being it's different. As a human being I get a big kick out of some of those books. I get a thrill. I'm not any different from the next man." He paused, with a reminiscent illumination on his face. "I been here at this job six years now. I used to hit the high spots. I suppose I've read more dirty books than any man in New England, and I could make the biggest collection of erotica in this country if I wanted to. Why, in the last two years I've seized 272 different titles—thousands of volumes—and I've read them all."

Then, with a genuinely persuasive pathos, he went on. "If everybody was like you and me everything would be all right; that is, it would if we could keep things to ourselves. But you know how it is. You'd do it yourself. I do it myself. As a human being I get a pretty big thrill out of this stuff. I read a dirty book and if it's any good I get a kick. But what do I do? Do I keep it to myself? No. I pick out the juicy spots and tell my friends about them. I hand it around and circulate it. It's only natural. You'd do the same. The same with a dirty picture. If it's got its good points, it's real hot, you want to show it off. Of course you do. Everybody does. I do it myself. And that's just where the trouble comes in. You know and I know that sort of thing can't go on. That sort of stuff gets into the hands of young boys and girls—and what happens? They're too innocent and too immature to handle it the way you and I do, so their minds get polluted. Why sometimes . . ." He paused; his eyes beaded and glistened. "Why, sometimes it's the contact of innocence with this filthy stuff that sinks a boy into foul habits for a lifetime. Naturally the government steps in here; and that's my job. I don't let anything get by me if I can help it. I act in my official capacity and there's an end to it. But I just wanted you to know I'm a human being."

"Of course," he went on—and somehow the more he talked the more rasping his voice seemed—"there's books and books. I don't see anything wrong, personally, with a book like Balzac's *Droll Stories*. Those are what you might call snappy stories, that's all. I don't mind them, and mostly I let them get by, especially if they're going to a reputable house. There's some editions that are illustrated, though, and the pictures are too hot. They make a raw book out of it. That makes a difference, and I have to call a halt there. And Straponola, there's nothing wrong with that. *Droll Stories* and Straponola, those are just snappy stories, and that's all—that is, the best of them. I wish they were all like that."

The gesture was not mightily convincing and had a small air of oratory. I said he must have some difficulty in deciding whether or not to confiscate a particular book. He answered with surprising confidence.

"Oh, no. As a matter of fact, I find it easier all the time. It's much easier now than it used to be. You see, well," he said, and then, with that pleased look people wear when proposing conundrums, he asked if I were married, and after my negative he went on: "Well, I am, and that makes a big difference. You'd be surprised. I've been married quite a while now, and the work gets easier all the time. You'll find out what I mean when you get married yourself. I mean you'll be able to decide things like this much better. Why, before I was married, sometimes I'd go easy on the stuff. But marriage makes a big difference. You learn what things are and what they aren't."

I missed the point and inquired if he might not be more explicit. How exactly did his domestic economy affect his judgment of books? How exactly would he decide upon a book in any given instance? It would seem to me, I said, very difficult to devise a system which would apply to more than one book—books being so very different among themselves and serving such contradictory purposes. In any event I admired his courage.

He took me up quickly, gleefully, with that assurance which substitutes in public life for spontaneity as well as for the more intellectual virtues. "It's easy," said he, "and takes no courage. I just figure out whether I can read the book aloud in mixed company. If I can, it gets by; if I can't, it don't, and that's all. You don't need to go any further."

I could not help imagining this small, energetic man in the middle of a great mixed circle of spinster aunts and avuncular beards—all on squeaky wooden benches—reading aloud from, say, the *Ulysses* of James Joyce. So satisfying was this image that I very nearly kept the peace; but I did offer a trifling suggestion on the ground that some books were what was called literature.

"Literature!" he said, and in his mouth it was an expletive of magnificent proportions, an exhaustive, bursting flatulence. "Literature! Don't speak to me about literature. Or classics." I have not heard a word sound more thoroughly obscene than this simple, if controversial, word "classics." He went on: "Yes, I know. People come in here and they call up and they write letters and try and tell me a thing is literature. I know the argument." He put on a finicky tone. " 'You can't suppress this book because it is part of our classic heritage. . . .' That's tripe. Why, I've had people come in here and tell me that Aristophanes' *Lysistrata* is a classic. It's a treatise on pederasty. Pederasty." He spat the word at me.

I said I thought the play was a little more than that. "No," he said shortly, "that's all it is: pederasty. But I've had worse books than that called classics. Books you never even heard of. Do you know what a classic is? No. Well, I'll tell you. And it's straight. A classic is a dirty book somebody is trying to get by me.

"And as for literature. I'm a student of literature myself. I enjoy good literature, and when I was younger I took a course in comparative literature myself. So you see, I know what I'm talking about. And if somebody don't like what I say, why they can take it to the Secretary of the Treasury, and maybe, by the time they get through, they'll learn better."

At this point I reminded him that a few months previously *Candide* had been refused entry, and that later the ban had been raised. Indignant innocence—or was it hurt pride?—raised a husky voice.

"Some swell banker friend of Mellon's put up a howl. That's why that's that. But it don't happen often. There's very few times I get overruled, very few times. I can count them. But about *Candide,* I'll tell you. For years we've been letting that book get by. There were so many different editions, all sizes and kinds, some illustrated and some plain, that we figured the book must be all right. Then one of us happened to read it. It's a filthy book, and I think the ruling ought to have been upheld. And it would have been if that banker fellow hadn't got into it."

As light-heartedly as I could, I mentioned to him the vote taken in the Senate at the instance of the Senator from New Mexico, and suggested that if the action were sustained he might shortly be out of a job, as the censorship of books on the ground of obscenity would then be altogether removed from the tariff.

He was very confident on this matter. "It won't go through. If the Senate doesn't reverse itself, the House will take care of it. The Senate just wasn't thinking what it was about. If that got through everything would be upset and we wouldn't know where we were at. I said so myself to my own Senator. On Armistice Day after his speech, I went up to him and I said, 'Bill, did you know what you were voting for when you voted to amend that book section in the tariff?' He looked at me kind of funny. Then he smiled and said no, he guessed he didn't. 'Well,' I said, 'I'll tell you. You voted to overturn the whole machinery of government. You voted to change the whole procedure of the courts.' I don't think he'll vote the same the next time it comes up."

There was one question I had been very much wanting to ask him, but had been afraid of the answer the oracle might give. He seemed in such a pleasant mood after the story about Senator Bill that I thought I might risk it, at least in a declarative form. So I described my experience over a term of five years in the book business with the demand for such books as his office had refused entry. Bankers, lawyers, scholars, men both socially and professionally reputable, I said, almost exclusively made up the list of customers. Much better men, I said, than either he or I, as I was sure he would admit. Should not their taste and knowledge, their position and reputation, be given some consideration in matters of this kind? Why should we except their judgment on this point alone?

He was ready for me. My verbosity had but let him gather breath. "That's just where you find the dirtiest minds, in the men higher up. I know. When I was younger, I used to hit the high spots. I used to go all round. I've seen all kinds of people. And I never saw a workingman, anyone who worked for a living, who was a pervert. It was all the other kind, men higher up, wealthy men, bankers and lawyers. You work for a living and you'll be all right. I know. I tell you I've seen them all. The wealthy class is full of perverts. Look at me," he cried, shoving his hands in my face. "Did you ever see a pervert with dirty hands? Did you?"

I looked quickly down and made sure mine were gloved; else I had been suspect. Again he said it, with a ferocious intonation. "Did you ever see a pervert with dirty hands?"

Though we could not agree on this point, we parted amicably. As I walked up the street I looked into the windows and wondered. And I also wondered whether it was because Utah is so far from any customs office that Senator Smoot is enabled to speak so righteously of censorship in the tariff.

A Poet's Lent

Review of *Doctor Donne and Gargantua:*
The First Six Cantos, by Sacheverell Sitwell
(1931)

The best that can be said of this poem is that it gives a good text to the critic. Hardly a superficial fault of texture, hardly an essential weakness of conception, but appears egregiously and flourishes at length in these eighty pages of expensive verse. It is a traditional poem even to its subject—according to its author it deals with the conflict of good and evil. A tradition is something handed down, something inherited or won, from the past; and this poem, certainly, goes a long way toward preserving out of the past and presenting in all baldness the principal maladies of English poetry.

In the first place, the poet has not thought about his subject sufficiently for his thoughts to reach the condition of feelings. He merely sets, in the preface which is outside the poem, the conflict of good and evil, the spiritual and the physical—presumably in the arena of the soul rather than in the world around us. Gargantua and Doctor Donne represent the opposing forces, and the narrator of the poem (who is also evidently God) supplies the impetus to action, and will in time hand down the judgment. Since both protagonists are morally nondescript, the judgment, when it appears, will be relative. So far, all effort and experience take symbolic form. Gargantua is bent on getting a mandrake root with child, and Doctor Donne is engaged in catching a falling star. If Gargantua succeeds he will, by *obiter dictum*, have solved the sexual problem; and Doctor Donne will have made man equal to God. Eden's innocence will be restored.

Blake might have made something of this machinery, because

241

the intensity of his observation was great enough to be carried over into the intensity of his vision. In transcending experience he would have taken it with him almost bodily, so that the process of his poem would have been the purification, without diminution, of his experience. Mr. Sitwell does nothing of the sort. He begins with symbols, he begins with transcendence, and takes all that he symbolises, all that he transcends, quite for granted; so that he ends where he began, in verbiage. Verbiage is not words, only their shells, without inner meaning. Instead of purifying experience as it presents the sensible modes of good and evil, Mr. Sitwell adulterates it. Instead of poetic symbols, heavy with the ambiguity of unseen things deeply felt, he gives us fairy tales that fail to convince.

So much for the solemn ambition buried in these cantos. The failure is the failure of any poet who *aims* to transcend himself or his subject. Successful transcendence should be inevitable, the reflection in the most faithful mirror.

Taken as fairy tales, the poem is even poorer than when taken as metaphysics. We are accustomed to allow for dead places, reaches of uninspired verse, in most long poems, but there is no compelling reason to excuse a grown-up poet (I do not say a mature poet) for continuous bad writing. Particularly from second-rate poets we expect, in the absence of great feeling and vision, a constant care for rhythm, metre, image, rhetoric—in short for technique. Else no one but a case-book psychologist would need to read the verse at all. Mr. Sitwell does not take this care, content usually with weak whimsy flattened out in bad verse. A curious reason for this is laid down almost in the form of a principle in the preface:

> Certain brusqueries of style, have been purposely and conscientiously left as they stand, for they act as a foreshortening and curb the sentimentality which it is not easy to avoid in a long poem.

Like most school-boy excuses, this one but points the flaws it is meant to hide. It may be that by conscientiously writing passages of pedestrian verse and by omitting the great labor of composing transitions, Mr. Sitwell has avoided some sentimentality; but what is more important, this same conscientious laziness brings out violently a great deal of sentimentality that *is* in the poem, without any help at all from what is not there.

By sentimentality I mean any one of three things: emotional language in excess of its impetus; a stock response to a stock situation; or a stock response to a unique situation. The second of these need not concern us, when it occurs in verse there is no cure for it. But the first and third are susceptible of treatment, because in both instances something real exists with which the poet can deal without deceiving himself or anybody else.

When the emotion is in excess of its impetus, the cure is a question of either working up the material—the impetus—to fit the emotion, which is done by presenting the feelings that make up the emotion more intensely; or by working down, so to speak, the emotional language until it fits the material without exaggeration or superfluity. The kind of emphasis desired determines the choice. When there is a stock response to a unique situation, the cure would usually consist in doing without the response altogether, in presenting the feelings which are the elements of the situation as barely as possible, thus leaving the emotion to take care of itself. In either case the cure is a matter of writing, of choosing words well, of making good verse from the point of view of the craftsman. It is in performing such tasks that a poet should write "purposely and conscientiously," because only good verse can express honest feeling—whether deep or trivial. If the poet does not always write the best-shaped verse he can, he will never escape writing sentimental verse. All his work will be, indifferently, either over-written—too pretty, too ornamental, and irrelevant; or under-written—too flat, too vague, and insufficient.

Mr. Sitwell in the present poem, and I think largely because of the means he has chosen to escape it, has constantly fallen into all three sorts of sentimentality. It is all either over-written or under-written. The saddest thing is that the essential weakness and cloudiness of the poem destroys the pleasure that ought to be taken in the fine things there are in it, the occasional rich sonorities of line and sweet delicacies of association. For Mr. Sitwell is actually a poet, as may be seen by this as well as by past performances. Perhaps this is his Lenten poem, the poet denying himself.

An Active Poem

Review of *Dream and Action,*
by Leonard Bacon
(1935)

The title of this poem is explained in the couplet from Verlaine which forms one-half of the epigraph:

> Aujourd'hui, l'Action et le Rêve ont brisé
> Le pacte primitive par les siècles usé.

But the poem itself is not so explained. It reads like a romantic scenario with dialogue for a movie of adventure in the Dutch East Indies and Abyssinia. One does not need to imagine at what points the lions and elephants would be brought in. Movies, however, are not composed in octaves with snappy rhymes, nor do they often employ the poetic clichés which serve beyond their time for Mr. Bacon. In short, this is an active poem, full of waste-motion, din, conventional cleverness, verbal fireworks, and dullness around the corner, just like Life. It has a Kiplingese virility, tinged with the Y. M. C. A., which equals Robert W. Service.

The poem has, however, a subject; it is a narrative of the life and death of the legendary Arthur Rimbaud. It begins with the famous quarrel between Verlaine and Rimbaud, which ended with a flesh wound for the boy and prison for the man, and works through sixty pages to Rimbaud's death from cancer in a Marseilles hospital. The end of the quarrel provides the poem with a refrain or burden. The bullet which struck Rimbaud liberated him forever, or almost forever, from the labour of writing.

> The wounded boy lay quiet. Strange reality
> The whole of his attention seemed to claim.
> Looking at his enemy, like one set free,
> He said, "Good bye! Farewell to poetry!"

The last phrase is repeated on suitable occasions throughout the book and acquires, like any formalized gesture, a label of meaning which has all the force and emptiness of a slogan.

But the lines above were not quoted for their dramatic implication alone. They may serve also as a sample of the quality of the verse and the quality of the feeling with which the narrative is invested. The substance is definitely indicated, the language despite the inversion is simple and conventional, the imagery is hypothetical (that is, you can so easily suppose the scene that it does not require presentation), and the poetry, whatever poetry is, is left for the reader to supply. This is a fair description of the day-to-day verse of such men as H. I. Phillips and James J. Montague, without the saving grace of timeliness. Now it is possible that verse of this description is necessary to get over the rough places and the uninteresting places (the places better unwritten) in a narrative poem, but for it to appear as the qualification of the initial and fundamental crisis of a poem is only a boast of weakness. Nor is there any competence, much less strength, in the following rendering of a crisis:

> He reached the summit and the end of his rope,
> And dropped as Dante and dead bodies drop,
> Though he had more effective cause, by Jimini,
> Than harking the sorrows of the house of Rimini.

Although Mr. Bacon perhaps did not intend that they should, these lines do not bring to mind the fifth Canto of the Inferno: "e caddi, como corpo morto cade," which perfects an experience; they sound like post-haste rhymes to make the end of a stanza.

The jacket of this book provides the information that Mr. Bacon is a writer of rollicking narrative and satire, and challenges a comparison with *Don Juan* and *John Brown's Body*. It is true that some of the bad places in *Don Juan* are as bad as the average stanza of this poem, but aside from that, comparisons remain invidious.

The reader may wonder, if such strictures are necessary upon it, why the book should be reviewed at all; and the answer is that on the back of the jacket Mr. Bacon receives high praise from the anonymous *Times, Sun,* and *Saturday Review,* and from Babette Deutsch and the Benét family. Mr. Bacon is one of those who carry the burden of our academic poetry, which is a serious and honorable burden to bear; and it has been the sole intention of this review to point out that he carries it a little too jauntily, with the ease and itch of a journalist.

Statements and Idyls

Review of *Horizons of Death,*
by Norman Macleod
(1935)

The art of poetry is amply distinguished from the manufacture of verse by the animating presence in the poetry of a fresh idiom; language so twisted and posed in a form that it not only expresses the matter in hand but adds to the stock of available reality. Since we no longer live at the stage where the creation of idiom is the natural consequence of the use of language, many of our best practitioners have necessarily to manufacture a good deal of mere competent verse in order to produce a few good poems.

Of the forty-two short poems Mr. Macleod has here collected, six seem to me of fresh idiom and good within their magnitude, nine good but for various reasons incomplete, and the rest of indifferent manufacture. Internal evidence, and the presumption that this is only a selection of the author's poetry, suggest that so far as materials, insight, and perception are concerned, many of the poems I cannot admire are as good as those I accept: as good, that is, from the author's point of view. We may assume that they express, for him, his feelings about his impressions. He is a personal poet. Had he worked the other way round and conceived himself the laboring medium through which his subject matter might be delivered to objective form and independent idiom, then not only would his average have been higher but his magnitude greater. And there would, further, be no doubt, as there must be now, as to exactly which the good poems are. As it is, we must depend on the accident of unanimity and a common language, which, like the accident of instinct, is only dependable in familiar circumstances or as a last resort.

If we consider the poems with these remarks for text, we see why even the best of them are not surpassing, why their magnitude is not greater than it is. Take four poems, not at random or merely for excellence, but four which add up the variety of Mr. Macleod's work: "The Reaping of Oats," "Newsreel," "The Lost Ones Back from New Mexico," and "Sons of Soil."

"The Reaping of Oats" is one of a number of idyls each of which notes under a given head a series of sense-feeling images which build up to the presentation of a landscape mood. The feelings are profoundly entertained and are full of implication, and the phrasing is often lovely with affection and discrimination; and there is no question but that the poet is genuinely at home with a genuine subject which he has felt as poetry. Yet the poem is not complete, it does not compose but remains essentially the series of notes it was in the beginning, held together only as an order or succession on the printed page. This is because the poet has been content to record the elements which gave him the emotion, personally, in "real" life or elsewhere, and has failed to carry over its uniting force in the relation between the elements on the printed page.

Since we cannot fail to grant that both the subject and the apprehension of it are poetical, the trouble must lie in the presentation, and I think it may be put technically as the difference between an arrangement and a composition. Composition is central and uniting, arrangement is centrifugal and serial. In poetry, that which is composed is independent and complete, and the effect of composition is obtained by the application of external form and by a kind of precise ambiguity in the use of words so as to display the relations between what they stand for, and thus release the emotion of the parts being together; which is the labor of obtaining a fresh idiom in a form.

"The Lost Ones Back from New Mexico" may be compared on this point with any of the idyllic poems. It is composed, rather than merely arranged; the emotion is secured integrally to the poem, and I think that this is done by the slight fresh twist of the language, guaranteed or placed by an adequate rhythm. The use of the word "portables" in the seventh line alone mars a choice of words which unites the human emotion with the landscape that aroused it.

"Newsreel," the most ambitious poem in the book, attempts to present our miserably convulsed social scene exactly as if it were a landscape—that is, in poetical terms alone; and its merit is obvious if put against such poems as "Out of Esthetic Air" or "Himalayas of Aspiration" which, no less sincerely, are felt rhetorically or politically. The power of the poem probably comes from uniting in composite images the social theme and the sense of environing and participating landscape.

"Sons of Soil" is short enough to quote:

> Color of soil is on their faces now,
> Their knowledge and the cool long curve of the loam
> In productive bearing:
> They are at home
> With the tradition of life germinating
> As men progress from the past into the future,
> And their muscles can ripple
> As their brains for social thought.

This is poetry of bare statement and has everything a poem needs except the focussing power of an imposed form. Here the form is accidental, which is the best way of describing the order of free verse to which the poem belongs, and thus the poem is left exposed to the accident of the poet's thought. We are led to this tentative observation: none of Mr. Macleod's verse adheres to a pattern; even the purest of his free verse reaches for iambic support; but the poems which have most power are those which more nearly approach a blank-verse norm. The harder the form, the freer the content. For the rest, it should be clear that the problems of poetry cannot be discussed except in the work of those who, like Mr. Macleod, actually write it.

Samples of Santayana

Review of *Obiter Scripta:*
Lectures, Essays and Reviews, by George Santayana
(1936)

The kind of unity in this book is like that of the bibliography which
the editors supply at its back, a unity that seems at first sight specious,
accidental, almost random, the unity of a procession or a lifetime.
Because the bibliography lists all of Mr. Santayana's writings, we are
able, in running over the titles, to think of all of them together,
presided over by his name, as one thing, despite their variety and
apparent mutual irrelevance. Similarly, the items in this book—which
run from literary criticism on Shakespeare and Proust, through dialec-
tical essays on "Symbolic Knowledge" and "Some Meanings of the
Word 'Is,' " to lectures on "The Unknowable" and "Ultimate Religion"—provide sample enactments of the unity felt in the bibliography. The variety is all Mr. Santayana's, and the apparent mutual
irrelevance only represents the equivocal forms in which a single
mind, if at all vital and awake, must express its interests. If this unity
is specious it is yet a fact and all we have, and it may reflect a
substantial unity as the interrelations of the different items deepen to
make a single emphasis.

That emphasis is moral—on the goods of rational life; and poetic—an imaginative deliverance of experience in discourse; and it is
for the most part drawn, as its maker hoped, "without violence from
the inevitable lights and insights of common sense." Samples are not
enough to furnish the whole orthodox philosophy in view. Samples are
only representative indices of a whole philosophy; but samples are also
tastes or savors and may have an effective esthetic unity of their own;

and there is no less of representative virtue if the reader takes what he is capable of taking of these essays for its own sake in passing. "Some Meanings of the Word 'Is,'" for example, doubtless represents the extraordinarily sustained dialectic of *Skepticism and Animal Faith*, but it may be taken here for an example of nothing but itself: a compacted philosophic metaphor at lyric intensity, significant, like poetry, for the idiomatic *quality* of the meaning it catches. "Significant speech is a lasso thrown into the air, lucky if it catches some living thing by a leg or by a horn."

Another essay, "Philosophic Heresy," which attacks by characterizing "the whole plague of little dogmatisms, that would harp universal harmonies on a single string," had best be taken neither as a sample nor esthetically, but for its immediate practical point. Our age, full of conflict and aggressive social needs, is, being without it, frantic for faith as a guide and stabilizer of action; and we suffer everywhere from single insights and formal expressions of single aggressive needs—what we call "ideologies"—set up with absolute authority. Such heresies, like private passions, are perhaps inevitable for immediate action. If Aristotle himself was a heretic—in that he ignored physics and "cast the universe in the molds of grammar and ethics"—there seems no likelihood any of us can escape, in persuading ourselves to action, a worse if different heresy.

Yet, as we are critics of action, valuers of experience, as we are philosophers in the old, wisdom-loving sense—and not mere advocates—we ought at least to sample the remedy for heresy which Mr. Santayana proposes, and which his philosophy attempts to enact. That is, to confess the notorious truth that a "system of philosophy is a personal work of art which gives a specious unity to some chance vista in the cosmic labyrinth." So confessing, our heresies become graphic and legitimate myths. If opinion is chastened and action is less, there is also less tragic waste in either realm, and a better chance for the "plain deliverance of a long and general experience" upon which the arts of action and philosophy ought both to be founded.

A Critic and His Absolute

Review of *Primitivism and Decadence: A Study of American Experimental Poetry,* by Yvor Winters (1937)

"This study originally began," says Mr. Winters in his prefatory Note, "as a sympathetic elucidation of the methods of the Experimental poets; it developed of necessity into an elucidation of their shortcomings." The last two sentences of the book perhaps represent the standard against which the shortcomings are measured.

> It will be seen that what I desire of a poem is a clear understanding of motive, and a just evaluation of feeling; the justice of the evaluation persisting even into the sound of the least important syllable. Such a poem is a perfect and complete act of the spirit; it calls upon the full life of the spirit; it is difficult of attainment, but I am aware of no good reason for being contented with less.

With such a standard, and with poetry being what it is—so ambitious and so careless—judgment is likely to be harsh and sympathy to disappear. It does not matter much if Mr. Winters cannot tell us—and he cannot—what justice is or what it has to do with syllables, what spirit is or whether it is capable of acting; we know what he means by translating his words into our feeling, our general sense, of what constitutes great poetry; which is exactly what Mr. Winters does himself. The best of his book, indeed all that is good in it, is when he gets back from his expressed standard into his feeling for the working of poetry among its syllables and images without any conscious regard for his standard at all. The worst of his book is when he climbs onto his standard and hauls tight while he whips: the standard, like all standards, rears, paws, and stands still, lathered for nothing.

But it was a good standard and came out of a good feeling, hard to keep up without help, for the great and beautiful qualities, which are yet not the only qualities of good poetry, of control and order and lucidity; and all that Mr. Winters has to say about these qualities or their absence in the poetry of Hart Crane, Marianne Moore, Eliot, Pound, Stevens, and Williams is acute and practically helpful in the evaluation of their poetry. He exhibits and elucidates facts, sometimes facts about poems, sometimes facts about the appreciation of poems, and sometimes a confusion of the two kinds of facts. No man is always right in his appreciation of poetry; mistakes are forgiven because they are better than indifference and because, too, the truth is—which Mr. Winters amply demonstrates—that few poems are ever right or clear about their own facts. When Mr. Winters is actually talking about the work of the American experimental poets, how it failed and even how it could have been improved, when he talks about meter and convention or any technical matter, he makes only normal mistakes and produces a great many pertinent and stimulating facts. Pertinent because they illustrate the poetry in question; stimulating, because the experienced reader will see at once that many of them have at least a partial application to all the poetry he reads. This is all that is required and all that ought to be asked of a critic: that he supply facts in terms of his feeling.

Unfortunately, neither critic nor reader is often willing or able to keep such close discipline. Other considerations are desperate to cry out. The mind makes invasion; the sensibility is violated by ideas, and all is lost, at just the wrong times, for the sake of principles, formulas and terminologies. Mastery is replaced by authority; recognition by categorical imperatives. Perhaps the mind will not otherwise do its work of getting the sensibility on paper; it will be literal and logical or nothing; it fears like its own death seeming to lean on the wayward, the provisional, the profoundly disorderly and disconcerting sensibility which actually gives it life; it insists, at any expense of its own values, on the application of absolute principles. That is one reason why criticism must be rewritten every generation—absolutes are momentary; and that is partly why the poetry criticized is sometimes permanent—in the degree that it leans only for appearance upon the absolutes of its time, as Shakespeare leaned on kings. Mr. Winters' system of absolutes, his coinage of intellectual counters, is not much better than other systems or much worse; but it is more bare-faced, candid and uncompromising than most; hence more irritating and I should say easier, in a good cause, to ignore. When he translates his absolutes back into the genuine but ultimately provisional elements of his feeling for poetry, he will be always at the level of his best in this book; he will then never allow a formulary about syllabic form to elevate the relatively dead poetry of Bridges and Sturge Moore above the living poetry of Eliot and Yeats, and I doubt if the poetry of Elizabeth Daryush will appear for judgment at all. Meanwhile, Mr. Winters' willing readers will make a rough translation—a mere paraphrase—for him. Other readers, to their own and Mr. Winters' loss—will prefer the pleasure of irritated rejection.

In Our Ends Are Our Beginnings

Review of *The World's Body*, by John Crowe Ransom,
and *The Triple Thinkers*, by Edmund Wilson
(1938)

One difference between Edmund Wilson and John Crowe Ransom is easy to put. Mr. Wilson is never satisfied unless he can show what lies behind and about a body of literature—its milieu both in society and in the person of the author—and he sometimes proceeds from that point to translate his sense of milieu into a general idea or set of ideas. Mr. Ransom is discontented unless he can get into the literature itself—the technical medium in which it operates—and he sometimes proceeds from that vantage point to reduce, or heighten, his observations to the level of specific literary principles. Mr. Wilson has to do with ends, Mr. Ransom with beginnings. One consequence of their difference in aims is this. When you have finished one of Mr. Wilson's better essays (I do not say his better criticisms) you may feel that he has done so well by his method that you do not need to read the works with which the essay dealt: the essay has replaced with its own values all the values that it mentioned. When you have finished one of Mr. Ransom's essays on particular poems or poets, you will feel, I think, that you have been put into contact with the work itself: the essay replaces nothing; rather, the essay itself disappears, and you find yourself impelled to get the book off the shelf and test out your new knowledge.

A good deal that is illuminating may be drawn out about the critical work of both men by pushing this pair of distinctions a little further into the field of particulars and considering two papers from their latest collections of essays. In *The Triple Thinkers*, Mr. Wilson has a small piece about A. E. Housman. Housman was a poet who had a profound and damaging influence upon the sensibility of his readers, an influence which T. S. Eliot, if he saw it that way, would call diabolic, and which the mere unbeliever must call the influence of the deeply dishonest, wilfully incomplete, and ultimately facile imagination. Such a poet needs showing up in his poetry. Mr. Wilson shows him up as a scholar and as a man: it is a malevolent miniature that he provides of a man with a closed mind, given to trivial and disproportionate fanaticisms, to irrelevant invective, and to paranoiac pride. The miniature seems a likeness, self-complete, obscured only by a general comparison with Gray, Pater, Carroll, Fitzgerald, and T. E. Lawrence: "the monastic order of English University ascetics." Finally, in a sentence which applies to the total Housman, including the poetry, Mr. Wilson remarks that he "never arrived at the age when the young man decides at last to try to make something out of this world which he never has made." Now the curiosity about Mr. Wilson's patient and lucid exposition is double. Although Housman was primarily important, to Mr. Wilson as to the rest of us, as a poet, references to the poetry are made only to illustrate the man, and are made, as it were, in prose. Quotations, that is, are printed with the lines run together but with the initial capitals retained: a bastard and irritating presentation that witnesses, at best, a momentary insensibility on Mr. Wilson's part. Secondly, unless I am misled, Mr. Wilson's implication is that the poetry remains *somehow* valuable despite his argument. Mr. Wilson's essay circles imaginatively about his subject, rearranging its elements to suit his image, but never coming in contact with it. There is no criticism in his essay; there is nothing there to criticize; in the end, it is just Mr. Wilson's dramatic imagination at work.

Let us take now, in Mr. Ransom's *The World's Body,* his essay on Edna St. Vincent Millay, who like Housman is a poet of wide and damaging appeal and whose fundamental immaturity, if worn with a difference, is equally a radical imaginative quality. She too needs showing up as a poet. Mr. Ransom sets about his task with a more than Southern gallantry, with that honest gallantry which consists in keeping the eye, for all the polite gesture of voice and word, precisely upon the object: Miss Millay's published verse. Mr. Ransom's eye focuses successively upon that which, in Miss Millay's work, is overwriting at the expense of strength; writing "which is 'literary' and impeaches the genuineness of the passion"; writing where tropes of such loose development are employed as by their musical nonsense to constitute a "parody of honest poetry"; writing which is a mere act of fancy. There follows, with examples, a discussion of the intellectual reach, the imaginative scope, of Miss Millay's poetry compared with four other modern poets: in which Miss Millay is limited by the evidence to that poetry which deals with "the love of natural effects, the worship of Nature, the delight of the senses, the concerns of the elemental passions, and . . . the guilt of civilized man." Finally, when she is rid of her affectations and writes within her limitations, "she has a vein of poetry which is spontaneous, straightforward in diction, and excitingly womanlike; a distinguished objective record of a natural woman's mind." Mr. Ransom provides three examples of success: the poem called "Elegy," which fixes upon the voice of a dead girl as the symbol of the irreplaceable; "The Poet and His Book," in which Miss Millay envisages her poetic immortality as "a series of precise and living actions"; and lastly "The Return," which "pictures Earth in a sort of Mother Hubbard character, receiving back the sons she sent out to failure, but too busy to give them much attention, and unaware of any reason why they should have failed." "The Return" is for Mr. Ransom nearly perfect. He ends his essay by defining the imperfection, which lies in the two words, comfort and comprehend, in the last line: "Comfort that does not comprehend"—a line which apparently means that in the grave the sons of Earth "obtain her loving comfort but not her understanding." I quote Mr. Ransom's conclusion. "The [poetic] act seems inadequate, and I look for the trouble, saying confidently: Metre. I think that is the trouble. Let us remember Procrustes, who will symbolize for us the mechanical determinism of metrical necessity, a tyrant against whom only pure-hearted and well-equipped champions will consistently prevail. Procrustes, let us say with absurd simplicity, finds the good word *comforter* too long for the bed. So he lops off her feet."

It seems superfluous, but a pleasure, to point out that here we have Miss Millay's poetry, as it were, by the feet—those it walks on as well as those lopped off. We know as far as Mr. Ransom is able to tell us what Miss Millay's values are and we can test his account in the verses themselves. Mr. Wilson's account of Housman, on the contrary, cannot be tested except by its inherent plausibility and persuasiveness, much as we test a poem or a novel. Mr. Ransom is a literary critic, Mr. Wilson an imaginative essayist.

This is not to say that Mr. Wilson's essay is without critical value; by the accident of his taste and intuition and the discipline of his mind—by the accident of approximate unanimity between him and his readers—it has great implicit value. It is value at one remove; with Mr. Wilson we do not know where we are except on his own say-so—behind the poet. With Mr. Ransom we know where we are all along—in the poetry—and are not required to take anything on trust. Mr. Wilson may go further when he is right; there is always room for fresh creation. Mr. Ransom has the advantage that by sticking to his texts he will never go so far wrong as to write Mr. Wilson's "Is Verse a Dying Technique?" Mr. Wilson thought he answered yes; actually, all he says is that the novel is a growing technique.

One more difference is this. Mr. Ransom ends his book by a declaration of the necessity for the technical study of literature in order to know what its integrity, that we seize, actually is. Mr. Wilson ends his with an essay on "Marxism and Literature," which if it has other than a controversial content is concerned with the problem of the literary man, the artist, in uniting his social and aesthetic vision. His final hope is that as "the human imagination has already come to conceive the possibility of re-creating human society," so it may re-create arts that "will deal with the materials of actual life in ways which we cannot now even foresee." Mr. Ransom probably does not share that hope because he probably does not see Mr. Wilson's problem; but if such a transcendence occurred, Mr. Wilson would have to test it out by Mr. Ransom's method before crowning it with his own. It is the World's Body of which in the end the Triple Thinker thinks—as Mr. Wilson may remind himself that Flaubert, who made the phrase, inexhaustibly knew.

A Good Reminder

Review of *In Defense of Reason,*
by Yvor Winters
(1947)

Mr. Winters has here put together the three volumes in which his critical work of the last twelve or fourteen years first appeared in small editions and from small presses. To these he has added an essay on Hart Crane's "The Bridge." Together they make a unit which Mr. Winters is right in calling a Defense of Reason. That is what his work comes to; and that, therefore, is what this review chiefly intends to estimate. For surely there can be no dodging the fact that Mr. Winters's criticism is powerful, informed, consistent, and for the most part just—with only those errors caused by too great a rigidity in the structure of his intellect. Nor, as surely, can there be any doubt as to the enlightening accuracy with which he examines the technical matters, especially the metrical matters, of verse; he belongs with Bridges and Patmore; his prosody is loving and exemplary. That is, it is clear that Mr. Winters's criticism is of great use in getting at American literature both for what it says or tries to say and for how it says or fails to say it. Why is it, then, that his criticism is not in general use? What is so formidable about this body of literary thought that it is more ignored than fought, more fought than understood? Is it that we duck blows that we cannot return?

The answer lies in the habits of our age. Mr. Winters's criticism is judicial; we have a horror of judgment because we do not know what it might destroy in our potential selves. Mr. Winters's judgments are in accordance with explicit standards; we have a necessary preference, in the world we live in, for all the implicit standards we do not

259

measure up to. Mr. Winters's standards have a tendency to be applied through law; we tend to feel that law either satisfies brute force or results from statistical averages and feel no kin whatever to the *ius gentium:* to the predictive and judicial force of our common nature. Mr. Winters believes in the supremacy of reason, under God, in human affairs; he is therefore orthodox and a monster in the wilderness; for we are not, with regard to Mr. Winters's point of view, either reasoning or reasonable men. He is as alien to us as only the thing we ignore in our hearts can be: the thing we forget we still are.

In the effort to forget a persistent thing we tend to make it something else. We try to make Mr. Winters seem what we mean by an absolutist rather than what he means by it; we make a substance out of a method, and confuse his judgments with the means—his convictions of possibility—by which he makes them. Mr. Winters is an absolutist, but only in the sense that he conceives—like the noble and necessary lies of Plato—that absolute truths must exist, which the mind may approach in apprehension and to which its judgments must attempt to conform; but he does not believe that he is in possession of the absolute, or even that he is possessed by it. He is a moralist and a rationalist; he believes in the serious value and understandableness of the major human enterprises, among which he puts the arts in first rank, and his absolute truths are the ideal forms of his allegiance. He is *therefore* against hedonism, relativism, determinism, romanticism, and that peculiarly modern theory of the division of the mind's labor on experience known as aestheticism. He will isolate nothing, except for analysis, but insists on seizing as much of the whole of experience as may be in an act of rational imagination or imaginative reason. It is not only that he by instinct repels confusion and insists on discerning order in chaos, but that he has a mastering conviction that there *is* relation and there *is* order in chaos and that these are definite and particular and are accessible by moral and rational means. It is thus that for him poetry becomes a precise instrument for the high contemplation—for the deed of high understanding—of a moral, rational, and purposeful life. I am not certain that he would accept it, but I would like to add that under his view poetry might be held not only to make rational statements about life and to judge it morally but also to create, or elicit, motives in life otherwise lacking or felt only as hidden promptings.

What happens when this point of view is applied to American literature? It is shown as coming everywhere short of its own intentions, as everywhere lost, or agonized, in its possibilities; short, because it could not make rational statements of what it was about; lost, because it refused the illumination and propulsive force of deliberated form. For rational statement it substituted pseudo-statement, that is, statements not correlated to the experience represented; and for deliberated form it substituted what Mr. Winters calls "the fallacy of expressive form," that is, the conception that a thing must have its own form even to that extremity where chaos is expressed by chaos. Thus the triumphs of American literature come about by tours de force, by the identification of the artist with his experience, or by accident.

Of course I exaggerate. And Mr. Winters exaggerates, but not as much as people think; he exaggerates a real thing. Surely it is enlightening to keep his point of view in mind when one thinks how much of modern American literature is either case-history or deals with the artist or outsider as the hero against the world; or again when considering the prevalence of specialized art, specialized criticism, and their consequence in the cult of initiates acting the old part of audience. Mr. Winters only exaggerates to make his point; and if we cannot accept his point as theory we cannot escape it as fact. His work is a very good reminder of the rational and formal qualities present, and highly valued, in almost every living literature except our own. Reading him, the old habits prompt and stir us.

Conrad Aiken: The Poet

(1953)

I

The newly collected poems of Conrad Aiken run to so many hundreds of pages no one reader can easily digest them in bulk. Nor can any one reader discriminate the best from the better and the better from the worst with any certainty even of personal choice. Digestion and discrimination must be the gradual labor of many readers. Yet it is good to have all the poems in one place; they make a bulk, and bulk is a great part of Aiken's quality in much the same way it is part of the quality of Swinburne, or Hugo, or Carducci, or Sir Walter Scott, each in his different way. It is not for isolated poems that these poets are remembered; anthologies cannot do them justice or even give a proper sample taste.

Some poets concentrate, compound, and construct their experience into words. Others, like Aiken, expand and extend and exhaust their experience. Their unity is in all their work, not in single efforts, where indeed the unity may evaporate. This is because such poets, and especially Aiken, work in a continuous relation to the chaos of their sensibilities (Houston Peterson called his book about Aiken *The Melody of Chaos*), and each separate poem issues with a kind of random spontaneity: the least possible ordering of experience, what is possible within the devices of prosody (such as the couplet, the quatrain, the sonnet, and so on), never the maximum possible ordering under what Coleridge called the coadunative powers of the mind. There is no generalizing power of the mind. Yet all the poems together make a generalization.

Perhaps we cannot say what that generalization is, though we may feel it. Who can say what the sphinx generalizes? —or a change in weather? —or Jacob wrestling in the stream? Yet we know very well, and try our best to say. So with Aiken. We must see if the shifts and alternations in his weather do not make a climate which generalizes them. Luckily Aiken himself supports this effort. If he did not exactly choose he somehow found it necessary to write in the mode of imagination here described.

In his autobiographical narrative called *Ushant,* Aiken gives an account of a prophecy of his life made to him by an eccentric "Unitarian-minister-and-clairvoyant" one morning in a Bloomsbury boardinghouse. "You have the vision, the primary requisite," said this gentleman. "You will be a true seer: it is, I fear, in the communication that you will fail. You will always tend to rush at things somewhat prematurely: you will see beyond your years, ahead of your maturity, so that continually, and unfortunately, the immaturity of your expression, a certain glibness and triteness, will tend to spoil your excellent ideas, leaving them to be adopted and better expressed—better organized because better understood—by others." And he went on: "You will touch [life] at almost every possible point; and, if you do die spiritually bankrupt, you will have known at least nearly everything—known and seen it, even if ultimately without the requisite power, or love, or understanding, or belief, to harmonize it into a whole, or set it into a frame. . . . You will want to taste your own spiritual death."

To this, and the rest of it, Aiken gives full assent: "How devastatingly true!" We all have such an uncle in the cupboard who says such words in our ears, if we listen: it is under such words that we see the divisive nature of our politics, our culture, and our individual selves. Aiken has written one version of the poetry of that condition, just as Eliot has written another version, which Aiken will not quite understand, thinking Eliot's version a betrayal of his. "That [Eliot's] achievement was unique and astounding, and attended, too, by rainbows of creative splendor, there could be no doubt. Indeed, it was in the nature of a miracle, a transformation. But was it not to have been, also, a surrender, and perhaps the saddest known to D. in his life?"

D. is Aiken objectively observed, spun out, developed, and coiled round himself as endlessly as possible within a single volume. And that volume, *Ushant,* is the best key we have to what Aiken the man was up to in creating Aiken the poet. From *Ushant,* then, it is easy to clarify and support what Aiken (or D.) undertook to believe the prophetic Unitarian from California meant in the Bloomsbury room. At one place Aiken says D. had a bias for form as form, "that inventions of form must keep a basis in order and tradition" and must be related to "a conscious and articulated *Weltanschauung,* a consistent view." On the next page he remarks that through Freud "at last the road was being opened for the only religion that was any longer tenable or viable, a poetic comprehension of man's position in the universe, and of his potentialities as a poetic shaper of his own destiny, through self-knowledge and love." The combination (of the philosopher and the maker) was expressed in the two volumes of "Preludes" which he here calls "serial essays towards attitude and definition."

But there are three other sets of remarks which would seem to clarify the way in which Aiken actually approached his double problem. One is where he refers to himself as the priest of consciousness in flight. A second is where he develops the notion that the true theory of art is, necessarily, the unwritten book; that the true aesthetic is of the impossible, where the act of initiation is taken as an end in itself. The third set of remarks summarizes his underlying philosophy: "One must live, first, by seeing and being: after that could come the translation of it into something else. This constant state of his 'falling in love,' falling in love with all of life, this radiant narcissism, with its passionate need to emphasize and identify, this all-embracingness, must find something to do with itself. Subject and object must be brought together, and brought together in an apocalypse, an ecstasy, a marriage of heaven and hell."

It might be supposed that everyone has a little more life—a little more seeing and being—than he can quite manage; but there is no need to quarrel with Aiken about that. What is interesting here is the "radiant narcissism" which is the radical quality of all his acts of apprehension, or at any rate of those which get into his poems and other fictions. His autobiography is itself an act of radiant narcissism. What he writes shines with the expanded light—perhaps the idiopathic light, perhaps the light of self-healing or idio-therapy—of what he has seen and been; and the hope is that, with the aid of the traditions and forms of poetry, it may be light for others also.

Aiken's life is a self-feast mediated in poetry, and what is so attractive about his poetry is that each of us, by letting his own egoism shine a little, may eat of himself there. This is also why he can speak of his world as a "rimless sensorium," and why the Unitarian prophet was right in telling the young Aiken that he would never set life into a frame.

But not everybody needs to make frames. If Aldous Huxley complained in 1920 that Aiken would have to find "some new intellectual formula into which to concentrate the shapelessness of his vague emotions," he was not reminding us of Aiken's obligation so much as he suggested our own. So long as this Narcissus remains radiant it will be our business to find a frame or frames for the radiance. The Narcissus is only ourselves at a desirable remove: the heightened remove of poetry in which even our worst selves seem authentic and our best impossible of attainment. For it is poetry like this which teaches us we could never put up with our best selves.

II

What then does Aiken do—what is his radiance—between the double blows of life and theory? What is his music and how does he sing it? He sings on two trains of thought or themes and he sings like the legendary bard, improvising old tunes as if they were his own by discovery or inheritance, or both. To expand into clarity and towards judgment these phrases will be the remaining task of this essay. What are the themes and how does a bard sing?

One theme is the long, engorged pilgrimage of the self coming on the self: the self creating the self as near objectively as possible. The second theme has to do with the dramatization—in theatrical terms, so far as a poem can be a theater—of the selves of others. *The Jig of Forslin* edges towards a fusion of both themes: where the self comes on a dramatization of the self, full-fledged and self-creative. *Turns and Movies,* his next set of poems, represents the second theme; *Senlin,* a few years later, represents the first. If there is a single theme in Aiken's work, it is the struggle of the mind which has become permanently aware of itself to rediscover and unite itself with the world in which it is lodged.

When the soul feels so greatly its own flux—the flow of itself recalling and eddying upon itself—it becomes very difficult to reassess the world other people inhabit. Very difficult and of absolute necessity. Bertrand Russell wrote his most lucid book, *Introduction to Mathematical Philosophy*, while in prison during the First World War as a conscientious objector to that world. In Aiken it is the self that is such a prison; one bursts out of it without ever leaving it, and one bursts into it without ever having been there. It is the contest of our private lives with the public world.

No theme could be closer to us; almost every mode of the modern mind tends to make the private life more intolerable and the public life more impossible. Only what used to be called ejaculations of the spirit suggests the blending of the tolerable with the possible. Arnold thought poetry could do the job of religion, but Arnold had never heard of psychology (psychiatry, psychoanalysis, and psychosomatics). Aiken could not help having Arnold for an uncle, but he had "psychology" for his other self, the hopeful and destructive brother of his heart.

In his poems there is always the cry: "Am I my brother's keeper?" But it is both brothers who cry, not one: sometimes they cry alternately, sometimes together. The attractive force of Aiken's poetry lies in these joined cries; they make the radiance of this Narcissus. Narcissus is only the personal, anecdotal, and legendary form for that frame of mind known as solipsism: the extreme subjective idealism that believes the mind creates the world when it opens its eyes. It lies in the background of the whole movement in modern art called expressionism (the feeling that what one says commands its own meaning) and is related to make the artist or outsider, as such, the characteristic hero of modern literature. Solipsism is the creative egoism, not of the primitive savage who believes in nothing he does not see, but of the civilized and excruciated consciousness which claims credence for everything it does see and, by the warrant of sincerity of feeling, everything it might see.

This is why we speak of so many levels of consciousness, all of them our own, and for that reason all valid; but none of them dependable for others, none of them showing to others any surety of motive. Dostoevsky invented buffoons who acted out of caprice. Gide invented criminals who made *actes gratuits*. Kafka invented his hero

"K" who could not act at all. Aiken's work belongs in this train of thought with his deliberate egoism, his structure by series and repetitions and involutions, his preludes to attitude and definition, the emphasis on the incomplete or aborted act of the incomplete or aborted ego. Your solipsist, because for him no action can ever be completed, is bound to be violent in expression.

Readers of Aiken's novels will easily understand the application of these remarks to all his work. Indeed the long poems will come immediately to seem themselves novels in a philosophico-lyric mode. The chaos under the skin of perception has become both part of the body, its bloodstream, and united with the mind, its creative matrix. For the mass of Aiken's work is deliberately pre-morphous; it is prevented from reaching more than minimal form. He attempts to preserve the chaos he sees and he attempts to woo the chaos he does not see. The limit of form which attracts him is the form just adequate to keep the record with grace: the anecdote, the analysis, and the prelude. He has the sense that as things are finally their own meaning (as he is himself), so they will take up immediately their own form.

This is true with the poems, and increasingly so from the earlier to the later volumes. *Turns and Movies* is a series of dramatic monologues, hard, rapid, and anecdotal, rather like *Satires of Circumstance* or *Time's Laughingstocks* by Thomas Hardy, full of murder, open and hidden hatred, wrong marriages, and burning infidelities: an effort to grasp the outside world by its violent sore thumbs. *Punch: The Immortal Liar,* the next volume, is Aiken's first conscious effort to fuse the two halves of his theme, and we get the violence of the inner man seizing that of the outside world. *Senlin,* four years later, is philosophical, meditative, musical, and repetitive, the free onward solipsism of the pilgrim trying to come on himself.

Something like one of these sets of attitudes can be applied to any of the original volumes. *Festus* is part of the pilgrimage. The *Charnel Rose* is a kind of theatrical or *Turns and Movies* version of romantic love. In *John Deth* we have the solipsist working towards annihilation, as in *Osiris Jones* we have him working towards epiphany. *Priapus and the Pool* is free erotic expressionism moving into philosophy. *The Kid* is an historical version of *Turns and Movies,* a frontier version of the civilized soul, remarking tradition as he goes. *And in the Human Heart* is an effort to make the inner violence transform the outer through love. *The Preludes of Attitude and Definition* exhibit in infinite variety both the tension and the distension of the two violences, what keeps the soul together in every moment but the last in its lifelong series of fallings apart.

The attitude breeds the vital chaos of definition. (Which may remind some readers of Aristotle's remark that there is an optimum definition for any point at issue, and one should never define more than necessary. In Aiken's preludes the right amount is reached when the vitality of the chaos is reached.) Lastly, though not last in chronology, the *Brownstone Eclogues* most clearly fuse, join, and crystallize the two violences of Aiken's theme, and it is from them therefore that an example will be drawn.

But a single quotation will not be enough. There is a poem in Aiken's mid-career which is a kind of anterior example of the meaning of the passage chosen from the *Eclogues*. The earlier poem has a lucky title for the purpose. It is classical, Freudian, and as anomalous as the next breath of air you breathe: altogether universal is "Electra" in the human heart. In "Electra" is the trespass of one human upon another; in the eclogue is the trespass into the human of the nonhuman out of which everything human is made. Here is the passage from "Electra":

> 'Under this water-lily knee' (she said)
> 'Blood intricately flows, corpuscle creeps,
> The white like sliced cucumber, and the red
> Like poker-chip! Along dark mains they flow
> As wafts the sponging heart. The water-lily,
> Subtle in seeming, bland to lover's hand
> Upthrust exploring, is in essence gross,
> Multiple and corrupt. Thus, in the moonlight'
> (She hooked a curtain and disclosed the moon)
> 'How cold and lucent! And this naked breast,
> Whereon a blue vein writes Diana's secret,
> How simple! How seductive of the palm
> That flatters with the finest tact of flesh!
> Not silver is this flank, nor ivory,
> Gold it is not, not copper, but distilled

Of lust in moonlight, and my own hand strays
To touch it in this moonlight, whence it came.'

This is what humans make when their egoisms trespass impossibly into each other's flesh. Here is the passage from *Brownstone Eclogues;* it is the complete poem called "Dear Uncle Stranger":

All my shortcomings, in this year of grace,
preach, and at midnight, from my mirrored face,
the arrogant, strict dishonesty, that lies
behind the animal forehead and the eyes;

the bloodstream coiling with its own intent,
never from passion or from pleasure bent;
the mouth and nostrils eager for their food,
indifferent to god, or to man's good.

Oh, how the horror rises from that look,
which is an open, and a dreadful, book!
much evil, and so little kindness, done.
Selfish the loves, yes all, the selfless none;

illness and pain, ignored; the poor, forgotten:
the letters to the dying man, not written—
the many past, or passing, great or small,
from whom I took, nor ever gave at all!

Dear Uncle stranger, Cousin known too late,
sweet wife unkissed, come, we will celebrate
in this thronged mirror the uncelebrated dead,
good men and women gone too soon to bed.

This is what trespasses into the human, "the bloodstream coiling with its own intent," and it is precisely what makes possible the creation of "the finest tact of flesh." The one trespasses upon as it illuminates the other. The two together make the original warrant for the ego to make whatever artifacts it can. Narcissus is not all of us but at some sore point we are all of us Narcissus. Aiken's theme is his radiance.

III

So for his theme. How does the bard sing? In the easiest language and the easiest external forms of any modern poet of stature. He sings by nature and training out of the general body of poetry in English. He writes from the cumulus of cliché in the language, always, for him, freshly felt, as if the existing language were the only reality outside himself there were. There is hardly ever in his work the stinging twist of new idiom, and the sometimes high polish of his phrasing comes only from the pressure and friction of his mind upon his metres.

It is hard to make clear, in a period where so many poets play upon their words and so many readers think the play is all there is, that this superficially "easy" procedure with language has long since and will again produce poetry—even the difficult poetry of the soul wrestling with itself. But it is so with Aiken, and it is worth while to end these remarks by trying to make this matter clear. Aiken depends on the force of his own mind and the force of metrical form to refresh his language. The cumulus upon which he really works is the cumulus of repetition, modulation by arrangement, pattern, and overtone. He writes as if the words were spoken to let the mind under the words sing. He writes as if it were the song of the mind that puts meaning into the words.

Thus, as in popular songs, the words themselves do not matter much, yet matter everything *and* nothing to those who sing them and those who hear them. This is to say Aiken takes for granted that his words are real; he never *makes* his words real except by the agency of the music of their sequence. No method works all the time, and when Aiken's method fails, you get the sense of deliquescence in his language, as if any words would do because none would work. To understand the successes of the method takes time and familiarity. In his language, but not in his conceptions, he depends more on convention than most poets do in our time, almost as much as Dryden or Pope. The point is, if you look into his conventions you will find them right, just, genuine, and alive. What more do you want? You have brought with you what was required.

Finally—for poetry is an affair of skill at words—Aiken demands of you, at a serious level, the same skill that newspaper poets demand at no level at all. Your newspaper poet merely wants to say something to go with what he feels. Aiken is looking hard to find, and make real, the emotion that drives, and inhabits him. Aiken, as Croce might say, has a vast amount of the same talent the newspaper poet has so little of. The amount of talent makes all the difference. The existence of poets like Aiken make poetry possible.

Obscuris Vera Involvens

Review of *W. B. Yeats and Tradition,*
by F. A. C. Wilson
(1958)

Literature, which has always wanted to be itself and also, when ambitious, something bigger than itself, has nevertheless always depended on and ended in something other than itself. In the commonplace of this fact, whenever it is not our wisdom to ignore it, lie all our troubles about conceiving an adequate poetics, and from it spring many of our difficulties in the detail of our criticism. The great example in western Christian culture and its posterity is the problem of how to read the Bible; whether literally or allegorically, and by what letter or by what allegory. Basil Willey, in his *Seventeenth Century Background,* suggests that this problem alone has prevented an effective Poetics; and indeed something of the sort seems true with regard to post-Reformation literature, and especially to literature since the French Symbolist movement with its novel private systems of allegory and its novel and arbitrary doctrines of statement: with, so to speak, its new and different scriptures with no public rule of interpretation and with no acceptable terms in which argument can take place. That the problem may be in essence artificial is immaterial; it is how a good part of our minds seems to work whenever we wish to describe their operation or to assess their value. What ought to have been mere machinery has become the dominant feature of understanding.

These remarks are in direct response to Mr. F. A. C. Wilson's examination of the hidden, or as he calls it the "ulterior," symbolism, mysticism, and system in certain plays and poems of W. B. Yeats. These he relates to what he calls Tradition, but I think he would have been nearer right if he had called it the genesis and mechanism of certain works of Yeats, or better still the iconography of certain works. We should not then have run the risk of thinking we were talking about a philosophy or a discipline of mind and might have been nearer the grounds of intimacy with the poetry: the intimacy which is the condition of generalizing judgment and particular enjoyment. Iconography points to the thought or feeling or belief which was merely indicated, or generalized, in the poem so that the reader knows what to bring with him. Genesis is similar, but at a more personal level, and uncovers for us, partially and problematically, what seems to have been happening in the poet's mind when he was putting the poem in order. Sometimes the two come together. I have two statuettes of identical iconography on my desk: embracing figures with elephant heads. One would do for an attractive door-knob and gain patina from the hands that used it. The other unites in the instant of meditation the tenderness, sexuality, and predatoriness of life religiously observed. This icon has the patina of its genesis and needs never be touched except by the mind.

Yeats's iconographic poems and plays are of both kinds, and I should suppose that the ultimate use of Mr. Wilson's study would be in the discrimination of the kinds; but this is not an end which he himself pursues. He is rather concerned to prove that there is an ulterior or anterior body of knowledge of which the reader must be in provisional possession, and which he must regard with sympathy if not with full credit, before he can resolve that poetry. He is particularly bent on upsetting the validity of the kind of treatment which Yeats's poetry has received under the New Criticism as exemplified by Cleanth Brooks and John Crowe Ransom on the ground that this criticism does not possess the hidden knowledge. The bulk of the book is devoted to the description and application of such of the hidden knowledge as is pertinent to a few of the plays and a handful of the poems. From Mr. Wilson's point of view he is right, and since it is the point of view of many people (all those who crave cognition before they will admit apprehension) we should be grateful to him for his exegesis. His treatment of "Byzantium" will infect the teaching of half the colleges in America. My fear is, the infection will replace the poetry in minds the least wary, and for a very simple reason. In most poets of difficulty the field of allusion is to particulars within the general body of knowledge, and when we have found it out we know what within our individual experience, our individual thought, it illuminates. In Yeats the field of allusion is partly general and we are at home with it, but it is also in a significant part to an idiosyncratic and esoteric congeries of knowledges, for the most part dubious in themselves and legendary or even forged in their provenance and with eroded contours in their intellectual physiognomy. The risk is that the sense of the poem will be lost in favor of the knowledges which may or may not have got into the poem at all. Thus the poems will grow into something which is not literature at all, but a ritual game. It is Yeats who is responsible for this, not Mr. Wilson, but only in a part of his work; Mr. Wilson is responsible only for the effect, which he may not have meant, that all of Yeats's work is like this. My own view is that poetry may and often does in Yeats's systematic poems contain many matters other than itself, and that Yeats's special knowledges are present as more or less alien matter which we may need but which we can neither admire nor justify in themselves. Sometimes they injure the poem, sometimes they make the poem possible, and sometimes they do not matter to the poem, but are only parallel, and doubtfully, to something in Yeats's mind: like the full content of the mind at any given moment.

A few of these risks may be illustrated from Mr. Wilson's book, where the reader will decide according to his temperament how useful he will find the book and whether for the poetry or for a game which our age seems bent on attaching to the poetry. One way or the other the book will remain useful.

The first example is from material not very far removed from our regular field of allusion. Mr. Wilson is discussing *The Herne's Egg* and says that Yeats borrowed principally from Balzac's *Seraphita* for his play. To him Yeats's character Attracta *is* Seraphita, and this he argues in a series of parallels. Seraphita says: "My marriage was decided upon at my birth; I am betrothed." Attracta says: "I am betrothed to the great herne." And Mr. Wilson goes on: "A character in Balzac's novel describes Seraphita, shortly before her transfiguration: 'To me she is a sorceress who bears in her right hand an invisible instrument to stir the world with, and in her left the thunderbolt that dissolves everything at her command.' Yeats preserves the exact image: 'Nor shall it end until / She lies there full of his might / His thunderbolts in her hand.' " There is more of this but too long to quote, and I do not see that the parallelism grows any closer; in fact, I do not see that there is any parallelism at all, not even so much as there is between Perdita, Marina, and Miranda, for these at least lay all in Shakespeare's mind. Of Balzac we know that he was interested in the romantic possibilities of Alchemy and Masonry and certain forms of mysticism but was hardly a model for initiation into any of these; and for the rest, we know that Yeats read Balzac; facts of which we may legitimately remind ourselves in a study of Yeats's mind.

For my next example I choose the Sibylline Books, with which all those of us with any classical leanings should be approximately familiar as a legend if not as a source. According to Mr. Wilson, Yeats used the Sibylline books in *The King of the Great Clock Tower* and *A Full Moon in March,* or at any rate they were present in his mind. I cannot be sure from his text just what Mr. Wilson's reference is. Yeats's "intention," says Mr. Wilson, "is to suggest that the fact of Caesar's death at the Ides of March, and of his subsequent apotheosis, led a large part of the Roman empire to regard him as the Messiah prophesied in the Sibylline books. For, he says, the Roman empire had not yet lost the conviction that the expected saviour would rise from the dead at a full moon in March." Then he quotes from *A Vision:* "Did the Julian house inherit from that apotheosis and those prayers the Cumean song? Caesar was killed on the fifteenth of March, the month of victims and saviours. Two years before he had instituted our solar Julian calendar, and in a few years the discovery of the body of Attis among the reeds would be commemorated on that day. . . ." Mr. Wilson says that "The symbolism of *A Full Moon in March* has to be related to the general theory set out in passages such as this." My dictionaries tell me that the reeds were Cybele's and that Attis was celebrated on the 22nd of March and that his vegetation was the pine tree. It is further noteworthy that the original Sibylline books were burnt in 83 B.C. and that the later or restored versions were corrupt and full of forgeries. Virgil (Aeneid VI, 100) says of the Cumean Sibyl: *obscuris vera involvens.* Here again I do not blame Mr. Wilson; he has made the best of a confused job by Yeats; but I remain troubled by the nature and scope of the authority appealed to. Of what mixture of beliefs does our poet wish to persuade us? My copy of Mr. Wilson's book is covered with marks indicating queries of this sort.

Some of these marks seem to query what might merely be fun, though it seems not: as the commentary on the goatherd's song from "Shepherd and Goatherd" which runs some six pages into a Platonic interpretation which to my mind cannot be needed except for fun. I select only the oddest: that there may be an influence in this song of "Castiglione's famous saying 'Would that I were a shepherd that I might look down daily upon Urbino.' " No amount of checking that I can do brings this quotation into any relation to the song or the poem to which it is applied except a relation of fun. But other marks point to something more serious, as this the final commentary on *A Full Moon in March:* "The consummation of virginity lies in its 'desecration,' just as the consummation of the divine order lies in its reconciliation with the fallen world." No doubt Yeats meant this or something of this sort; but his own lines had said something much better precisely to the extent that this explanation is not thought of. Again, there is the commentary on "Chosen" which runs over five pages, which befouls us in a platonic and neo-platonic theology over matters which the poem had already made superbly plain. I refer especially to the commentary on the second stanza of this poem and this I must quote for its own beautiful force:

> I struggled with the horror of daybreak,
> I chose it for my lot! If questioned on
> My utmost pleasure with a man
> By some new-married bride, I take
> That stillness for a theme
> Where his heart my heart did seem
> And both adrift on the miraculous stream
> Where—wrote a learned astrologer—
> The Zodiac is changed into a sphere.

Mr. Wilson attacks the last three lines and carries us through Parmenides, Plato, Plotinus, Aristophanes, and Macrobius (where a short note might have been in order), and yet says nothing about the preceding six lines which give the last three their only excuse for *poetic* being. If the commentary is pertinent to the poem at all, then one must say that Yeats ate a "crazy salad with his meat." Otherwise one says that this poem contains both the icons on my desk at once and it may be that we shall have to handle the second in order to contemplate the first; but I should rather choose at once the horror of the daybreak.

Mr. Wilson prefers not to discriminate and is willing to leave judgment to those who come after him and build their judgment on his own ground. I would make a beginning towards such judgment by comparing "Byzantium," which gets a whole chapter of commentary, and "Sailing to Byzantium," which gets nothing for itself and only a few lines to set it with "Byzantium." Mr. Wilson's commentary makes me believe for the nonce that "Byzantium" is machinery all but the last line, and this I had not thought before, or not so strongly; but it also makes me believe that "Sailing to Byzantium" is much the finer poem of the two, which I had always known without any matter of belief entering in; the poem has no machinery moving for its own sake, but all moves the actual thought in the mind. "Byzantium" brightens only under the friction of exegesis, except for its last line: "That dolphin-torn, that gong-tormented sea," which is a poem itself. "Sailing to Byzantium" brightens in its own fire, shines in its own darkness. Its machinery, its system, its heterodox mysticism as Mr. Wilson would call it, only makes the words more solid with the action of the thought.

This is how one would wish to look at all Yeats's poems, remembering that Aristotle thought that the shape of poetry is life-like and was the most universal form of knowledge, and that Croce thought poetry was the substance out of which philosophy was raised and was in parallel relation to, but not identical with, all the other modes of our knowledge and action; and remembering, too, that Bergson found in poetry the turbulence that reminds us what we must do to keep alive. If we keep all this in mind, we will not mind much that Yeats, in some of his poems, took his philosophy or theology first, and in some other poems made theological commentary on earlier poems, and indeed we will not mind familiarizing ourselves with as much as necessary to get at the poems. In my opinion, that is all Yeats did; for he is not recognizably either a philosopher or a theologian, and I hardly think much of a magician. So we will accept the loose parallel of Balzac and the image of the Sibyls, but neither with more than the authority Yeats *made* of them. We will accept in the same way

Porphyry's Cave of the Nymphs—as a kind of shorthand coherence for Yeats's images; but we will not take Porphyry's philological examination of the Odyssey. So, too, we will take as usable the figures and tropes from alchemy and from the Kabbala, for these are much like the obsessive images in ordinary life, and perhaps also the sense of the Deus Absconditus, for we are all moved by hidden things; but we have no need to accept the trappings any more than we have to accept sortilege in reading Virgil—unless we take them as the incentive to the opportunism of the lively mind. It is the same with the Rosy Cross and Theosophy, with Boehme, Swedenborg, and the systematic part of Blake. For if we do accept them as systematic authorities we shall be looking in poetry for what is not there.

Philosophy herself is impossible in the presence of too many accepted systems, and poetry is impossible in the presence of too many accepted machineries. I will not say, thinking of Yeats, that a hierarchy is necessary among his special knowledges but certainly some sort of order is desirable in which to consider them outside the poetry. Within the poetry we can take these systems and these machineries as adventitious aids in the great job of putting down our spontaneity—or, better still, to provide room for direct or ultimate perception to expand. As there is an optimum of definition, so there is an optimum mixture of beliefs in the sense of tenets, articles, doctrines; though there is no optimum in beliefs as accessions to experience—as we see gloriously in Dante. If you pass much beyond the optimum in either definition or doctrine you are likely to come out with puerile visions and sterile revelations. One thinks of what William James describes as the puerile saints of the middle ages (those, for example, who never raised their eyes) as compared to the virility of St. Francis; or one thinks of the sterility of those positivistic analytic techniques in philosophy, sociology, or psychology, which reduce thought to language but which seldom raise thought to language, as compared to the constant fruitfulness of the speculative daring of Niels Bohr, Plato, Pascal, or J.-H. Fabre—whose language is everywhere interpenetrated with the force of their own thought and rides on *that* élan. One thinks of Yeats, and sees that he shifted between the extremes of the puerile and the virile, the sterile and the fruitful, and that his élan was in between, in the poetry.

Yeats had a mind so active that he needed many ideas and beliefs to restore it from its great fatigues, and he took them so far as possible from out of this world where he could give them or find in them what authority he wished without feeling that he had damaged them or separated himself from their virtues. But, in consequence, when he was driven to make a system he made a confusion. This is a partial judgment on a part of Yeats's work and I am brought to it by Mr. Wilson's book; by the memory of Dante's discipline; and by the pressure of Yeats's other work—this last most of all. It is true that a great part of Yeats's work is infected—a flush of the skin—by his system, as we are all infected by our private vocabulary; but the greater part of his work seems free of it except at the kind of ulterior level where it does not matter—as there is always an unknown physics in *any* poem as in any soil, which only adds zest to the use of either. Here our great delight is in looking with an attention beyond the reach of our conscious skills; with precisely the skill no machinery ever reached.

Edwin Muir:
Between the Tiger's Paws

(1959)

Young Englishmen when asked how they felt about the poetry of Edwin Muir answered by and large that they had not troubled to make an opinion about it because it had little relation to the serious venture of poetry at this time. There was an intonation of voice that, if prompted to make an opinion, would make a bad one. Young Americans when asked returned a restive blankness, rather like the puppy who does not understand what is wanted, and the Americans, in this case, were nearer right than the English if only because they had nothing at all to go on, and the Englishmen (so we like to think) ought to have known better as a race of people given to the making of verse: of making something into verse; a habit which has occasionally produced poetry. I would say that the Americans needed instruction, while the English needed correction about matters of fact. There is something wrong about habits of writing poetry which insist on valuing highly only the professional poetry which springs (when it does not merely make a bog) from those habits. The professional poet and his poetry should be seen as the collapsing chimaeras they mainly, and of necessity, are; then we could scratch where we itch. Then, too, we could enjoy for the hard and interesting things *they* are, the verses made by quite unprofessional poets like Edwin Muir out of honest and endless effort and the general materials of their language. In doing so, most of us who write would even appreciate ourselves better and would do better what we did and would above all appreciate better the true great poet and how he differs from us only, and enormously,

280

in degree. *"Onorate l'altissimo poeta; l'ombra sua torna, ch'era dipartita."* Your small poet shares in that honor.

It is only degree. Think of Edwin Muir and listen to these words. "Through all [these images] there runs a feeling, a feeling which is our own no less than the poet's, a human feeling of bitter memories, of shuddering horror, of melancholy, of homesickness, of tenderness, of a kind of childish *pietas* that would prompt this vain revival of things perished, these playthings fashioned by a religious devotion. . . ." No words could better be applied to the praise of Edwin Muir than these; I would alter nothing and add very little, as the remainder of these remarks, of which they will form the burden, will show. But the words were not written about Muir but about a passage in the *Aeneid* to exemplify the complex images which inhabit all poetry and the spirit which animates them, and they were written by Benedetto Croce. They touch on the point of projection where Muir and Virgil join in kind however distant they may be in degree.

Virgil wrote the will of the Roman Empire when that empire was young. Muir, sturdy in his own way, has written an individual, a personal—an English, a Scotch—footnote to life in the true empire at a time when the notion of a good empire seems no longer plausible or possible but only an image for longing without hope. There is nothing either official or evangelical or prophetic about him, and least of all is there any plea for the kind of greatness we call grandeur, public or private. There is, rather, all Virgil's piety—the childish *pietas*, as Croce puts it—directed inwards upon the force of his own mind and thence outwards upon the nature—the naturalist's nature and human nature—that has affected him. Piety is that medium of conduct in which we feel and then achieve a harmony in the clashing of necessities: that harmony which I find myself calling over and over the concert of conflicts; and which is so difficult to achieve without the mediating presence of some form of empire, Roman or not. This difficulty in achieving harmony indeed seems the characteristic difficulty of the human condition in our times, and it sometimes seems possible only to think it in verse.

To say that this is what Muir has done, is another way of saying something about the attractive force of Muir's verse: he has made his harmony in the thought—not the numbers, the *thought*—of his verse: verse for him is the mode of his thoughtful piety, the mode of the mind's action where his piety is not only enacted for him but takes independent action on its own account and for us: when it does, it becomes poetry. This differs from the usual run of things. Usually, poetry gets along very well only reflecting thought already entertained or so to speak without any primary thought at all. I do not say that Muir's mode is any better, only that it is worth distinguishing how it is different from, say, the poetry of Ezra Pound or that of Pope. Pound's thought is in his cadence and numbers; Pope's versification cuts off the roots of his thought; Muir's thought is in the verse itself—hence the sense in the most regular of his verses of a continuous vital irregularity, whereby we know how alien and independent is thought that has taken on its identity, and how full of war any harmony is in its incarnations.

There is a passage in the chapter on Rome in Muir's autobiography which bears on the point. It is not, of course, verse, and rings in the "other harmony" of prose. But it leads of a certainty towards poetry, purely and without infection; which is one reason I quote it, with the second reason that my own sense of Rome is in good part Muir's and that in his language he has discovered for me a grand version of the experience I stood convicted of in Rome. I refer to the current of thought which he communicates in the word Incarnation. Rome is where all manner of things take to the grace of the body, body in their meetings and body in their conflicts, a concert altogether.

"We saw the usual sights," he says, "sometimes enchanted, sometimes disappointed; but it was Rome itself that took us, the riches stored in it, the ages assembled in a tumultuous order, the vistas as street corners where one looked across from one century to another, the innumerable churches, palaces, squares, fountains, monuments, ruins; and the Romans themselves going about their business as if this were the natural and right setting for the life of mankind.

"The history of Rome is drenched in blood and blackened with crime; yet all that seemed to be left now was the peace of memory. As we wandered about the Forum we could not summon up the blood-stained ghosts; they had quite gone, bleached by centuries into a luminous transparency, or evaporated into the bright still air. Their works were there, but these cast only the ordinary shadow which everything set up by mankind gathers at its foot. The grass in the courtyard of the Temple of the Vestals seemed to be drenched in peace down to the very root, and it was easy to imagine gods and men still in friendly talk together there."

So far the harmony is easy and no more than sensitive to contrive. "But," he goes on, "it was the evidence of another Incarnation that met one everywhere and gradually exerted its influence." Here Muir reminds himself of the life neighboring the Scotch churches of his boyhood in the persons of their ministers. "In figures such as these the Word became something more than a word in my childish mind; but nothing told me that Christ was born in the flesh and lived on the earth.

"In Rome that image was to be seen everywhere, not only in churches, but on the walls of houses, at cross-roads in the suburbs, in wayside shrines in the parks, and in private rooms. I remember stopping for a long time one day to look at a little plaque on the wall of a house in the Via degli Artisti, representing the Annunciation. An angel and a young girl, their bodies inclined toward each other, their knees bent as if they were overcome by love, 'tutto tremante,' gazed upon each other like Dante's pair; and that representation of a human love so intense that it could not reach farther seemed the perfect earthly symbol of the love that passes understanding. . . . That these images should appear everywhere, reminding everyone of the Incarnation, seemed to me natural and right, just as it was right that my Italian friends should step out frankly into life. This open declaration was to me the very mark of Christianity, distinguishing it from the older religions."

The harmony is harder here since it has to do with how harmonies are come by, with the art of the art, the passion of the passion, the story of the story. It is like—as a direct experience—St. Thomas' definition of allegory where the words signify things which themselves then signify further, yet there remain with us only the primitive words or the plaque on the wall. The allegory which Rome provided for Muir out of the monuments and fountains of human ruins and aspirations, and which he records in his prose, is a kind of prefiguration of the allegory—the effort to make things speak further for themselves than our mere words can signify alone—which he completes in his verse.

I should like to point out that these allegories are not—as so many of our allegories are nowadays—puzzles or evasions or deliberate ambiguities or veilings of purpose, and they do not require interpretation according to anything but the sense of intimacy in experience approached or observed with piety in order to accept what is there. All that is needed are the common terms of our tradition together with some familiarity with the habits of English verse and a responsiveness to a handful of literary allusions which are, or used to be, universally permitted and expected. I mean the allusions which are very nearly a part of the substance of our mind, so early were they bred in us by education and conversation: the allusions we can make without consciousness of their meanings, but which, when we do become conscious of their meanings, are like thunder and lightning and the letting go of breath. A thing is what it is, and is its own meaning, which might seem to us, as it did to Dante in his *Paradiso,* a condition of blessedness, though in our context of reading and writing we take tautology as the face of obfuscation and irrelevance. Ripeness is all. A thing is what it is, and when you can say so you will have made an allegory of direct statement—a statement so full of itself that it promises an ultimate comprehensibility; it prefigures what is in its nature to be fulfilled, either backwards or forwards, as is just.

Here is such an example of direct allegory, the last quatrain of "The Good Man in Hell":

> One doubt of evil would bring down such a grace,
>> Open such a gate, all Eden could enter in,
> Hell be a place like any other place,
>> And love and hate and life and death begin.

This looks backwards, through a little theology, into our most backward selves where we abort, but need not, human action in the hell of the wilfully wrong affirmation: it is that lethargy of sensation, or boredom of perception, which feels only the wrong good. Here is another allegory, which though it returns to Homer, had better be said to look forward. The poem is called "The Return" and it may be that the final phase of our pilgrimage, whatever earlier routes it took, is always a return; at least it would seem so to those of us in middle age or beyond. To the Ulysses who wanes in each of us in long hankering there is Penelope waxing ahead: the *gnostos,* the home-coming, the return, which constitutes by magic certainty like the octave in music, the farthest reach of the journey.

> The doors flapped open in Ulysses' house,
> The lolling latches gave to every hand,
> Let traitor, babbler, tout and bargainer in.
> The rooms and passages resounded
> With ease and chaos of a public market,
> The walls mere walls to lean on as you talked,
> Spat on the floor, surveyed some newcomer
> With an absent eye. There you could be yourself.
> Dust in the nooks, weeds nodding in the yard.
> The thick walls crumbling. Even the cattle came
> About the doors with mild familiar stare
> As if this were their place.
> All around the island stretched the clean blue sea.
>
> Sole at the house's heart Penelope
> Sat at her chosen task, endless undoing
> Of endless doing, endless weaving, unweaving,
> In the clean chamber. Still her loom ran empty
> Day after day. She thought: 'Here I do nothing
> Or less than nothing, making an emptiness
> Amid disorder, weaving, unweaving the lie
> The day demands. Ulysses, this is duty,
> To do and undo, to keep a vacant gate
> Where order and right and hope and peace can enter.
> Oh will you ever return? Or are you dead,
> And this wrought emptiness by ultimate emptiness?
>
> She wove and unwove and wove and did not know
> That even then Ulysses on the long
> And winding road of the world was on his way.

This poem needs no commentary by way of discussion, for it invites the comment of attachment, of intimacy. It is a plaque of incarnation affixed to the wall of the mind, where, looking, you could be yourself. There is no end to the journey that is at hand. Let us say that this is a poem of great tenderness, the tenderness of human action which stretches between one being and another and stretches most in absence, most of all in the absence in the same room, and yet is the tenderness, which is the life, of actual possibility, confirming it even in the snapping point of failure. In our beginnings are our ends, all a return. To repeat, if the good man in hell broke lethargy, Penelope creates the live waiting which is also attention commanded. Each is annunciation bringing incarnation.

If so the poems themselves are epiphanies, like those green ones Stephen Dedalus meant to write, for epiphany—the showing of what is already made—is as far as the mind can go with what is wanted or needed. The verse makes only the analogous incarnation of the thing—its mere behavior—into words and forms that sometimes become poetry. But the secondary often leads us back to the primary, to what is still first; so let us look a little at the kind of poet Muir is, at his equipment in verse, and at the ideas and habits of mind that beset him in his epiphany of his grand theme.

As to the kind of poet to which Muir belongs, it is the kind we all are in our salutations, our aversions, and our reveries—when we cry out, turn aside, or let the dreams within us work themselves into shape beyond our normal shaping powers. He is like all of us in those moments when we put meaning into our words. Only he is better than most of us mainly are, for the shapes and meanings last for others' use: common currency in motion. There are no monuments here, either of imagination or ambition, and no bids for power and domination. There are, rather, gestures of recognition, and intimations of the forms of all these. We are in their presence, as Shakespeare says water is in water, or as Burns says the snowflakes are on the black river. Only it is not Shakespeare and not Burns. This is what is meant by saying that Muir is not a professional poet, not even a public poet. Neither the open nor the overweening career was ever his. This is not Milton, who knew and overpassed his powers, but Milton's secretary, the Member from Hull, Andrew Marvell, who pursued his best possibilities and was several times seized by powers beyond himself—the same powers that sometimes seize us. Or let us say that Muir is like Traherne, who rehearsed traditional mysteries, rather than like Donne, for whom none of the traditions and no mere rehearsal was ever enough. Perhaps Muir is like George Herbert without a parish or a doctrine or any one temple to construct. He made secular what was his own, which was indeed how he saw it even when it was supernatural in its mode of contact, in annunciation and resurrection. His poems and no doubt his life were topical only to himself, and we make him our topic in the common place between us. He made a commonplace book in our own language.

Such is Muir's kind of poetry, and there ought to be a name for the kind. No doubt Mr. Northrop Frye will provide us with a good one (for he knows how we take hold of things better by a name than by the substance), but in the meantime we can say that it springs from an old and natural tradition like sunlight or breathing and is about as hard to do without until we take our summers on the moon. I think there would neither be great poetry nor amusing poetry nor the grand folly of private poetry if there were not also, aware of all these, the steady poetry of the kind written by Muir. This poetry is a kind of thinking in verse, which is a very different thing from versifying thought, for the verse is the vital mode rather than the mere metrical mode of the thought, and is thus the substance of what we remember as well as the memorable form. It is a thinking in verse—as thinking in algebra or in farming or love—which so far as it reaches form is poetry live with the action of the mind, and which when it does not reach form has the dullness of the active mind failing. Almost none of our brains, as Darwin knew, are good for very much thinking, in verse no more than otherwise. Thoughts that fail in poetry are like dogs that have lost the scent.

Some brook has run between or a swamp sogs under the feet and the life runs out of the flurry of action. Where the hound gives up and denies his interest the poet goes on willy-nilly, more dogged than any dog, so long as there is any verse to help him pretend a course or a spoor. Somewhere, across some gap or dark of occasion, what is lost may be recovered. I take it Muir means something like this in another language—which has the desperateness of the certainty of what approaches saying and cannot be said—when he ends his autobiography in the following way: "In the infinite web of things and events chance must be something different from what we think it to be. To comprehend that is not given to us, and to think of it is to recognize a mystery, and to acknowledge the necessity of faith. As I look back on the part of the mystery which is my own life, my own fable, what I am most aware of is that we receive more than we can ever give; we receive it from the past, on which we draw with every breath, but also—and this is a point of faith—from the Source of the mystery itself, by the means which religious people call Grace." Muir was looking back at the perennial mystery, and perhaps the perennial philosophy, of his whole life; I was looking at the mystery of the practice of writing verse. There is some place where the looks cross.

One such place perhaps may be seen in the type of verse which Muir characteristically writes when the verse comes nearest to thought—when the words contribute to and indeed almost occasion the thought. The words precipitate, they do not distil the thought. Muir makes no epigrams in the modern sense in words which in themselves flash the wit; as a poet he is singularly little in love with words, and his words never make us blush. He makes no apothegms nor gnostic sayings either; there is no special penetration and no special mystery of knowledge; he observes by habit, rather, that way of words that goes with ritual and makes runes: he makes an old script, an older and different alphabet, out of the general mystery and the common intuition, inescapably present, when looked at, in our regular vocabulary of word and myth and attitude. He has the great advantage of the power to re-create or transform them. His own poems make the best commentary on the distinction I want to set forth. Here is the end of "Ballad of Hector in Hades":

> Two shadows racing on the grass,
>   Silent and so near,
> Until his shadow falls on mine.
>   And I am rid of fear.
>
> The race is ended. Far away
>   I hang and do not care,
> While round bright Troy Achilles whirls
>   A corpse with streaming hair.

One does not even need to have read the *Iliad,* unless as a child; everything to do with Troy is part of our natural possession—a gift of our past—and all our languages have so constantly, if irregularly, re-possessed themselves of it that every fresh statement of it, every variation or addition, has a natural authenticity. Hector and Achilles might well have been taken up by Freud along with Oedipus and Narcissus, for at least within our Psyches we all run in great heat round that wall, and it makes little difference whether the other fellow is Hector or Achilles. In the eschatology of the Psyche Hades is not so judgmatical as the Christian hell, and our roles continue to reverse themselves, nightmare to nightmare, as they do in ordinary life. Our nightmares are the playmasters of our minds and none are so masterly as our Greek nightmares. Homer has them all in their urgent and obliterative forms; Ovid their urbane forms; Muir, when he tackles them in his verse, their therapeutic and reminding forms. Surely, there is no cliché of nightmare so universal, touching so sharply upon us all, as the corpse with streaming hair; Achilles (and it could have been Hector) in this poem is only a *figura* for the figures with whom we are in perpetual pursuit in our private Hades. It is our nightmares wake us as we have lost our next to last breath, and with what is left we make a rune or die, and there is a wide emptiness all around us, in which our senses and our decisions swim in common vertigo, accusing and self-accusing. This is the rune for the corpse with the streaming hair; and I will only remind you that the Duke of Clarence, just before he was visited by his murderers, saw in that dream of his which "lengthened after life" (*Richard the Third,* I, 4) "A shadow like an angel, with bright hair / Dabbled in blood." Clarence, like Hector, spoke from the private Hades of the Psyche, and he, too, made a rune.

From "The Enchanted Knight" I quote the first and the last two stanzas.

> Lulled by La Belle Dame Sans Merci he lies
>> In the bare wood below the blackening hill.
> The plough drives nearer now, the shadow flies
>> Past him across the plain, but he lies still. . . .
>
> When a bird cries within the silent grove
>> The long-last voice goes by, he makes to rise
> And follow, but his cold limbs never move,
>> And on the turf unstirred his shadow lies.
>
> But if a withered leaf should drift
>> Across his face and rest, the dread drops start
> Chill on his forehead. Now he tries to lift
>> The insulting weight that stays and breaks his heart.

No one needs to know Keats's poem, anymore than Keats needed to know the literary and folk sources for the belief in the fatal

destructiveness of love in one of its roles upon which his poem—
and Muir's—depends. The belief had a cave home in some furthest source within us—perhaps in some anterior metamorphosis
of the Psyche in which love and its inspirations exacted their cost
more vividly than now and charged daring more quickly with its
natural end. As we think in an earlier form of ourselves, so we
use a different alphabet of feelings; and in that form and that alphabet we believe preciously in what in its present form we greet
only with the attraction of horror. The verse restores the early
form by giving its thoughts a mode of action. All Muir's poem
except one word is a rune and ritual celebration of that dread
lady—Robert Graves's White Goddess—who takes back in one
moment not only her gift to her lover but also his life itself; the
one word is the word "insulting," a modern and moody word, by
which the poet expresses his rebellion against the tradition and
his denial of the ritual, the while it breaks him down. It is as if
Muir thought for a moment like Dostoevsky, where the last gasp
of the individual is in insult and injury and laceration. The history of the word insult is present here whether Muir knew it or
not: as a frequentative form of the verb *insilire,* to leap upon.
The rain of insult is perpetual while life lasts. This poem, then, is
a rune in old ballad form, to express and purge the nightmare of
the White Goddess.

The poem called "The Island" goes beyond the condition of
rune and makes a spell out of the glamor or secret art of grammar.
The island of the title is not Muir's birthplace the island of Orkney,
but Sicily, the visible merging place for all our histories, teeming, as
it does with living people, with the races and beliefs and arts of other
times, especially teeming with beliefs, some now quite lost to conscious memory. In Sicily erosion and fertility compete in every mode:
"Harvests of men to give men birth." All this is only less so in the
Island of Orkney, for we survive as it were only in islands. Here is the
end of the poem.

> And self-begotten cycles close
> About our way; indigenous art
> And simple spells make unafraid

> The haunted labyrinths of the heart,
> And with our wild succession braid
> The resurrection of the rose.

Possibly it should be emphasized that it is the indigenous art and the simple spells that make the braid. Indigenous art is innate art, a spell is a saying with magic power when said in a special way and special form. To make the indigenous simple is to make the spell of rational imagination with which both to purge and to involve our wild succession.

That is to say, in the work of a man like Muir whose mind has no temptation either to remake the world or to reason it out of existence, the rational imagination here makes its maximum task to recapture tradition in direct apprehension, to find in what happens to him an illumination in the linkage of the chances that have gone before with the abstractions that persist. It is as if, with Muir, allegory were the indigenous and final art. As he says,

> Or so I dream when at my door
> I hear my soul, my visitor.

And when he says this he reminds us of Emily Dickinson and how we might reassess her along the same lines but with a different and perhaps larger stretch than those that contain Muir. Muir is a Dickinson with a different lack. But both poets resorted naturally to all the tradition to which they were exposed, and they made their resort to find abstractions in which their problematic—even their unseemly—sensibilities could be united with their selves. Muir's resort was to the Greek and classical, to the Christian, and to the monstrous forms or postures of the Psyche that precede all our taxonomy, and it is these forms that he set about putting to the commonest musics he could find: the sonnet, the ballad, the anecdote, and in the commonest diction he could hear—not the language of the street, but the general language of literature. The two provided means for the discernment of the memorable, since it was in the service of memory both had grown up. Here one thinks of Valéry's remark, that one keeps in memory only what one has not understood, or of that poet's other remark that Reason (and this is her warrant of office) admires the monuments (the cities of imagination) that she could not herself have built. In Muir it is sometimes the actual damaged monuments of true cities only in our lifetime truncated from their stories, like the city of Prague, which he loved, and which is the subject of the poem, "The Good Town." Plato, Augustine, Dante and (in a small persistent pang) Baudelaire did this, and so Muir. Cities are like annunciations, visits of the soul on our grandest human scale in monumental analogy to the everlasting devastations of the moment seized:

> Whether the soul at first
> This pilgrimage began,
> Or the shy body leading
> Conducted soul to soul,
> Who knows? This is the most
> That soul and body can,
> To make us each for each
> And in our spirit whole.

These lines, which end a poem called "The Annunciation," make a wooing of that goddess, other than the White Goddess who makes us die, who makes us live, the personal city within the great. There is a poem called simply "Song"—the simple spell of indigenous art— where the two cities are in piety joined. It is the song of the thought Muir put most in his verse.

> The quarrel from the start,
> Long past and never past,
> The war of mind and heart,
> The great war and the small
> That tumbles the hovel down
> And topples town on town
> Come to one place at last:
> Love gathers all.

One observes here that Muir's most direct statement reaches to the purest abstraction. He is like this even when his concern is in the immediate mood of the crash of melancholy and joy. I would cite, for they are too much to repeat here in full, the twinned poems called "Dejection" and "Sorrow," but must quote the ends of both anyhow.

. . . For every eloquent voice dies in this air
Wafted from anywhere to anywhere
And never counted by the careful clock,
That cannot strike the hour
Of power that will dissolve this power
Until the rock rise up and split the rock.

. . . If it were only so . . .
But right and left I find
Sorrow, sorrow,
And cannot be resigned,
Knowing that we were made
By joy to drive joy's trade
And not to waver to and fro,
But quickly go.

It was just said that these things are in piety joined, and piety is not an artichoke to be pulled apart for the eating, with the most part discarded, for we have here, in the language of Croce and Virgil which we began by quoting, "a human feeling of bitter memories, of shuddering horror, of melancholy, of homesickness, of tenderness, of a kind of childish *pietas,*" and we must not tamper with it like psychiatrists but become intimate with it without assault like fellow-humans. It is with piety that we recognize our familiars, even when they are horrors or our inmost selves, but most when we see we should be nothing at all without them. It is with piety that we make the best order out of our stories. If we need an abstraction or a generalization to grasp and share what Muir's thinking in verse is up to it is in our best conception of the piety of the story. For there is a piety in Muir—and like humility, in a hair's breadth it will be pride or humiliation—towards nature, the cross, the Greeks, death, time, love, old age, and to the obsessions of all these and their nightmares. For our nightmares only smother us where we have paid too much attention to our real life.

Now to repeat, since even a story to be true must repeat itself, wherever Mr. Muir himself is, the inner motion of his poetry still draws from the "carnival of birth and death," as he calls it, of the Orkney sea-farm where he grew up. Muir is an island man and is full of natural piety—a phrase Wordsworth put into poetry. But where

Wordsworth observed it, and sought it, Muir's poems exert his natural piety, as a function of his being, exert it equally to the hill and the plough, to the stars and to his Visitor the Soul, never forgetting the one when he greets the other. His poetry participates without prejudice in the warfare between the two elements of the tradition which moves him. I do not think this warfare very different from the war of the journey and the war of the pity which inhabited the mind of Dante, and I think it is in this sense that Muir is a traditional poet; he deals with the wars of our journey and our pity. His order—whether in his prosody of ballad and sonnet and blank verse or in his themes of the human condition—his order is as old as the terms of experience and the reach of thought; but everywhere there is the wildness of fresh disorder which is the current of life in his order. If the wildness is reminiscent of eternity both before and after, so much the better. The regular is most wild.

All this is vivid in the poems themselves. Here is the other of the two poems he has called "Return." (The first was that with which we began about Penelope awaiting Ulysses.)

> And the voices,
> Sweeter than any sound dreamt of or known,
> Call me, recall me. I draw near at last,
> An old old man, and scan the ancient walls
> Rounded and softened by the compassionate years,
> The old and heavy and long-leaved trees that watch
> This my inheritance in friendly darkness.
> And yet I cannot enter, for all within
> Rises before me there, rises against me,
> A sweet and terrible labyrinth of longing,
> So that I turn aside and take the road
> That always, early or late, runs on before.

And here are the last distichs of "Epitaph" and "Self Despite."

> If now is Resurrection, then let stay
> Only what's ours when this is put away . . .

—————

> So I may yet recover by this bad
> Research that good I scarcely dreamt I had.

In Mr. J. C. Hall's introduction to the *Collected Poems* Stephen Spender is quoted as saying that Muir witnessed everywhere in Rome the climactic symbol of Resurrection. To this Mr. Hall puts a foot-note. "Edwin Muir tells me that the symbol which impressed him in Rome was that of Incarnation, not Resurrection." To me, both seem right, and the two fragments of verse which I have just quoted attest it. In the poems both Resurrection and Incarnation—the rediscovery and the bodying forth—are going on at the same time. That is why so much of the poetry is nearly not words at all but the action of the mind itself taking thought of Resurrection and Incarnation, the carnival of birth and death. Like Prospero, that great persona of human piety, this poet would still his beating mind.

> This love a moment known
> For what I do not know
> And in a moment gone
> Is like the happy doe
> That keeps its perfect laws
> Between the tiger's paws
> And vindicates its cause.

Between the Tiger's Paws Muir stills his beating mind.

Homo Ludens

Review of *The Literary Works of Matthew Prior,*
edited by H. Bunker Wright and Monroe K. Spears.
(1959)

So far as a combination of incompetence and great interest can
judge, this edition of Prior, the first since the Cambridge edition of
1907, gives every desirable reading use. It is handsome, as the price
and the fact that it is in the Oxford Text series testify. The text is
followed by 263 pages of factual commentary which at every point
I have checked is helpful. I am happy to possess and use such an
edition. If there are errors they will take equal errors and equal
scholarship to correct. It is to be hoped that the editors, or one of
them, may go on to write the grand interpretive note called a biography—not a long book to drown in, but a monograph of say a
hundred pages, which might be published with the letters. Prior's
poetry is that of an interesting man, and the interest, I think, runs
both ways, and into the interest of public history as well as private.
He was a Foreign Service Officer, a Secretary to statesmen, and had,
for example, something to do with the Peace of Utrecht; he also
attached the loyalty of his mistresses, especially of the one who was
the character in the title of "Jinny the Just," and is the sweet company kept in the poem which used to be called by those who loved
it (though not, it seems, by Prior) "The Secretary." In this edition
the letter is restored to the anonymity of "Written in the Year
1696." Under one title or the other it ought to appear in every
anthology as one sample of what Prior was up to at his best: to play
lightly with genuine sentiment in such a way that it adds to the

sensibility. Since it is missing from the anthologies (including Auden's, an incomprehensible omission) just here on my shelves, I venture to quote it entire. It should, after all, be one of those commonplaces which each man may refresh for himself, and for which women should feel grateful.

> While with Labour Assiduous due pleasure I mix
> And in one day attone for the Busyness of Six
> In a little Dutch Chaise on a Saturday Night
> On my left hand my Horace and   on my right
> No Memoire to compose and no Post-boy to move
> That on Sunday may hinder the softness of Love:
> For her, neither Visits nor Parties of Tea
> Nor the long winded Cant of a dull Refugée
> This Night and the next shal be hers shall be Mine
> To good or ill Fortune the Third we resign:
> Thus Scorning the World and superior to Fate
> I drive on my Car in processional State.
> So with *Phia* thrô *Athens Pisistratus* rode
> Men thought her *Minerva* and Him a new God
> But why shou'd I stories of Athens rehearse
> Where People knew Love and were partial to Verse
> Since none can with Justice my pleasure oppose
> In *Holland* half drownded in Interest and Prose:
> By *Greece* and past Ages what need I be tried
> When the *Hague* and the Present are both on my side
> And is it enough for the Joys of the day
> To think what *Anacreon* or *Sapho* wou'd say
> When good *Vandergoos* and his provident Vrough
> As they gaze on my Triumph do freely allow
> That search all the province you'l find no Man there is
> So blest as the *Englishen Heer* SECRETARIS.

The reader will supply the name of any Jane he will in the blank space the fourth line provides for the King's Secretary's use. He will not likely provide the following extract from Prior's "Heads for a Treatise upon Learning." He is advising no man to write poetry unless he must, and remarks that he himself felt the compulsion all his life long. "But I had two Accidents in Youth," he goes on, "which hindered me from being quite possest with the Muse: I was bred in a Colledge where prose was more in fashion than Verse, and as soon as I had taken my First Degree was sent the Kings Secretary to the Hague, there I had enough to do in studying French and Dutch and altering my Terentian and Virgilian Style into that of Articles Conventions and Memorials, So that Poetry which by the bent of my Mind might have become the business of my Life, was by the happyness of my Education only the Amusement of it, and in this too, having the prospect of some little Fortune to be made, and Friendship to be cultivated with the great Men, I did not launch much out into Satyr, etc. . . ." This was written a quarter of a century after the poem, and is true only under the shaping force of memory. But there are resemblances or linkages that show clearly (and there are others which may be looked up, at the leisure and curiosity of the reader), and one is the effect the lightness of punctuation makes in both verse and prose as a notation for the special music of Prior's language. At best it is speech-making music on the page where usually it is made in the throat. Prior was a great experimenter in prosody, and his prose pieces contain much live and pertinent matter, and there are others even in the verse itself, as in the opening of "Frederic," where he argues that he is writing verse "in the ancient guise, free, uncontroll'd." Nor can I help giving this on the other prosody of the conceiving mind:

> That CUPID goes with Bow and Arrows,
> And VENUS keeps her Coach and Sparrows,
> Is all but Emblem, to acquaint One,
> The Son is sharp, the Mother wanton.
> Such Images have sometimes shown
> A *Mystic* Sense, but oft'ner None.

This is from the first Canto of "Alma," and I have given it here for an ulterior reason, that it is written in octosyllabics and may be put against the anapaests of the poem about the Secretary, and these are the two meters where Prior did most for English verse. One could wish for the sake of those who practise the trade of verse, the applied or practical art, that Ezra Pound had commented Prior's verse in the same spirit that he commented Golding and Marlowe and Crabbe forty years ago to the great advantage of those who have ears to read with; one wishes it the more so, because some of the Cantos are the best anapaests of our time and parts of "Mauberley" practice the expansion of the octosyllable. Since Pound did not do so, there is always Saintsbury who gives a long section to Prior in his *Prosody* and shows how he carried on from Dryden and made Swinburne possible. (One does not make a meter all by oneself; to be used, they must be recognized and attended as a convention, all the brilliant work of our linguistic friends notwithstanding, for the habits of language are only primary to the use of language by poets. As Gascoigne said, "Verse that is too easie is like the tale of a rosted horse.") But to make a nutshell of it in the kingdom of bad dreams, Saintsbury singles out from "The Secretary" one couplet:

> This Night and the next shal be Hers shal be Mine
> To good or ill Fortune the Third we resign

which it is a double pleasure to repeat, and he singles it out because, I suppose, the meter of it touches upon, and moves, the sense, as the pulse does the voice. "And with it," he says of this couplet, "the lighter English poetry entered, for all purposes, and not merely for theatrical or musical ones, into the possession of a new medium." A little later, as a kind of preliminary conclusion about Prior, there is this: his "accomplishment, and still more his example, in the domiciling of the anapaest and the octosyllable are his greatest achievements." Of course Saintsbury was speaking of the state of English verse at a particular time—of how it is possible at a given time to employ public aids in solitary efforts—and that is a conception alien to general present considerations. We forget that in poetry our reversionary interests may be our life-blood. It is worth doing better than we do when we cannot soar. Here is a quatrain from the "Child of Quality" which succinctly says it as a part of all our enterprise.

> Nor Quality, nor Reputation,
> Forbid me yet my Flame to tell.

> Dear Five Years old befriends my passion,
> And I may Write 'till she can Spell.

Which to my taste is better than Arnold who as you remember thought we ought to write criticism that poetry may come. I of course bar the great critics, but they will not trouble us by their quantity; their quality would lead us otherwise to write verse, especially when education and career lead us to Articles Conventions and Memorials. Who would not rather have read, let alone written, "Jinny the Just," "Paulo Purganti," or "The English Padlock" than any but the best criticism whatever?—for of the poems we are all intimate and hopeful of their subjects, and in the other, to use a figure Prior used thrice, we tug a rope of sand.

Reading Prior complete after thirty years raises, like a land mist towards evening in October, a nostalgia for what must be an unknown delight in our time and language: a general habit of good light verse in which the play of music and sentiment may sometimes be very serious play indeed, and I would say the same thing of light prose, rather than that which coys or cloys us something that buoys us. Our trouble is that we have gone ambitious and care nothing for the fame we can earn, care nothing, or little, for any accomplishment that does not make or break the ambition. I do not mean that there is not a great deal of light verse written; but that the most of it is written abominably, not at all like that of John Betjeman or Phyllis McGinley (to make two admirable exceptions), but that most of it is written without the caress of detail that makes the detail sing. One's ambition should sometimes be for the verse and not for the self, for making not for aggrandizement; and one should suffer the shame of deserved defeat in the bad rhyme and spasmodic meter, where one most commonly observes it, in our limericks and other gnashings of the language; for bawdiness is nothing without clenching rhyme and the ordonnance of meter; and we have, as Prior shows, a body of meter in our language worth attending and a possibility of rhyme worth expanding. I think of people who swim, skate or dance well—and I think of people who write light verse (to say nothing of those moved by their first ambitions) only to remember the Thursday Amateur's

Night which fell like crockery between the Features and wish to God, and all the gods, that they were amateurs in any sensible reception of that word. *Homo Ludens* is the amateur I like best. Prior's anapaests on Jinny the Just tell us what that is:

> While she read and accounted and pay'd and abated
> Eat and drank, play'd and work't, laught and cry'd, loved and hated
> As answer'd the End of her being created.

A Poetics for Infatuation

Shakespeare's Sonnets
(1961)

There will never be, I hope, by some chance of scholarship, any more authoritative order for Shakespeare's sonnets than that so dubiously supplied by the 1609 quarto. It is rather like Pascal's *Pensées,* or, even better, like the *order* of the Psalms, as to matters of date or interest. No one can improve upon the accidentally established order we possess; but everyone can invite himself to feel the constant interflow of new relations, of new reticulations—as if the inner order were always on the move—in the sonnets, the *Pensées,* the Psalms. Thus the vitality of fresh disorder enters the composition and finds room there with every reading, with every use and every abuse we make of them. Each time we look at a set of things together but do not count them, the sum of the impression will be different, though the received and accountable numerical order remains the same. If we complain of other people's perceptions it is because we feel there is greater vitality in our own; and so on. We had better persist with the received order as a warrant that all of us have at least that point in common.

That point is worth a good deal more with Shakespeare's sonnets than with Pascal or the Psalmist. It is thought that the text follows that of original manuscripts or fair copies, and no intuition bids me think otherwise. Furthermore, till private interests rise, the sequence we have seems sensible with respect to their sentiments, and almost a "desirable" sequence with respect to the notion of development. Anyone who feels weak about this should try reading the sonnets backward all the way; they will turn themselves round again from their own force. At any rate numbers 1 to 17 make a preparatory exercise for the theme which emerges in number 18 and continues through number 126. With number 127 there is a break, not to a new theme but to a new level or phase of the old theme which lasts through number 152. The remaining pair of sonnets sounds a light echo on an ancient model, but with fashionable rhetoric, of the devouring general theme.

That theme is infatuation: its initiation, cultivation, and history, together with its peaks of triumph and devastation. The whole collection makes a poetics for infatuation, or, to use a slight elaboration of Croce's phrase, it gives to infatuation a theoretic form. The condition of infatuation is a phase of life; not limited to sexual attraction, though usually allied with it, it also modifies or exacerbates many matters besides—especially, it would seem in these sonnets, matters having to do with the imaginative or poetic powers. The story of Pygmalion is one of several ultimate forms of infatuation, and Pygmalion is a name for sonnet after sonnet because the problem of personal infatuation is turned into a problem in poetics. If I cannot have my love I will create it, but with never a lessening, always an intensification of the loss, the treachery, the chaos in reality. To say this is to say something about what is overriding whenever we think either of infatuation or poetics. The maxim was never made overt but it was latent—in the undercurrent of the words—throughout much of the Renaissance: if God is reality, I must contend with him even more than I accept him, whether as lover or as poet. So it is in the sonnets. Like all of Shakespeare, they contain deep grasping notions for poetics; and this is precisely, as we master these notions, how we make most use of his poetry. We beset reality.

Let us see. The first seventeen sonnets are addressed to a beautiful young man who seems unwilling to settle down and have children. They could be used by any institute of family relations, and they must have been a great nuisance to any young man who received them. The most they tell him is that he cannot stop with himself (which is just blooming), that he cannot conquer time and mortality and reach immortality (which do not now concern him), and indeed that he can hardly continue to exist unless he promptly begets him a son. If these sonnets were paintings by Titian they would swarm with naked children—little Eroses, or putti—but Venus would be missing. There is no bride in the marriage. The argument of these first sonnets proceeds with an end in view; the prudent member speaks; but there is no premise, and no subject. There was no real "young man" in these poems—though he could be invited in. As they stand, Shakespeare was addressing not a young man but one of his unaccomplished selves; the self that wants progeny addressing one of the selves that does not. The voices of the children in the apple trees can be heard whenever this set of the sonnets stops in the mind: a deep strain in us all. Perhaps it is this strain in the feelings that makes Shakespeare the poet address the other fellow as the unwilling father—the chap who never answers. Montaigne's thoughts on the affections of fathers for their children (II, viii) reach the same sort of point Shakespeare dandles a little, but cannot yet accept, in sonnets 15 to 17. "And I know not whether I would not rather have brought forth one child perfectly formed by commerce with the Muses than by commerce with my wife." Sonnet 17 goes only so far as to offer both immortalities, the child and the rhyme.

In 18 ("Shall I compare thee to a summer's day?") there is a rise in poetic power and the poetic claim is made absolute. At the same time the "young man" gains in presence and particularity, and the emotion begins to ring. The "other" self has been changed. Where the lover had been using verses around a convention, now the poet is using love both to master a convention and to jack up his self-confidence. This is of course only the blessed illusion of poiesis: that what poiesis seizes is more certain as it is more lasting than any operation of the senses. The couplet illuminates:

> So long as men can breathe or eyes can see,
> So long lives this, and this gives life to thee.

There is a burst of splendor in the tautology of *"this."* Every essence is eternal, but Shakespeare wants his eternity in time (which as Blake says is the mercy of eternity). He keeps both "thy eternal summer" and his own "eternal lines," and these are the tautology of *"this."* But the sonnet contains also premonitions of the later Shakespeare, especially in the seventh and eighth lines where *we cannot trim sail to nature's course,* and it is this sentiment which haunts the whole poem, its special presence which we get by heart. Shakespeare hung about not only where words were (as Auden says the poet must) but also where sentiments were to be picked up. A good poem (or bad) is always a little aside from its particular subject; a good (or bad) hope from its object; or fear from its horror. Shakespeare could take the nightmare *in* nature as an aspect of unaccommodated man—whether on the heath in *Lear* or in the waste places of private love. At any rate, in this "this" sonnet there is a change in the theoretic form one makes in order to abide nature, a change from convention to poiesis. Poetry seizes the eternal essence and the substance (here the poem) ceases to matter. We *give up* the fertile self; one illusion succeeds another, one self another self. The last illusion would be to create or find the second self of second sight. For this a poem is our nearest substitute and furthest reach.

Sonnet 19 ("Devouring Time, blunt thou the lion's paws") comes, for this argument, as a natural digression, where Shakespeare announces and explicates the doctrine of rival creation (creation not adding to but changing God's creation). If in this sonnet we understand time to be God in Nature, the matter becomes plain. We save what is ours, we save what we have made of it: beauty's *pattern* to succeeding *men.* Only the pattern saves and salves. Even the phoenix burns in the blood; only in "my verse" shall the phoenix of my love "ever live young." Perhaps this is to take the sonnet too seriously, for it may be only an expression of vanity—yet vanity may be as near as we come to expressing our doctrine, and vainglory, in this world of time, as near to glory. Poetry is a kind of vain glory in which we are ever young.

Sonnet 19 is not only a digression, it is a nexus to number 20 ("A woman's face with nature's own hand painted"), where the notion of verse—or love—ever young sets up a fright. That in us which is immortal is never free of time's attainder. Nothing in us is free, for there is no necessity with which we can cope. We cope with what passes away, necessity leaves us behind. Whenever immortal longings are felt, one begins to learn dread of the immortal. Who has not seen this in the pupils of his beloved's eyes?—that if the immortal is the ultimate form of paradise, it is the immediate form of hell. *One's firmest decision is only the early form of what transpires as a wrong guess.* In the sonnets Shakespeare deals with the reckless firmness of such untranspired decisions, and I would suppose this sentiment to be in vital analogy to the puzzle-phrase of sonnet 20—"the master-mistress of my passion"—a phrase at the very heart of the dialectics of infatuation (which is a lower stage of poetics, as our master Plato shows in his *Phaedrus*). Master-mistress of my passion! It is the woman in me cries out, the smothering cry of *Hysterica Passio*, which Lear would have put down as a climbing sorrow. The notion is worth arresting us. Poetics, hysteria, and love are near together—and the nearer when their mode is infatuation. In sonnet 20 Shakespeare "found" (we may find) the *fabric* of what we call his sonnets—his second-best bed—the fabric, the Chinese silk or Egyptian cotton or West of England cloth or Scotch voile or some animal fur to your choice—some membrane to your touch. Shakespeare is *il miglior fabbro* in another sense than either Dante or Eliot had in mind; he found the fabric of raised feeling. But when I say "found" I do not mean that Shakespeare (or we) thought it up. It was the other side of the lamppost or when you opened the bulkhead of the cellar in your father's house. I cannot speak of the particulars: but I fasten for one moment on the rhyme (lines 10 and 12) of "thee fell a-doting" and "my purpose nothing." What is that aspirate doing there in that completing rhyme? Is it the breath of doting in nothing? It was behind the lamppost and in the cellar; and what did Hamlet say to his father's ghost? If that is not enough to get from a rhyme let us go back to the distich of lines seven and eight. Here bawdiness is compounded with metaphysics in the new simple: the master-mistress:

> A man in hue all hues in his controlling,
> Which steals men's eyes and women's souls amazeth.

There is a rhyme of meaning here if not of sound between "controlling" and "amazeth," and the one confirms the other; it is one of the many places where Dante and Shakespeare rhyme—I do not say they are identical—in what they signify. In Canto XIX of the *Purgatorio* Dante converts a thought into a dream of the Siren, and in that dream things change as he wills, all hues are in his controlling, for the object of attention changes complexion or color; its colors—as love wills—*come amor vuol, così le colorava*. The second line in Shakespeare's distich is the confirmation. The hues attract, draw, *steal* men's eyes, but penetrate, discombobulate, *amaze* the souls or psyches of women. There are infinite opportunities but no direction. A minotaur lives at the heart of this dream which if it lasted would become bad, but the dream wakes in the last line: "Mine be thy love, and thy love's use their treasure."

If you do not like the minotaur with Theseus and Ariadne, then let us repeat that word which superbly rhymes with itself: Narcissus. If so we must leave Narcissus at once and come again to Pygmalion. Narcissus and Pygmalion are at the two extremes of every infatuation. Of Pygmalion alone we had a hint in sonnets 9 and again in 15 to 17; but in sonnet 21 we begin to move toward the poetic Pygmalion making not Galatea but Narcissus. In short we come on Pygmalion and the Rival Poet, the poet who cannot tell the truth but only its convention. Pygmalion works in private on the making of his Narcissus. We follow the Rival Poet; he can only be the will o' the wisp of another self—in reality the anticipation of this self, and so on. We are among the executive hypocrisies by which we get along. Treachery becomes a fount of insight and a mode of action. Indeed, there is a honey-pot of treachery in every loving mind, and to say so is no more than a mild expansion of these lines:

> And then believe me, my love is as fair
> As any mother's child.

When there is infatuation of soul or body in it, love is always my child. Sonnet 22 has two examples, one of the child, the other of the treachery. There is:

> For all that beauty that doth cover thee
> Is but the seemly raiment of my heart

where the child exaggerates, perhaps corrects, certainly gets ahead of the father; and, for the treachery,

> O therefore, love, be of thyself so wary
> As I, not for myself, but for thee will . . .

lines which tell that wonderful, necessary lie without which we could not tolerate the trespass we know that our affections make upon others: I love you on your account, not mine, for yourself not myself: a lie which can be true so far as Pygmalion and Narcissus make it so.

When I say love, I speak of Eros and Philia but not of Agape who is with the sun and moon and other stars, and under their influences torn to other shreds. I think, too, of Rilke's Prodigal Son who ran away because he could not abide the love around the house. Shakespeare, however, in the couplet, lets the pride of lions loose—the very first *terribilità* in the sonnets:

> Presume not on thy heart when mine is slain:
> Thou gav'st me thine not to give back again.

In short, you are nothing but what I created. Put out that child.

However accidentally it is achieved, the sonnets proceed, at least from sonnet 23 through sonnet 40, in an order wholly appropriate to the natural consequences of the position reached in sonnet 22. If we insist on what we have made ourselves, nothing else can serve as much. As we find this and that unavailable we find ourselves subject to the appropriate disorders that belong to our infatuation and the worse disorders—the order of the contingent or actual world—which seem to attack us because we think we have no part in them. The disorders are all familiar; it is the condition of infatuation that makes it impossible for us to ignore them and undesirable to understand them: our intimacy with them frights us out of sense, or so to speak raises the temperature of sense a little into fever. So we find Shakespeare, in his confrontation of the young man, feeling himself the imperfect actor, inadequate to his role and troubled by himself and the world, and all for fear of trust—of himself or of others.

> So I, for fear of trust, forget to say
> The perfect ceremony of love's rite . . .

The rival poet is in the twelfth line, "More than that tongue that more hath more express'd"—where "more" becomes an ugly accusation indeed from a man "O'ercharg'd with burthen of mine own love's might." To self-inadequacy is added, as if it were a double self, a new, and worse, and inextinguishable self-love, which at one moment asserts eternal strength and at the next fears impotence and cries out for fresh "apparel on my totter'd loving." Infatuation does not fill every moment and would not exist at all if one were not half the time outside it. The *miseria* of infatuation is in the work necessary to preserve it *together* with the work necessary sometimes to escape it; and *ennui* is always around the last and next corner—the last and next turning—of *miseria.* It is *ennui* that gives infatuation its sharpest turn. Sonnet 29 ("When in disgrace with fortune and men's eyes") is a poem of *ennui*, but is also (and perhaps consequently) a true monument of self-pity—of ambition, career, profession, as well as infatuation: all places where one finds oneself "Desiring this man's art, and that man's scope." It is in T. S. Eliot's "Ash-Wednesday"— *his* monument to self-pity—that this line is used with the word "art" changed to "gift." Love is only a refuge as it was only an excuse for perceiving all this. It may be less Christian of me but I prefer Shakespeare's word and if I had to make a substitution I would use "deep skill." Sonnet 30 ("When to the sessions of sweet silent thought") carries on this theme of self-pity which no writer of the first rank— and I think no composer—has been able to avoid, and makes in the first quatrain a human splendor of it. The splendor was so great that nothing could be done with it; so he made a couplet. One engages in self-pity to secure an action or to preserve a sentiment. The sentiment is in the second quatrain, the action in the third, but the human splendor is in the first. As for the couplet, its force is much better expressed in the third quatrain of sonnet 31, which otherwise fits poorly in this set, unless as a digressive generalization.

> Thou art the grave where buried love doth live,
> Hung with the trophies of my lovers gone,
> Who all their parts of me to thee did give:
> That due of many now is thine alone.

It seems an accident of *expertise* that the next sonnet should be a complaint—the special complaint of the lover as poet—that this poet cannot join the decorum of style with the decorum of love. Who knows better than the man aware of his infatuation that style is impossible to his love? The content of infatuate love, while one is in it, is of a violence uncontrollable and changeable by a caprice as deep as nature, like the weather; which one might not have thought of did not the next sonnet deal with violent change in actual weather and the one after that with changes in moral and spiritual weather. The third (number 35) makes something of both weathers and brings us to the civil war of love and hate, from the sense of which we are hardly again free in the course of the sonnets, whether those to the young man or those to the Dark Lady. It is that civil war of love and hate, no doubt, which inhabits sonnet 36 ("Let me confess that we two must be twain") but appears in the form of the perennial guilt felt in any unrequited love. This kind of guilt is what happens to the motive for action that cannot be taken.

> I may not evermore acknowledge thee
> Lest my bewailèd guilt should do thee shame.

The next batch of sonnets (37 through 40) makes something like a deliberate exercise in poetics on the analogy of substance and shadow, with love (or the young man) as the tenth Muse who brings presence to the other nine. But they also show (in 40) the first dubious form of the jealousy that is about to rage at large, quite as if it had been what was being led up to all along. Jealousy is perhaps the tenth Muse, and has the advantage that she can be invoked from within, the genie in the jar of conscience, needs no help from outside, and operates equally well on both sides in the civil war of love and hate, outlasting both. *Jealous,* it should be remembered, was once an active verb in English (as it still is in French), having to do with an intense, usually unsatisfiable craving, especially in its defeated phase. It is the right verb for infatuation in its later and virile stages when all but the pretence of the original force of love is gone. It is of this sort of thing Thomas Mann is thinking when he speaks (in *The Story of a Novel*) of "the motif of the treacherous wooing" in the sonnets, and of their plot as "the relation of poet, lover, and friend"—a relation made for jealousy.

Indeed from sonnet 41 on there is little left truly of love but infatuation and jealousy in a kind of single distillation, sometimes no more than a flavor and sometimes the grasping substance of a poem. Jealousy becomes a part of clear vision and by the special light it casts alters the object of the vision. The threefold relation makes jealousy thrive and encourages her to create. There is an intermittence of life as well as of the heart, and it takes place in those moments when jealousy reigns absolutely, which it succeeds in doing more frequently than any other of the emotions under love. But the moments of sovereignty are never long; she never rules except by usurpation, and by pretending to powers and qualities not her own—as truth and necessity. In her bottom reality she is a craving, zeal without proper object, and indeed as sometimes in English the words *jealous* and *zealous* have been confused; so have what they signify. In the sonnets the occasional return to the purity of infatuation is almost like becoming whole-souled. Again, as before, the accidental order of the sonnets provides a fresh reticulation. After the jealousy of 41 and 42, there is the invocation of dreams and daydreams in 43 and the invocation of thought in 44 and 45, with, in 46, "a quest of thoughts, all tenants to the heart." These remind us that there is a desperation of condition, deeper than any jealousy.

Dreams are a mode and daydreams are the very process of creation. Nathan Sach's remark, which ought to be famous, that "daydreams in common are the form of art" can perhaps be amended to read "the form of life"—especially when connected with an infatuation which, as in these sonnets, takes over so much else in life than its asserted object. There is much to be said about daydreams as the poetic agent of what lasts in poetry, but not here; here the point is to emphasize that dreams and daydreams—"darkly bright, are bright in dark directed"—show a deep poetic preference at work; this sonnet does not wish to *change* reality so much as to rival it with another creation. Similarly, addressing ourselves to sonnet 44 ("If the dull substance of my flesh were thought"), there is a great deal to be said about the way the poetic process illuminates the nature of thought; here the immediate interest, and it should not be pushed much out of its context, is in the ninth line: "But, oh, thought kills me that I am not thought." May not this be pushed just enough to suggest that thought and daydream are in the very closest sort of intimacy? Shakespeare seems to grasp what I assume to be the fact that thought takes place elsewhere than in words, though there may be mutual impregnation. I believe there is some support for such a notion in Prospero's phrase (*Tempest*, IV, i, 164, New Cambridge Shakespeare): "Come with a thought; I think thee, Ariel: come." This is rival creation triumphant.

The three sonnets 49–51 could be taken to represent that awful ennui in infatuation when both thought and daydream fail. The idea—image, not thought—of suicide seems at hand, the only refuge from the ennui of the unrequited. The idea lurks between the words, lending a thickness. But the ennui itself gets bored into a return to the old actions and the old patterns of action, together with the doubts and stratagems appropriate to each, in the contrary stages—the breathless ups and exhausted downs—in the history of any grasping infatuation. Consider the variety—the disorder pushing into order, every created order dropping away—in sonnets 53 through 65. The paradox of substance and shadow presides, but is constantly recognizing other speakers. It is essential to infatuation that it cannot feel sure of itself except by assertion, and every assertion carries its own complement of doubt and therefore its need for reassertion. In one's love one makes, or finds, the ideal; and at once the ideal draws on, breathes in, everything in the lover's mind; then the beloved, so to speak, is surrounded, attended, or ignored as the case may be. It is certain among all uncertainties that when Shakespeare speaks of the constant heart (at the end of sonnet 53), what is signified is the pulsing shadow of the veritable ideal. But, to repeat, consider the variety of these assertions. There is the poetics of beauty and truth, where my verse distils your truth, and with this belongs the immortality of ink. Then there is the feeling of apathy in perception, that slipping off of infatuation where one *knows* it to be self-sustained if not self-created; but to know this is to feel the pinch that sets one going again, when we get infatuation fully occupied *and* conscious of itself. This releases the possibility, which sonnet 57 seizes, that one may so rejoice in jealousy that it becomes a masochistic generosity, a martyrdom for love of the enemy and the self—not God. Surely then there is the need to ad lib at the edge of love, playing with eternal recurrence, with the poetics of time, and risking the assertion of self-love (in argument to the beloved) as a form of objective devotion. Then comes the most familiar recurrent assertion of inky immortality, with the poetics of history and ruin and the mutability of nature herself (as we might say in the second law of thermodynamics) as new modifiers. Such is a summary account of the variety of pattern and shifting pattern. The next sonnet (66) speaks sharply to the whole procession, what is past and what is to come. It is the center of the sequence.

It is better at the center than it would have been at the end, for as it is now the reader can put it in wherever he arrests a particular reading of the sonnets. It is a center that will hold, I think, wherever it is put. "Tir'd with all these, for restful death I cry." In form it is not a sonnet, nor is it so as a mode of thought, but it exists formally to the degree that it is among sonnets, and as mode of thought it depends on, and is in answer to, the feelings that inhabit these sonnets: it is like a principle issuing order for their values. It is an advantage that the poem has also an independent existence as a catalogue and a naming of the convertibility of goods and ills in the world that makes us—a convertibility to downright domination. The lines are in the Roman sense classic in their modelling and so familiar in their sentiment that we can nearly ignore them as one more cry: All that's upright's gone! But let us look at the lines not as familiars but as strangers—or if as familiars, familiars we detest. Each line from the second to the twelfth exhibits clichés for what in any other form we could not tolerate and as clichés can dismiss if we read lightly. But once we bend our attention we see that these are insistent clichés, like the ornamental dagger on the desk which suddenly comes to hand. The cliché insisted on resumes its insights, and perhaps refreshes and refleshes itself as well. To re-expand the cliché, so that it strikes once again upon the particular and the potential experience it once abstracted and generalized, may well be a part of the process of wisdom; it is certainly the business and use of serious poetry—a business and use of which Shakespeare was prime master. Our sense of his mastery only redoubles when we remember what we can of the powerful clichés his work has germinated in our language. In the present poem the clichés were not germinated by him but were modified by the order he gave them and by the vocabulary—mastery of the force in words—of the last four in the catalogue.

> And art made tongue-tied by authority,
> And folly, doctor-like, controlling skill,
> And simple truth miscall'd simplicity,
> And captive good attending captain ill.

Do not these items precipitate us at once from the public life which presses us so much but in which we are actually so little engaged directly into the actual life which absorbs both our private momentum and all our free allegiance? These are lines where our public and private lives meet and illuminate, even judge, each other. They strike our behavior down with all its inadequacies to our every major effort; yet this behavior, and its modes, are how we keep alive from day to day—though it is how we should die lifetime to lifetime. The reader may gloss as he wills the generals of these lines into the privates of his life; but I think he might well gloss in the light they cast on the secret form of the mastering infatuation we have been tracing in these sonnets. These are the circumstances of any love which makes a mighty effort. Here it seems better to gloss only the apposition of "simple truth miscall'd simplicity." What is truly simple is only so to those who are already equal to it; a simple is a compound, like a compound of herbs, of all that we know which bears into the nearest we can manage of a single substance. Here, in this line, a truth achieved is miscalled perception not begun. Hence the rightness of Shakespeare's couplet.

> Tir'd with all these, from these would I be gone,
> Save that to die, I leave my love alone.

Love is the simple truth achieved, and not to be able to love is to be in hell. This sonnet is a critique of love infatuated.

It is a pity not to arrest these remarks now, but there are other themes, and new developments of old themes, in the remainder of the sonnets, both those to the young man and those to the Dark Lady, which will fatten further into fate the truth of the love and of the infatuation here paused at in "Tir'd with all these." A few will do for comment, and the first will be one of the sonnets (number 73, "That time of year thou may'st in me behold") having to do with the imminence of death. I remember H. Granville-Barker talking at great length about the first quatrain of this sonnet. It illustrated his notion of why we need no scene painting when producing the plays. I do not know if these remarks got printed, or I would send the reader to them. Here are lines two through four:

> When yellow leaves, or none, or few, do hang
> Upon those boughs which shake against the cold,
> Bare ruin'd choirs, where late the sweet birds sang . . .

The reader will remember that the second quatrain is an image of sunset fading into dark and sleep, and that the third develops the notion that the ashes of our youth make our death bed and ends with the trope that haunted Shakespeare throughout his work, the trope that something may be "consum'd with that which it was nourish'd by." These two quatrains have no particularity in their imagery or their syntax, and are indeed vague generally, a sort of loose currency. But these quatrains are lent particularity and the force of relations by the extraordinary particularity (barring perhaps the word "choirs") and syntactical unity of the first quatrain. If the reader cannot see this, and see where he *is*, indefeasibly, let him read the lines over till he does, noting especially the order of "yellow leaves, or none, or few." Perhaps it will help if he remembers an avenue of beech trees with nearly all the leaves dropped, and the rest dropping, on a late November afternoon toward dusk; then even the "bare ruin'd choirs" become enormously particular. These words are the shape of thought reaching into feeling, and it is the force of that thought that was able to achieve particularity and order in the words. It is to achieve the eloquence of presence, and it is this presence which interinanimates the whole poem, so that what was merely set side by side cannot now be taken apart. I suggest that this is a model in something near perfection for how the order and particularity are reached in the sum of the sonnets if they are not counted but taken by the eloquence of full presence as one thing.

In support of this, the set of eleven sonnets (numbers 76 through 86), which are frankly on poetics, may be brought into consideration as studies of the interinanimation of poetry and love. One begins to think one of the things to be said about poetry is that it makes an infatuation out of life itself: the concerns of the two seem identical. At any rate these sonnets are concerned with style—where "every word doth almost tell my name"—with style whereby we both invoke and control the violent talents of the psyche. *Grammar* and *glamor,* as the dictionaries will tell you, are at some point one and the same; the one is the secret art, the other the public show; the one is the Muse, the other the Love. The rival poet—the "other" way of writing—also inhabits these sonnets, and I think his shadowy presence suggests that he never existed save as an aid to Shakespeare's poetics.

He makes possible, this rival poet, along with the mistress shared by the lover and the young man, the seeking of humiliation and hatred and personal falsity, and that very grace of shame (sonnet 95) which discloses what Dostoevsky's Dmitri Karamazov calls the beauty of Sodom together with the harshness of love in action. But he does not make possible, except as something to turn aside from, as a prompt to a reversal of momentum—the deepest change of tide, yet only possibly its fall—these two sonnets of transumption. (I will not say transcendence; it is not a word that belongs in Shakespeare's poetics. I prefer Dante's Latin adjective *transumptivus* to describe this aspect of Shakespeare's sonnets.) I mean sonnets 105 ("Let not my love be call'd idolatry") and 108 ("What's in the brain that ink may character"). The first sonnet is a Phoenix and Turtle poem, with these last six lines:

> "Fair, kind, and true," is all my argument,
> "Fair, kind, and true," varying to other words;
> And in this change is my invention spent,
> Three themes in one, which wondrous scope affords.
> Fair, kind, and true have often liv'd alone,
> Which three till now never kept seat in one.

I will not gloss the three words, except that they have to do with belonging and that together they make a mood which does not gainsay or transcend but is a crossing over from other moods by the ritual of repetition. The ritual is necessary and superior to the mere words— like Pascal's unbeliever who if he takes the devout posture may find belief—and when ritual is observed the distinction disappears between the hysterical and the actual. This, in effect, is the commentary sonnet 108 makes on the text and practice of sonnet 105:

> like prayers divine,
> I must each day say o'er the very same.

To cultivate one's hysteria and to cultivate the numen may often turn out to be the same thing, and the ritual for the one may be the observance of the other. In the end how far can the human need be from the power that moves it? And how different should be the approach? We repeat and repeat—almost as much as in music in the elsewhere of poetry we repeat—for the secret presences in words are felt, if not revealed, in repetition, and this is so whether it is the Lord's Prayer or the prayer that intensifies personal infatuation. As the good father who would convert us says, we cannot escape prayer. The immediate object of the prayer tends to disappear as the presence presses: fair, kind, true.

Only one other sonnet (number 116, "Let me not to the marriage of true minds") makes a comparable transumption, and again it comes with a reversal of the tide that has been flowing. That tide was undermining and reductive, subduing the lover's nature to what it worked in, reducing love at last to a babe in the couplet of number 115, as if this were the last form the hovering, transmuting eye of infatuation could show. But from Love is a babe we come in number 116 to "Love's not Time's fool." Like Cleopatra's speeches in Acts IV and V of her play, we need the right syntax of feeling to see how this sonnet escapes nonsense: it is a nonsense we would all speak at the next epiphany, whether of the same person or another. Such nonsense is the only possible company for the mighty effort to identify the ideal of love in the individual. It is the last accommodation of man alive, its loss its deepest discomfort. The second quatrain knows both:

> O no! it is an ever fixed mark,
> That looks on tempests and is never shaken;
> It is the star to every wandering bark,
> Whose worth's unknown, although his height be taken.

Some say the star is the North star, but I think it may be any star you can see, and lose, and find again when you use the same way of looking, the very star "Whose worth's unknown, although his height be taken." It is only the angle of observation that we have learned of the one thing always there. The pang is in the quick.

Beyond this there is nothing in hope or faith; but in cheated hope and bankrupt faith there are the sicknesses and nightmares of love infected by the infatuation it has itself bred. So it is with the remaining sonnets addressed to the young man. It is not the sickness of love-longing; it is the sickness when the energy has left the infatuation, though the senses are still alert and vanity still itches, and indifference has not supervened. The nightmare is double: the trespass of the actual beloved on the lover, and the trespass of the actual lover upon the beloved. These are the trespasses that bring us to ruin—if anything of the ever fixed mark can still be seen—and the amount of ruin in us is inexhaustible until *we* are exhausted. "O benefit of ill!" Nightmare is how we assess the trespass of one individual upon the other (which is why "trespasses" in the Lord's Prayer are nearer our condition than "debts"), and if we have dreams and daydreams in common, as Montaigne and Pascal thought, then it may be that in the terminal stages of an infatuation we sometimes have nightmares in common. Then the general becomes our particular. Let the first quatrain of sonnet 119 stand for these trespasses:

> What potions have I drunk of Siren tears,
> Distill'd from limbecks foul as hell within,
> Applying fears to hopes and hopes to fears,
> Still losing when I saw myself to win?

Number 126, the last of the verses to the young man, is not a sonnet but six rhymed couplets. Had it become a sonnet, or even added a couplet, it must have become a curse or even an anathema. Nothing is so mortal as that which has been kept too long in one stage of nature; we have horror even of a beauty that outlasts the stage of nature to which it belonged. Not even an infatuation can be maintained more than one and a half times its natural life. There is no relief so enormous as the surrender of an infatuation, and no pang so keen as the sudden emptiness after. Such is the curse, the anathema, upon Pygmalion and Narcissus these sonnets show; but they would show nothing were it not for the presence among them of the three sonnets—"Tir'd with all these" (number 66), "Let not my love be call'd idolatry" (number 105), and "Let me not to the marriage of true minds" (number 116). The first gives the condition of apprehension, the second the numinous ritual, and the third the limits beyond us in hope and faith for the mighty effort, which in one of our traditions is the highest of which we are capable from the *Symposium* and the *Vita Nuova* through these *Sonnets,* the effort to make something last "fair, kind, and true" between one being and another. There is a trinity here. What wonder then, as we find ourselves short of these powers, if in vain hope we resort to infatuation?

And not once but again, with what we call the Dark Lady as our object, and this second (second or hundredth) time with a prophetic soul for abortion and no hope of children at all. One knows at once one is among the mistakes of life which, unless we can make something of them, are the terms of our central failure in human relations.

Where with the young man it was a question of building something, if necessary with other means short, by the cultivated hysteria of infatuation, with the Dark Lady there is a kind of unbuilding going on, the deliberate exchange of pounds of flesh for pounds of spirit. It is like drinking too much. Every morning the rewards show as losses, and the more they show so, the more one is bound to the system. One's private degradation is the grandest Sodom. If it were not for the seriousness of the language and its absolute jarring speed, a sonnet such as 129 ("Th'expense of spirit in a waste of shame") could have been written of any evening begun in liquor that did not come off well; but there is the language and its speed, and the apprehensions from the central lonely place that this lover must seek what he must shun. The two sonnets, number 133 ("Beshrew that heart that makes my heart to groan") and number 134 ("So, now I have confess'd that he is thine"), together with 129, make a dread commentary on *philia.* In this lover's triangle, where each pair shares the third, mere sexual force—that treachery which moves like an army with banners—is superior to the mightiest effort *philia* can make alone. Once infatuation is simply sexual it is the great swallower-up of friendship or love. Sonnet 134 exacts not Shylock's pound of flesh, which he was refused because it would have cost spirit, but is sexuality exacting, and receiving, since it does not harm the body, the pound of spirit.

> The statute of thy beauty thou wilt take,
> Thou usurer that put'st forth all to use,
> And sue a friend came debtor for my sake;
> So him I lose through my unkind abuse.

The two sonnets are two maws for over-interpretation. Let us say sexuality is indeterminate and undeterminable; a force that has too much left over to absorb into its immediate end; or a force of which the sexual is only a part, but which sex raises to its extortionate ability. In the impasse of these sonnets, it would help nothing that the Dark Lady can be thought a third man, but it would hinder only those who wish to improve Shakespeare's reputation. But I suggest this only to return to the possibility, with which I began this paper, that the poetics of infatuation move among the coils and recoils of the various selves that thrive and batten upon the Psyche. This is the sixth line of number 133: "And my next self thou harder hast engross'd." Add to this only what evidence there may be in the two "Will" sonnets (135 and 136) where, other matters being present by chance, Shakespeare paid attention chiefly to the clenching of his wills in the general field of sexuality. Has no one suggested that this clenching of wills was Shakespeare's way of declaring his uncommitted anonymity? There is Thomas Mann's realm of the anonymous and the communal between us all. "Swear to thy blind soul that I was thy *Will*."

Dark Lady, Third Man, Next Self, or the Anonymous One, there is no question of the sexuality and human infatuation pressing to find form within and under and among the words of the sonnets. In this second set, without the mighty effort to lift us that was in the first set, without Pygmalion and Narcissus and the Immortal Ink, the spirit wrestles in the flesh that engorges it, and the flesh—one's own flesh—is convulsed in the spirit that engulfs it. The two journeys are remarkably the same—as are the tower and the abyss—both in itinerary and target. Deceit, distrust, humiliation, jealousy, the plea for annihilation, and self-pity, with occasional glories in general disaster and with the world of the real senses—like the light and sweet air in Dante's Hell—always at hand; these are the common itinerary, with all the other "tender feeling to base touches prone." The common target is repudiation—repudiation without an ounce of renunciation in it. "I am that I am." To say it once more, the sonnets illustrate the general or typical as the poetic, but there is a force under the words, and a force drawn from the words, which compels us to apprehend what had been generalized.

With that force in mind let us look at two sonnets just before the end. Number 151 ("Love is too young to know what conscience is") has perhaps as one of its points that love asserts a special form of conscience by escaping its general form (as we use the word in English) into what we know now as consciousness. (The reader who delights in such matters should read the chapter on *conscience* and *conscious* in C. S. Lewis' *Studies in Words;* he does not touch on this sonnet's conscience, but he does discuss several other Shakespearean usages which help us to apprehend our present mystery.) I myself think that the two sets of meanings are deeply present here, on the simple rule of thumb that a poet can never know exactly which power or powers in his words he is drawing on, and the clearer the intention (what was to be *put* into words, not what was already there) the greater the uncertainty of his knowledge must be; and besides, the words may modify and even correct his intention, as well as ruin it—else there were no reality in words and no rush of meaning either from, or to, or among them. When I say the two sets of meanings are present, I do not intend to mark an ambiguity, but to urge that two voices are speaking at once which can be heard at once. This is the compacting power of poetry, which commands us so far as we hear it. Love is too young to know what true consciousness might be, Love is too young to know the pang of judgment as to the good and evil nature of an act or thought or condition. "Love is too young to know what conscience is." The second line, "Yet who knows not conscience is born of love?" suggests that intimate consciousness leads to the pang of judgment, just as the pang illuminates the knowledge one did not know that one had. Children and saints, said Dostoevsky, can believe two contrary things at once; poetry has also that talent. Our common idiom, "I could (or couldn't) in all conscience," keeps the pair alive in what seems a single approach. The phrase "in all conscience" generalizes several sorts of behavior in a convenient single-ness of form, so that none of them can be dismissed. I remember the anecdote a sociologist told me about an inmate in Trenton State Prison. When asked why he had stolen a car, he promptly answered that his conscience made him. "Yet who knows not that conscience is born of love?"

As we go further into this sonnet the voices thicken with tumescence, both of the body and of "the nobler part" as well. Priapus, rising, empties the rest of the body and drains something of the spirit ("tender feeling to base touches prone"); there is a physiological and spiritual disarray for the sake of a momentary concentration where it would be out of order to call for order.

This, then, is the priapic parallel, the comment of consciousness and conscience together, now that Pygmalion and Narcissus are in another limbo, for all the sonnets, whether to the young man or to the Dark Lady. Pygmalion and Narcissus made human efforts, but Priapus is a god and undoes all efforts not his own. His comments are in his searching actions. We can see this in lines seven and eight:

> My soul doth tell my body that he may
> Triumph in love; flesh stays no farther reason . . .

The Greeks had a word for the bitterness of things too sweet, but Shakespeare has the verbal power for the sweetness of things too bitter. The soul in these lines cannot be taken as reason (the habit of ratio or proportion), and is unlikely to be the immortal soul which in the end must want another lodging and "deserts the body it has used." I think rather of the "blind worm" in Yeats's very late poems, and of the stubbornness of dreams prompting, prompting, prompting—for lines forgotten and stage business impossible. The lines may return to mind and action ensue. Because I think of the blind worm I think the soul here is the Psyche, who is much older than the soul and is so much further back in the abyss that she is prepared to identify life with the blind stubbornness of the worm if necessary. It is the Psyche that gurgles in the words of this sonnet. When the Psyche speaks, and is heard, everything merely personal collapses—all that the Psyche must regard with the disdain owed to the mere artifact. One hunts for a grave that is not an artifact, not even the headstone. It is the Psyche's voice, then, in the couplet, where everything is known together and all is pang, all consciousness and conscience, but as a condition not a commitment of life.

> No want of conscience hold it that I call
> Her "love" for whose dear love I rise and fall.

The labor of the Psyche is always toward the recovery of the animal life, since there can be none without.

But there is another voice than the Psyche's which makes another labor and another prayer. This is the labor and prayer of all we have made human in us, the prayer of the great lie—noble or ignoble—by which alone all that we create in ourselves or in society can survive. Consider sonnet 152 ("In loving thee thou knows't I am forsworn"); it is a repudiation, but also a reassertion.

> I am perjur'd most;
> For all my vows are oaths but to misuse thee,
> And all my honest faith in thee is lost:
> For I have sworn deep oaths of thy deep kindness,
> Oaths of thy love, thy truth, thy constancy . . .

Our oaths and promises are our best lies, if only because we know that the roughage of life will mar if not break them, but more because we know that they make our truth. We lie in search of truth: to build truth: and our great cities and monuments and poems are proof of our powers. They make us meaningful because they are that part of us which survives, what we admire in ourselves even to infatuation, whence our promises come.

> Tir'd with all these, from these I would be gone,
> Save that to die, I leave my love alone.

ACKNOWLEDGMENTS

continued from copyright page

"Dirty Hands: A Federal Customs Officer Looks at Art." *New Republic* 62 (2 April 1930), 188–90 (signed with the pseudonym Perry Hobbs). Reprinted in the pamphlet *Dirty Hands, or the True Born Censor* (Cambridge, Eng.: Minority Press, 1930).

"A Poet's Lent." Review of *Doctor Donne and Gargantua: The First Six Cantos,* by Sacheverell Sitwell (Boston: Houghton). *Poetry* 38 (June 1931), 162–66. Copyright 1931 by The Modern Poetry Association. Reprinted by permission of the editor of POETRY.

"An Active Poem." Review of *Dream and Action,* by Leonard Bacon (New York: Harper). *Poetry* 45 (January 1935), 223–26. Copyright 1935 by The Modern Poetry Association. Reprinted by permission of the editor of POETRY.

"Statements and Idyls." Review of *Horizons of Death,* by Norman Macleod (Parnassus Press). *Poetry* 46 (May 1935), 108–12. Copyright 1935 by The Modern Poetry Association. Reprinted by permission of the editor of POETRY.

"Samples of Santayana." Review of *Obiter Scripta: Lectures, Essays and Reviews,* by George Santayana, ed. Justus Buchler and Benjamin Schwartz (New York: Scribner's). *New Republic* 88 (28 October 1936), 357–58.

"A Critic and His Absolute." Review of *Primitivism and Decadence: A Study of American Experimental Poetry,* by Yvor Winters (New York: Arrow Editions). *New Republic* 91 (14 July 1937), 284–85.

"In Our Ends Are Our Beginnings." Review of *The World's Body,* by John Crowe Ransom (New York: Scribner's), and *The Triple Thinkers,* by Edmund Wilson (New York: Harcourt). *Virginia Quarterly Review* 14 (Summer 1938), 446–50. Reprinted by permission.

"A Good Reminder." Review of *In Defense of Reason,* by Yvor Winters (New York: The Swallow Press and William Morrow). *Nation* 164 (14 June 1947), 718–19. Copyright 1947, *The Nation.* Reprinted by permission of the Nation Associates, Inc.

"Conrad Aiken: The Poet." *Atlantic Monthly* 192 (December 1953), 77–82. Reprinted by permission.

"Obscuris Vera Involvens." Review of *W. B. Yeats and Tradition,* by F. A. C. Wilson (London: Gollancz). *Kenyon Review* 20 (Winter 1958), 160–68. Copyright 1958 by Kenyon College. Reprinted by permission of the estate of the author and *The Kenyon Review.*

"Edwin Muir: Between the Tiger's Paws." *Kenyon Review* 21 (Summer 1959), 419–36. Copyright 1959 by Kenyon College. Reprinted by permission of the estate of the author and *The Kenyon Review.*

"Homo Ludens." Review of *The Literary Works of Matthew Prior,* ed. H. Bunker Wright and Monroe K. Spears. 2 vols. (Oxford: The Clarendon Press). *Kenyon Review* 21 (Autumn 1959), 662–68. Copyright 1959 by Kenyon College. Reprinted by permission of the estate of the author and *The Kenyon Review.*

"A Poetics for Infatuation." *Kenyon Review* 23 (Autumn 1961), 647–70. Copyright 1961 by Kenyon College. Reprinted by permission of the estate of the author and *The Kenyon Review.*

For Excerpts

Excerpts from Blackmur's poems used in "Blackmur on the Dove's Wings" and "Blackmur's Craft" are reprinted from *Poems of R. P. Blackmur.* Copyright © 1977 by Princeton University Press. Reprinted by permission of the Princeton University Press.

Fitzgerald excerpts in "Robert Fitzgerald: Blackmur, Princeton, and the Early Gauss Seminars," ed. Edmund Keeley, are reprinted from *Enlarging the Change: The Princeton Seminars in Literary Criticism 1949–1951* by Robert Fitzgerald. (Boston: Northeastern University Press, 1985.) Copyright © 1985 Robert Fitzgerald. Reprinted by permission of the publisher.

Berryman excerpts in the introduction to Blackmur's texts by Joseph Frank are from *Love and Fame* by John Berryman. Copyright © 1970 by John Berryman. Reprinted by permission of Farrar, Straus and Giroux, Inc., and Faber and Faber Ltd.

Eliot excerpts in "Blackmur on Henry James" by Denis Donoghue are from "Ash-Wednesday" in *Collected Poems 1909–1962* by T. S. Eliot, copyright 1936 by Harcourt Brace Jovanovich, Inc.; copyright © 1963, 1964 by T. S. Eliot. Reprinted by permission of Harcourt Brace Jovanovich and Faber and Faber Ltd.

Yeats' poetry excerpts in "Obscura Vera Involvens" by R. P. Blackmur are reprinted with permission of Macmillan Publishing Company from *The Collected Poems of W. B. Yeats.* Copyright 1933 by Macmillan Publishing Company, renewed 1961 by Bertha Georgie Yeats. Dramatic excerpts are reprinted with permission of Macmillan Publishing Company from *The Collected Plays of W. B. Yeats.* Copyright 1934, 1952 by Macmillan Publishing Company. Copyrights renewed 1962 by Bertha Georgie Yeats and 1980 by Anne Yeats. Additional permission granted by A. P. Watt Ltd., on behalf of Michael B. Yeats and Macmillan London Ltd.

Macleod excerpts in "Statements and Idyls" by R. P. Blackmur appear by permission of Norman G. Macleod.

Bacon excerpts in "An Active Poem" by R. P. Blackmur are reprinted with permission of Harper & Row from *Dream and Action* by Leonard Bacon, copyright 1934 by Leonard Bacon.

Aiken excerpts in "Conrad Aiken: The Poet" are from *Collected Poems* by Conrad Aiken. Copyright 1953, 1970 by Conrad Aiken; renewed 1981 by Mary Aiken. Reprinted by permission of Oxford University Press, Inc.

Muir excerpts in "Edwin Muir: Between the Tiger's Paws" by R. P. Blackmur are from *Collected Poems* by Edwin Muir, copyright 1960 by Willa Muir. Reprinted by permission of Oxford University Press, Inc.